13.69

Festival Europe!

Fairs & Celebrations
throughout Europe

Margaret M. Johnson

Mustang Publishing Co.
Memphis, TN

For the Griswolds—
Carl, Mark, Kate, and Carl, Jr.
Thanks for sharing Europe with me!

Distributed to the U.S. book trade by National Book Network, Lanham, Maryland. Distributed in England and Europe by Gazelle Book Services, Lancaster, England. For information on other distributors, please contact Mustang Publishing.

Library of Congress Cataloging-in-Publication Data

Johnson, Margaret M., 1944-
    Festival Europe! : fairs & celebrations throughout Europe / Margaret M. Johnson
        p.   cm.
        ISBN 0-914457-41-1 (paperback : acid-free paper) : $10.95
        1. Festivals--Europe. 2. Fairs--Europe. 3. Europe--Social life and customs. 4. Europe--Description and travel--Guidebooks. I. Title.
    GT4842.J64   1992
    394.2'694--dc20   90-50867
                                                                CIP

Printed on acid-free paper. ∞

10 9 8 7 6 5 4 3 2 1

Maps by Elizabeth A. McCormack.
Note: Maps are not drawn to scale.

Acknowledgments

Throughout the course of writing *Festival Europe!*, a number of people have rendered assistance, from inspiration to translation. Others have provided help only they can know. I thank you all:

Carlton E. Johnson, the International Programs faculty of Western Illinois University, the European Travel Commission, M. Silver Associates, Chancery—Diocese of Rockville Center, Maureen and Walter Marlowe, Gea Hekman Polan, Stephane Legrande, Sally Gilhooley, Adrienne Greenbaum, Christina Engelbredt, Luciano Artusi, Bill Elia, Alison Carpluk, Bill Schiavo, Bob Coffey, Wayne Snell, Larry Iannucci, Ray Wurm, Darlene Cordingly, and the New York offices of the European Tourist Boards, which gave invaluable information and help.

I also wish to thank Rollin Riggs, in particular, for his help and faith in this project.

Margaret M. Johnson

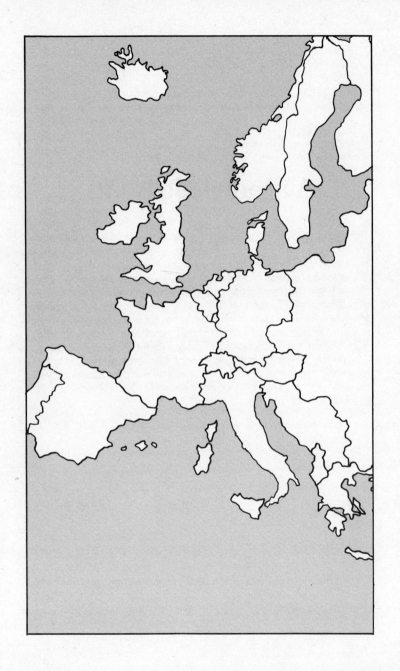

Contents

1

Introduction

Who doesn't love a parade, a pageant, a festival? There's something about the ritual of marching, music, and costumes that makes any celebration irresistible.

While sitting in the heart of Munich's Marienplatz, waiting for the copper figures of the *glockenspiel* to perform their daily tournament, a friend remarked that I should visit Frauenkirche, the gothic cathedral whose onion-shaped twin towers have been the city's landmark since 1525; or perhaps, he suggested, go to St. Peter's, Munich's oldest church, built in 1180.

"It's hard for us to believe," he added, "that these churches are centuries older than our own country!"

His remark seemed to epitomize what most travelers expect from Europe—ancient traditions, medieval treasures, religious processions, and a vast and varied sense of history. There's no place like Europe to really quench our thirst for the past.

"The past," of course, means different things to different people. First-time travelers want to see the "top sights" prescribed by Frommer, Fodor, Birnbaum, et al. In Rome, a tour of the Colosseum, constructed in 72 A.D., is a must. In London, you can't miss the Tower, the fortress continually occupied for 900 years. And in Athens, almost every tourist attraction was constructed sometime B.C.!

Every major tour company can provide an itinerary that will acquaint you with the "top sights." Tourists traveling independently can also see all the major attractions with great ease. Armed with any of the traditional guidebooks, "Dollarwise" or otherwise, anyone traveling to Europe today can easily find books that explain all the tourist "musts," provide hotel and restaurant recommendations, and even list transportation schedules, temperatures, and conversion charts of everything from money to shoe sizes.

But what about the "other" Europe—the Europe of medieval festivals, of processions and dancing, of jousting in 15th-century

7

costumes, of goat auctions, garlic fairs, and wine festivals? What about the procession and bareback horse race known as *Il Palio* held in Siena each July 2 and August 16? What about the *Backfischfest*, a folk and wine festival held in Worms in early September? What about the potpourri of the arts called the Edinburgh International Festival and its accompanying band and bagpipe spectacle, the Military Tattoo, held in the Scottish city for three weeks in August? Or the feasting and shucking that accompanies the first catch at the Galway Oyster Festival in late September? Or the Puck Fair that pays homage to a goat for three days in August in Killorglin, Ireland?

Other guides *might* mention such delightful events in passing, but this is the stuff of which *Festival Europe!* is made!

This book is based on the premise that few American travelers ever get to see the festive side of Europe, away from the obligatory monuments, museums, and cathedrals. Perhaps first-time travelers need the security and knowledge of having climbed the Eiffel or the Leaning Towers. But they needn't overlook the Bayeux Festival held to celebrate William the Conqueror's birthday, only two hours outside of Paris, or the *Festa dei Ceri* (Race of the Candles) or *Palio dei Balestriere* (Palio of the Archers) held in May in Gubbio, a few hours from Rome.

Festival Europe! is designed to help you discover the "other" Europe. No matter what your travel plans might be, no matter how long or short your stay, no matter what other guides or itineraries you may have at your disposal, *Festival Europe!* will enrich your journey by directing you to the history, parades, and pageantry that only Europe knows how to provide.

And because most travelers are governed by the time they are going and place they are visiting, *Festival Europe!* is arranged by country or group of countries, each with an annotated calendar of events from May to October, the most popular travel period. Often, suggestions for off-season activities and special events follow. And always, the primary focus of *Festival Europe!* is on festivities of the type Webster would define as "occasions for feasting or celebrating, especially a day or time of significance that recurs at regular intervals." It offers you the best of that "other" Europe.

I wish you a festive journey!

2

▮ Ireland

"The calamitous years burnt themselves deep into the imagination of the people and have haunted their descendants ever since."
—F.S.L. Lyons, *Ireland Since the Famine*

As a direct result of the failure of the 1845 potato crop, the subsequent epidemic of "potato fever," and the blight of 1846 and 1847, Ireland suffered one of the greatest tides of emigration ever witnessed. Between 1845-55, nearly 2,000,000 Irish left their homeland.

This desperate flood would not subside for several generations. In fact, according to Lyons, "the current that flowed to the far corners of the earth eventually numbered 475,000 to America, 70,000 to Canada, and 370,000 to Australia between 1841-1925." As severe as these figures are, the irony lies in the fact that the U.S. now boasts millions of people of Irish ancestry whose imaginations have been so haunted by tales of the old country that in 1990 alone, 440,000 North Americans traveled there.

Another irony exists in the fact that even with the famine—and later, "The Troubles"—the Irish still have cause, perhaps a need, to celebrate in countless fairs, festivals, and *fleadhs* throughout the tiny country. Irish journalist Stan Gelber Davies once wrote that "the whole culture of Ireland is based on conviviality. . . Other nations have local festivals, but I do not think any people have taken to the idea with our enthusiasm. There is scarcely a town, or even a village, anywhere in the island which has not thought of an excuse for an annual festival. . . It is how we live."

Unfortunately, sandwiched between a pony fair or a weekend *feis*, there are occasional political and religious flare-ups between the rival Protestant and Catholic residents of Northern Ireland. Amid the drinking and the dancing, there is occasional weeping, caused by the complicated, centuries-old battle between the Irish and the English. It eventually led to the founding of the Republic of Ireland in the south and the creation of Northern Ireland, made up of the six counties

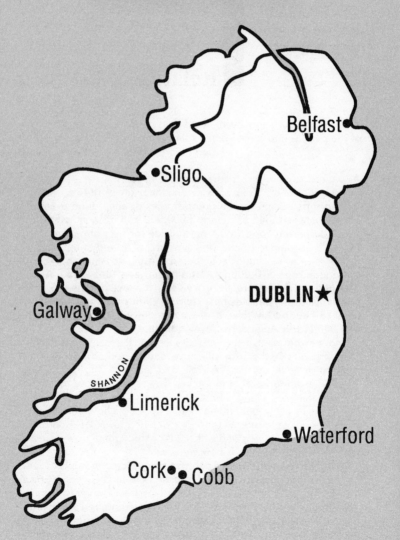

IRELAND

Belfast•

•Sligo

DUBLIN★

Galway•

SHANNON

•Limerick

•Waterford

Cork•• Cobb

of Ulster. On June 22, 1921, King George V opened the parliament of Northern Ireland as an official part of Great Britain, and from that day forward, the weeping has continued.

But because this book is about festivals and not politics, the two countries have been combined in what is appropriate geographically, if not ideologically. The Connemara Pony Show is treated equally with Ballycastle's Oul' Lammas Fair, and the Hibernian's Parade through Belfast on July 15 shares fair billing with the Orangemen's Battle of the Boyne celebrations on July 12. This chapter covers events from Dublin to Derry and from Belfast to Ballybunion.

Travel to the various festivals throughout Ireland is quite easy via the rails or the roads. Because the country is so small (only 300 miles long and 150 miles wide) and so close (only six hours to Shannon or Dublin from New York), Ireland is a logical and ideal beginning for your festival tour through Europe.

May

Cork—Choral and Folk Dance Festival

Founded in 1954, the Cork International Choral and Folk Dance Festival has now become one of the major European festivals. Since its inception, choirs and dance teams have come from all over the world to participate in unique programs of choral music and folk dancing. In the course of the festival, you may hear outstanding examples of the polyphonic, classical, or romantic periods, as well as examples of contemporary and avant-garde composers. (early May)

Killarney—Pan Celtic Week

This annual event draws Celts from Scotland, Wales, Cornwall, the Isle of Man, and Brittany back to join their Irish kin for traditional dancing, music, sport, and pipe band competition. Colorful and traditional. (mid-May)

Ennis—Fleadh Nua

This Comhaltas Ceoiltoirí Eireann festival attracts thousands of people from all parts of Ireland and abroad. It includes musicians, singers, dancers, wrenboys, biddy boys, strawboys—all woven together in a rich cultural pattern. A wealth of traditions gathered from all parts of the country are combined to evoke and embody what the organization calls "the real Ireland." (late May)

Dundalk—International Maytime Festival

Billed as the country's longest running festival (it began in 1964), Dundalk Maytime offers a full and varied program for 10 days, including the selection of the Maytime Queen, a variety of musical and social events, and an international amateur drama competition. As a border town, the people of Dundalk try to put aside economic blues, cross-border trade problems, and even terrorism in a determined effort to leave their troubles behind and celebrate with the 20,000 visitors who flock to the town each year. The drama festival draws amateur performers from America, Israel, and Europe, as well as all around Ireland. (late May)

Ballyporean—Welcome Home Festival

The tiny village of Ballyporean has the distinction of being the birthplace of former U.S. President Ronald Reagan's paternal great-grandfather. Since Reagan's visit here in 1984, the small town and pub named for him have become tourist landmarks. This festival is really just another good excuse for visitors to stop off at the quaint village for a round of parties and Irish fun. (late May)

Listowel—Listowel Writer's Week

Although the atmosphere of the Writer's Week may appear to be purely "academic" with its round of workshops, theater productions, lectures, and readings, there are countless events that offer pure entertainment. Musical concerts, art exhibitions, dance bands, and pub music all contribute to the highly festive nature of this basically "arty" festival. (late May/early June)

June

Dublin—Music in Great Irish Houses

For over 20 years, the salons of some of Ireland's largest and most beautiful 18th-century mansions around Dublin have housed this delightful musical event. Birr Castle, Castletown, Russborough House, and Royal Hospital Kilmainham have been venues for the series of chamber music concerts which run for 10 days. For more information, write GPA Music in Great Irish Houses, 4 Highfield Grove, Rathgar, Dublin 6. (early June)

Dublin—Bloomsday

June 16, 1904 is the day on which all the events of James Joyce's *Ulysses* took place. Since 1954, it has also been the day when Dublin remembers Joyce with a kind of Joycean feast day. Ironically, Joyce was once reviled by the city, whose rows of brown brick houses he called "the incarnation of cultural paralysis." Today, he's revered as a cultural icon and a priceless magnet for both students of Irish literature and visitors who wish to follow in famous footsteps.

Several events mark Bloomsday, including the ritual pilgrimage of Leopold Bloom along the *Ulysses* trail, public readings, costume parties and parades, and visits to locations associated with Joyce like his Martello Tower, the James Joyce Cultural Center, and Davy Byrnes Pub, where Bloom stops on his day-long odyssey. Joyce aficionados can begin the day like Bloom with a breakfast of kidneys at the South Bank Restaurant, or enjoy a special Bloomsday lunch at Davy Byrnes—gorgonzola cheese and burgundy, the meal Bloom had.

Dubliner John Ryan, organizer of the first event, says, "Every year I see more and more people coming for Bloomsday. . . To a great extent, *Ulysses* and James Joyce put Dublin on the map. He has given the city a literary identity that could be the envy of the world."

And poet Brendan Kennelly says, "In Dublin, every day is Bloomsday." But none quite like June 16.

Ballybunion—International Bachelor Festival

The essence of this festival is the *craic*, the good times which dominate the 10-day whirl of music, fun, and drink and which has overshadowed all other events since 1972 in this beautiful seaside town. Although the festival committee strives to promote a variety of activities aside from the main one—partying—the highlight is always the nightly Festival Club, which all 20 bachelors must attend. According to recent winner Dennis Wagner, "To participate you can't be seen with the same woman more than once. You must have a good time and be able to hold your drink. And above all else, if you defect and get married you must leave the club immediately and nominate someone else to take your place." Participant or not, the visitor to Ballybunion during this last week of June can't miss a unique taste of modern Irish folk culture. (late June)

Salthill—Harp Lager Festival

This festival, whose slogan is "Have a whale of a time," combines entertainment for all tourist tastes. In addition to the variety of food and drink available, the festival also includes a parade of horses and hounds known as the Galway Blazers, an all-breeds dog show, a "bonny baby" and "glamorous granny" competition, beauty pageants, dancing, and concerts. Very folksy! (late June/early July)

July

Buttevant—Cahirmee Festival

With its motto of "Cahirmee for Horse—Cahirmee for Fun," the annual festival has its origins in "the times of old when the Fair went on for days on end, with not alone buying and selling, but also such side attractions as athletics, chariot-racing, musical competitions, and hurling." A real Irish country fair that offers a week of native fun. (early July)

Enniscorthy—Strawberry Fair

While the strawberries—the guests of honor during this festival—are absolutely luscious, they are simply an excuse for community dancing, singing, and sporting events. Another good fair! (early July)

Portarlington—Festival Francais de Portarlington

The organizers of this event (partly sponsored by the Guinness Brewery) hope it will soon be on par with the top-ranked Rose of Tralee

Festival in Tralee. Activities include the Jewel of Arlington Competition, a snail-eating championship (!), an art exhibition, jazz sessions, and traditional Irish entertainment. (mid-July)

Dublin—Dublin Horse Show

Held annually since 1868, the Kerrygold Dublin Horse Show is recognized as Ireland's greatest equestrian and social event and draws countless visitors each year. Preparations start at the beginning of the year, when invitations are sent to foreign equestrian federations for the International Jumping Contests. Two prestigious awards are presented: the Aga Khan Trophy (The Nation's Cup) and the Grand Prix of Ireland. The Ballsbridge Showgrounds attracts horse lovers from all over the world to enjoy the pleasures of the show. For more information, write Royal Dublin Society, Ballsbridge, Dublin 4. (mid-July)

Edenderry—Edenderry Festival

Billed as ''the midland's latest, greatest, and most colorful nine-day festival,'' the program of events makes it a worthwhile stop for anyone traveling through this lovely, lakeland region 40 miles west of Dublin and 40 miles east of Limerick. Most of the ''typical'' Irish attractions are offered here as well. (late July/early August)

Keadue—O'Carolan Harp Festival

Harpers from the U.S., England, Germany, and Japan join Irish harpers at O'Carolan airs in Keadue for an event highlighted by the All-Ireland Harp Competition. Several thousand visitors can partake of the barn dance, ceili, and street music provided by the numerous musicians who travel to Keadue each year. (late July/early August)

Cobh—International Folk Dance Festival

Colorfully costumed dance troupes from around the world come to the seaside town of Cobh to perform native dances. Along with competitions held nightly, there's street entertainment throughout the town during the week-long event. (mid-July)

Adare—Adare Festival

Adare Manor, formerly the magnificent estate of the Earls of Dunraven and now a luxury hotel, hosts this 17-day event that features maestro Hugh Wolff and the New Jersey Symphony as the resident orchestra, with guest artists like Phil Coulter, James Galway, Stefan Grapelli, and Nancy Griffiths. This relatively young festival, created by Manor owners Tom and Judy Kane, is becoming a world-class showcase for the arts in Ireland. Performances, held in a 2,000-seat tent on the Manor grounds, feature primarily classical symphonic music, but the Festival also offers solo performers, evenings of jazz, and choral recitals. For more information, contact Adare Festival,

P.O. Box 910, Short Hills, NJ 07078 U.S.A. (toll-free phone 800-462-3273) or Adare Festival, Adare Manor, Adare, Co. Limerick. (mid-July)

August
Galway—Galway Arts Festival
Classical music, poetry readings, art exhibitions, and countless theatrical events are all part of this festival week. You can see performers from throughout Ireland and the world at a number of venues, but mostly at the Great Southern Hotel, located in the heart of Galway on Eyre Square. The Arts Festival is only one of a number of major events held in the lovely city during the summer. (early August)

Gorey—Gorey Arts Festival
A genuine potpourri of the arts is the best way to describe what goes on during the two weeks of the festival. One night it's jazz, the next it's rock; a puppet show, a photography exhibition, a reading of traditional Irish literature, live theater—little is excluded at Gorey. When you've had your fill of the arts, there are beautiful beaches to visit in this part of Ireland called "the sunny southeast." (early August)

Granard—An Bun-Fhleadh, Harp Festival
The annual Harp Festival is steeped in tradition, going back to 1781 when the event first took place here. Revived in 1981 by the late Canon Gilfinnan, it has been gaining popularity ever since, and over 20,000 people now attend. In addition to events related to the harp, the festival incorporates a variety of musical genres and has been called "a cross between a *fleadh cheoil* and an ancient musical festival." (early August)

Killorglin—Puck Fair
The occasion of a great round of events and festivities, the Puck Fair usually runs the same three days of August (10-12) when, according to historical records, Jenkin Conway received a royal patent in 1613 to "hold a fair in Killorglin on Lammas Day and the Day after."

While some say that King Puck, the great male goat that presides over the festivities, is inspired by pagan rites of harvest and fertility, he is nonetheless the main attraction. Some say he was introduced to the fair in 1808 when the local landlord, forbidden by law to levy tolls to cattle or sheep fairs, hit upon the novel idea of holding a goat fair to collect his money. Another legend has it that a troop of Cromwellian Roundheads routed a herd of goats, which obligingly stampeded toward Killorglin, thus warning the people of the approaching army. The grateful populace installed King Puck in honor of the goats who saved the town.

Whatever version is accepted has no effect on the final festivities.

From Gathering Day, when King Puck is paraded through the town and installed on his lofty platform; through Fair Day, when livestock are bought and sold; to the final event of Scattering Day, when the goat is released with ceremony and celebrations at sunset—the Puck Fair has no match for fun and Irish tradition.

Killorglin is 13 miles from Killarney Town on the Ring of Kerry route.

Birr—Birr Vintage Week
Now in its second decade, Birr Vintage Week continues to be the premier Midlands festival. The "vintage" aspect of the event is an antiques fair and a parade in vintage costume. The beautiful Birr Castle Demesne nearby offers a quiet sanctuary for those who need respite from the festival's round of parties. (mid-August)

Clifden—Connemara Pony Show
This annual event, organized by the Connemara Pony Breeders Society, brings together the finest of the breed of this unique Irish pony. The show is billed as an ideal place for potential buyers to make contact with owners and breeders. For those who just want a taste of Irish country life, the beautiful surroundings of wild Connemara provide the perfect setting. (mid-August)

Ballybrit—Galway Races
Ireland has a great tradition of horsemanship, whether at the country fair, the horse show, or the races, and the Galway Races are a long-established part of that heritage. The first Galway Plate was run in 1869 and remained a two-day event until 1962, when it expanded to a six-day meet. Now the races take place twice during the summer in August and provide a country fair atmosphere as well as authentic horse racing. (late August)

Disclaimer

While every effort has been made to include as many events as possible, there are, of course, many that are not mentioned. My intention is to offer a wide array of festivals that travelers might wish to include on their itineraries, while neither endorsing nor intentionally ignoring any. My hope is that *Festival Europe!* will be considered "comprehensive" while not possibly "complete."

Though I have made every attempt at accuracy, bear in mind that things may change between press time and the time of your visit. Neither the author nor the publisher accepts responsibility for any problems you may encounter as a result of an inaccuracy in this book.

I would welcome your criticisms, suggestions, discoveries, and advice. Please write me in care of Mustang Publishing, P.O. Box 3004, Memphis, TN 38173 U.S.A.

Various locales—Fleadh Cheoil na hEireann

This three-day gathering of Ireland's traditional musicians—ballad singers, accordion players, pipers, fiddlers, whistlers, and dancers—takes place annually at a different location. One of the most colorful and exciting cultural events on the Irish calendar, the competition to host the event gets fiercer each year. Recently, Sligo was honored as host city and boasted "the sound of a thousand blended notes to greet you!" Truly an international event, the *fleadh* (pronounced flay kyoh-il) usually draws up to 100,000 people to experience the "sessions" of the century both day and night. For more information, contact Comhaltas Ceoltoiri Eireann, Belgrave Square, Monkstown, Co. Dublin. (late August)

Tralee—Rose of Tralee Festival

She was lovely and fair/Like a Rose of the summer/Yet it was not her beauty alone that won me/O no it was the truth in her eyes ever dawning/That made me love Mary, the Rose of Tralee.

The lyrics of famous Irish tenor John McCormack become personified in Tralee each year, when young women from all over the world arrive to compete for the Waterford Crystal Trophy and the title "Rose of Tralee." Others visitors, nearly 100,000 each year, come to enjoy the range of activities that constitute this festival week. Fireworks, traditional music, races, and just plain merry-making are all part of the fun. With residents and visitors roaming the streets day and night, Tralee assumes a Mardi Gras flavor for the week. (late August)

Kilkenny—Kilkenny Arts Week

Like some of the bigger arts festivals held throughout the world, the Kilkenny show now has a "fringe," which includes exhibits of arts, crafts, photography, and sculpture, and also mime, music, and street theater. The main festival provides all you might expect, including classical music concerts in Kilkenny Castle and St. Canice's Cathedral; country music, jazz, and rock in local hotels and bars; and poetry readings and cabaret shows in restaurants and open-air venues. The week-long event offers a pleasant diversion from busy Dublin, only a few hours' drive away. (mid-August)

September

Lisdoonvarna—Matchmaking Festival of Ireland

The Matchmaking Festival, over 200 years old, is based on an ancient tradition of wealthy landlords taking their sons and daughters to Lisdoonvarna to enjoy the spa waters. The current festival grew from this tradition and now includes the four weekends of September, when the town swells from its usual population of 800 to more than 8,000. Every evening there are over 16 different forms of entertainment—music, singing, dancing, drinking—in addition to the matchmaking, of course.

Those seriously interested in finding a mate can complete an extensive questionnaire, which attempts to match people to potential suitors. According to local playwright and pub owner John B. Keane, who wholeheartedly supports the idea of the festival, "Marriage is a tough confrontation, so anything that can help can't be bad."

For those already perfectly matched, a visit to Lisdoonvarna can be fun nonetheless—for the eating, the drinking, and the enjoyment of a day at the Listowel Races (the second weekend). Another true taste of Irish country life! (throughout Sept.)

Clarenbridge—Oyster Festival

Billing itself as "the home of the world's most famous oyster," Clarenbridge hosts a week of events devoted to seafood. Starting with a fish-cooking demonstration, the week progresses through seafood luncheons, oyster tastings, and an oyster-opening competition, in addition to the pageantry surrounding the "Oyster Queen." Irish entertainment of all varieties accompanies the eating and drinking. For those who prefer less ceremonial homage to the oyster, many local pubs provide casual seafood dining. And for those who prefer another culinary extreme, the nearby Dunguaire Castle offers a medieval banquet, complete with entertainment. (See below.) (early Sept. weekend)

Cork—Murphy's Cork Folk Festival

Organizers of this "folk" event have come to realize that the word has several implications. Since they define it as a focus on "people, honest-to-goodness people," they have tried to combine a broad base of international music with music indigenous to Cork, hoping that the end result will please everyone. Sponsored by the Cork-based Murphy's Brewery (makers of Murphy's Irish Stout, which is never to be confused with rival Guinness), the weekend-long festival has attracted performers from Texas, Africa, England, plus countless Irish groups. (mid-Sept.)

Waterford—Festival of Light Opera

For two weeks each September, amateur companies from the British Isles come to Waterford to compete in operetta performances. Popular productions like South Pacific and The Merry Widow have been staged in recent years. Fringe events include a ball, several varieties of music concerts and competitions, sporting events, and general entertainment. For more information, contact Waterford International Festival of Light Opera, Theatre Royal, Waterford. (mid-Sept.)

Galway—Oyster Festival

Throughout the week-long round of events—all presumably devoted to the consumption of the renowned bivalve mollusk—there's little time to stop and rest. The opening event, the Irish Oyster-Opening Championship, draws participants from around the world, and the winners go on to the World Oyster-Opening Championship. There's truly never a dull moment in Galway! (late Sept. weekend)

October

Dublin—Dublin Theatre Festival

Irish Life magazine wrote that this festival "deserves recognition at least for its survival. Dublin may be a famous theatre city, having produced Sheridan, Wilde, Synge, Yeats, and O'Casey, but it has also been a touchy and hostile environment for the theatre." In 1957, when the festival was established by Brendan Smith, Alan Simpson was on trial for obscenity for producing Tennessee Williams' *The Rose Tattoo*. In 1958, the festival was nearly cancelled for staging works by "blasphemers" like James Joyce, Sean O'Casey, and Samuel Beckett.

Twenty-five years later, the festival has indeed survived, and it functions for two important reasons: to present the best of new Irish theater to the world and to present what's new in world theater to Irish audiences and performers. Theaters participating in the festival include the renowned Abbey, The Gate, The Focus, and The Peacock. For more information, contact Executive Director, Theatre Festival Office, 47 Nassau Street, Dublin 2. (first two weeks of Oct.)

Kinsale—Kinsale Gourmet Festival

Called "the gourmet capital of Ireland," the appealing little town of Kinsale has been increasing its reputation for fine restaurants by promoting them in the form of a festival organized by the Kinsale Good Food Circle. A £65 membership fee entitles patrons to free participation at all festival activities. Patrons must make their own reservations at the restaurant of their choice for each evening. One-day tickets are also available and entitle you to attend the official champagne reception and show at the festival club on Thursday, or the show at the club on Friday, or the Grand Dress Ball (a black-tie affair) on Saturday. (early Oct. weekend)

Ballinasloe—Great October Fair and Festival

In Ballinasloe today, the great link between past and present is the October Fair, and in the minds of the older citizens, the passing year is measured in terms of "before the Fair" or "after the Fair."

Local tradition says the big fair of *Beal Atha na Slua* (the Town of the Ford of the Hosts) began many centuries ago, but it did not get official recognition until 1722 when Frederick Trench applied "to hold a fair on his lands at Dunlo." Sheep and cattle were raised on the pastures, and the limestone in the soil made for strong horses. These same horses proved to be just what the armies of Europe needed, and for years buyers flocked to Ballinasloe to purchase them. The

Fair continued to grow until World War I, when horses were replaced by automobiles. But the tradition of The Fair did not die out, and a local committee made energetic efforts to revive it, which they have done quite admirably.

The Fair caters to all tastes. While still primarily an agricultural show, complete with horse fair, a pony-jumping competition, and a filly and colt competition, there are all types of merriment throughout the week to please urban and rural tastes. The "King of the Fair" presides over all functions in elaborate ceremonial robes, and there are stalls, games, rides, traditional entertainment, and best of all, the delightful people of Ballinasloe. (early Oct.)

Wexford—Wexford Festival Opera

Since its inception in 1951, this festival has often served as a place where promising operatic careers are launched. Staged in the Theatre Royal, a 19th-century, 550-seat opera house, the entire season is filled with warmth and ambiance. Top international singers and musicians present three productions of unusual operas, such as Haydn's *L'Isola Disabitata*, Massenet's *Griselidis*, and Albert's *Tiefland*.

The festival organizers are proud of the support they receive from the townspeople, who share in the production tasks. In addition to the operatic performances, there is a full recital program that runs from noon to midnight daily, plus a congenial atmosphere throughout the town, which makes it a highlight of the Irish social calendar and a tourist delight. For more information, contact Wexford Festival Opera, Theater Royal, High St., Wexford. (late Oct.-early Nov.)

Cork—Guinness Jazz Festival

For three days and four nights on the last weekend of October, Cork, Ireland's third largest city, becomes the jazz capital of Europe. Over 40,000 fans flock here from around the world to welcome the more than 100 bands and internationally acclaimed musicians who take part, including Ella Fitzgerald, Mel Torme, and B. B. King. Concerts and jazz sessions are held throughout the city in pubs, clubs, and hotel lounges. While jazz is hardly an Irish invention, there's a uniquely Irish feel to the festivities. For more information, contact Cork Tourist Office, Grand Parade, Cork.

Comhaltas Ceoiltoirí Éireann

Known simply as Comhaltas, this organization is Ireland's premier cultural movement. Founded in 1951, it has branches in each of the 32 counties of Ireland, as well as in the U.S., Canada, Britain, Luxembourg, and Australia.

Begun by a small group of men and women who decided to strike a blow for Irish culture, Comhaltas has grown to over 400 branches promoting the music, song, dance, and language of Ireland. More than 750,000 people attend Comhaltas events annually.

For a copy of the annual calendar of events write to Comhaltas Headquarters, 32 Belgrave Square, Monkstown, Co. Dublin.

The Irish Country Fair: Part of a Living Tradition

Like so many other things Irish, the holding of fairs goes back so far that its beginnings are delightfully entangled in myth and tradition. There will always be several stories about the origins of each; most people just choose the one that appeals to them best.

Whether originally a pagan ritual or simply a chance for neighbors to bargain on goods and livestock, the country fair has survived and flourished. As it has for centuries, the fair remains a big part of the Irish country social calendar.

At one time, fairs were held on Lammas Day, the first day of August, or later in autumn. The Gregorian calendar and local convenience have altered the dates slightly, but the three premier country fairs—the Puck Fair, Ballinasloe's Great October Fair, and Northern Ireland's Oul' Lammas Fair in Ballycastle—have managed to establish fairly consistent dates annually.

In Killorglin, the Puck Fair is usually August 10, 11, 12; in Ballinasloe, the Great October Fair takes place during the first week of October; and in Ballycastle, the Oul' Lammas Fair is held on the last Monday and Tuesday of August. For more, see their individual entries.

Medieval Castle Banquets

Ireland has always been renowned for its hospitality, a tradition as true today as it was in medieval times. In the 15th century, a nobleman's standing was measured not just on his possessions or his conquests, but on the hospitality he offered to friends and strangers alike. Visitors were greeted on arrival, wined, dined, and entertained in lavish style. They left singing the praises of their genial host.

Visitors to modern Ireland can enjoy similar graciousness at three beautifully preserved medieval castles, where you can become the guest of the Lord of the Manor, take on the mantle of the times, and enjoy a sumptuous banquet while being entertained by musicians, singers, and storytellers. *Céad Mile Fáilte* (''A Hundred Thousand Welcomes'') is offered twice nightly at Bunratty Castle (Co. Clare), Knappogue Castle (Co. Clare), and Dunguaire Castle (Co. Galway).

Bunratty Castle, Bunratty
The most complete and authentic medieval castle in Ireland, Bunratty is only eight miles from Shannon Airport. Built in 1469, the cas-

tle has been magnificently restored to its former glory, with furnishings and tapestries reflecting the style and fashion of the 15th century.

At Bunratty, you can share a banquet with the Earl of Thomond, drink fine wines, and sip its famous Bunratty Mead, while the renowned Bunratty singers entertain throughout the evening. Variety and spice resound at a Bunratty banquet. (Open year-round.)

Knappogue Castle, Quin

Beautifully restored in authentic medieval style, Knappogue was originally built in 1467 as the premier castle of the McNamara tribe, which dominated the area for 1,000 years. Knappogue offers its visitors good food and flowing wine. There's music and dance, with mime and rhyme to round off a traditional evening of medieval entertainment. (Open May-Oct.)

Dunguaire Castle, Kinvara

Standing magnificently on the shores of Galway Bay, Dunguaire Castle has long been the proud monument of the 7th-century stronghold of Guaire, King of Connaught. The history of the castle and its associations with the area are tellingly illustrated inside its hallowed walls. In addition to its fine seafood and wines, Dunguaire provides dramatic entertainment from the works of greats like Yeats, Synge, and St. John Gogarty. An evening at Dunguaire Castle is a memory steeped in tradition. (May-Sept.)

Shannon Ceili, Bunratty Folk Park

For those who prefer a more down-to-earth, homey event, the Shannon Ceili is the perfect way to end the day. Authentic Irish stew, fresh soda bread, apple pie and cream, and a cup of tea top the ceili menu, while entertainment is provided by the fiddle, the accordion, the flute, and the bodhran. With its keynote simplicity, the ceili is one that reflects the other side of Irish entertainment, but "one that will surely touch the strings of your Irish heart." (May-Sept.)

Banquets and the Shannon Ceili are offered at 5:45pm and 9:00pm daily. Book in advance through B.M.I.T., 149 Main St., Medway, Massachusetts 02053 USA (800-982-2299) or Shannon Castle Tours, Shannon International Airport, Co. Clare.

Irish Holidays

New Year's Day, St. Patrick's Day (March 17), Good Friday, Easter Monday, June Holiday, August Holiday, October Holiday, Christmas, St. Stephen's Day (Dec. 26).

For literature and further information, contact the **Irish Tourist Board**. In the U.S., the address is 757 Third Ave., New York, NY 10017 (212-418-0800) or (800-223-6470).

Northern Ireland

May

Belfast—Civic Festival and Lord Mayor's Show

Fourteen days of civic celebrations include concerts, competitions, and exhibitions. The festivities begin with the Lord Mayor's Show, when Belfast streets are filled with floats and bands. (mid-May)

Ballyclare—Ballyclare Horse Fair

The horse fair is the highlight of the Ballyclare May Festival, which usually runs May 21-28. You can buy a horse or donkey (perhaps you'd better just watch) and see the time-honored tradition of horse trading at its finest.

June

Carrickfergus—Medieval Banquets

Much like its counterparts in the south (at Bunratty, Knappogue, and Dunguaire), Carrickfergus Castle offers marvelous feasting at the table of John de Courcy. Musicians and dancers in 12th-century costumes serve a traditional Irish meal. (weekends)

Ballycastle—Fleadh Amhran agus Rince

This traditional Irish festival of song and dance—a weekend full of genuine Irish music and high-stepping—is held annually in Ballycastle near the end of the month.

Belleek—Fiddle Stone Festival

Fiddlers from all over Ireland converge on this pretty village to play in honor of a famous 18th-century fiddle player. The fiddle event is part of a ten-day Beleek Festival with fringe events. (late June)

Glenariff—Feis na nGleann

Feis (pronounced "fesh") has origins in 19th-century interest in Ireland's native sports (like hurling), culture, and language. Dancing, music, poetry, arts and crafts, and sporting competitions make this feis a pleasant addition to the calendar. (late June)

Antrim—Northern Ireland Game and Country Fair

Held on the grounds of the beautiful country estate of Shane's Castle, this real Irish fair is considered a premier field sports event. It celebrates all aspects of outdoor sports and country life. (late June/early July)

July

Hilltown—Booley Fair
This event is billed as "five days of sheer nostalgia." The blacksmith, stonemason, and spinner demonstrate vanishing skills typical of Irish country life from a bygone era. There's also a sheep fair, concerts featuring traditional music and dance, and street stalls full of interesting things to eat, drink, and buy. (early July)

Belfast—Battle of the Boyne Celebrations
The biggest and best-known annual parade Northern Ireland, this march celebrates the historic Protestant victory at the Boyne River. Fought between two 17th-century kings, it is remembered in colorful style by the Orangemen, who march with bands playing and banners flying to the parade grounds to hear political and religious speeches. People take advantage of "the Twelfth" to eat, drink, and dance the night away. (July 12)

Scarva—Sham Fight
This traditional event has been staged here for 200 years. A huge parade with dozens of bands converges on this picturesque village for a symbolic re-enactment of the Battle of the Boyne. The "fight" is a joust between two horsemen in period costume, one portraying William of Orange, the other James II. (July 13)

Carrickfergus—Lughnasa Medieval Fair
The superb Castle of Carrickfergus is the setting for this weekend of medieval entertainment and traditional stalls. The name Lughnasa is derived from a quarterly feast of the old Irish year. (late July)

August

throughout—Hibernians Parade
On August 15th, the Catholic population of Northern Ireland celebrates the Feast of the Assumption with processions, open-air meetings, and Gaelic sports. Hibernians in green sashes march with banners and Gaelic pipers in saffron kilts.

Lisburn—Irish Festival of Good Beer
At least 12 great beers are yours for the tasting at Hilden Brewery during this annual three-day event. In addition to sampling, the festival offers competitions and various entertainment. (late August)

Ballycastle—Oul' Lammas Fair
The oldest of the traditional country fairs held throughout Ireland (north and south), this fair gained its charter in 1606. There are sheep and pony sales, but in general, it's a big social occasion, with a variety of entertainment throughout the day and even more at night. (late August)

September

Belfast—Belfast Folk Week

For this weekend, downtown Belfast is dedicated entirely to Irish folk talent—music, dancing, a songwriter's workshop, ceili bands, and, of course, those famous Irish fiddlers! (mid-Sept.)

Dromore—Dromore Horse Fair

This little cathedral town hosts a cavalcade of horse-drawn vehicles and big horses in a charming display of rural Irish life. (late Sept.)

October

Larne—Mounthill Fair

This traditional horse fair dates to the 17th century, and like so many others throughout the country, it provides a vast array of all types and breeds of horses. It's a colorful conclusion to the Northern Ireland calendar. (early Oct.)

Holidays in Northern Ireland

New Year's Day, St. Patrick's Day (March 17), Easter Monday, May Day (May 1), Spring Bank Holiday (last Monday in May), Orangeman's Day (July 12), Summer Bank Holiday (last Monday in August), Christmas Day, Boxing Day (Dec. 26).

For literature and further information, contact the **Northern Ireland Tourist Board**. In the U.S., the address is 276 Fifth Avenue, Suite 500, New York, NY 10001 (212-686-6250).

3

Great Britain: England, Scotland, & Wales

Like the Republic of Ireland and Northern Ireland, which share a common land but are divided politically, England, Scotland, and Wales are culturally separate, traditionally distinct, and linguistically unique. Therefore, a visit to London is a far cry from a visit to Llangollen or Loch Lomond, and a stay in Glasgow is quite different from an evening at Glyndebourne. Likewise, rugged events like Wales' Viking Festival (billed as a weekend where "hordes of Vikings gather to feast and fight") and Scotland's traditional Highland Games and Clan Gatherings are quite different from the English Maypole Dancing or 'Obby 'Oss festivities.

Aside from the countless music festivals, most British events stem from traditional, regal, or historical customs. Several groups like the English Civil War Society and the Sealed Knot are devoted to battle re-creations and jousting tournaments combined with costumed events and period entertainment. For any visitor to England, they are spectacular pages from history.

As you might expect, a score of events pay homage to literary sons like Shakespeare, Dickens, and Chaucer. And there are sporting events that reek of royalty and British tradition like Wimbledon, Royal Ascot, and the Henley Regatta.

To travel to Scotland is to immerse yourself in a spectacle of scenery and spirit, both festive and malted. Scottish Tourist Board material suggests "You can make every day your own festival on the Malt Whiskey Trail through Speyside, where some of Scotland's finest malt whiskey is distilled from the magical combination of carefully malted barley and pure snowmelt water from the Grampian Highlands."

The Highlands. What visitor would want to miss a Highland Clan Gathering replete with bagpipes and kilts, or the spectacle of the Highland Games that permeate the countryside in the summer? *Festival Europe!* lists more than 75 such events, including the most celebrated Braemar Royal Highland Gathering near Balmoral, Queen Elizabeth's summer home.

Scotland's cities, Glasgow and Edinburgh, often serve as the base for visitors, and both provide spectacular entertainment. Glasgow was named Europe's Culture Capital in 1990, and Edinburgh bears the title "Festival City" for its renowned International Festival and Military Tattoo. Theater critic Clive Barnes said, "The diversity and abundance makes the city for three weeks a year the center of the cultural world." Along with its Fringe, the entire city is so filled with activities of international renown that you could spend an entire vacation in Edinburgh and never be bored.

Wales is a land of song, a land of history, a land of fun, whose friendly citizens have won world fame for their poetry and song festivals called *eisteddfodau*. After a visit to the 40-year-old Llangollen International Musical Eisteddfod, the poet Dylan Thomas wrote, "The only surprising thing about miracles is that they sometimes happen." In Wales, this and other miracles have been occurring for centuries and continue to enhance the festival calendar.

England

May

Padstow—'Obby 'Oss Festival

The Padstow May Day event, reputed to be the oldest dance festival in the country, perhaps in all Europe, marks the coming of summer and dates from pre-Christian times, when the horse was worshipped as a fertility god. Beginning at midnight on May 1, the May Song is heard around town, and at 10:30am the stable door opens and the 'Oss appears—a black canvas-skirted monster, six feet in diameter, with a witch-doctor's mask. The 'Oss scares and charms those who come to see him, while his colorfully dressed followers sing and dance to old Morris tunes and drums. The day-long event ends at 9:30pm, when the singing and dancing cease and the 'Oss dies, only to be reincarnated again next May Day. Padstow is 11 miles north of Newquay.

Minehead—Sailor's Hobby Horse

Like its counterpart in Padstow, the Mindhead (Somerset) May Day celebration is so old that, according to villager John Leich, "there's no accurate record of its commencement." The Sailor's Hobby Horse, constructed in the village and festooned with ribbons, is carried throughout Minehead and dances to the sound of melodies and drums. If you fail to give the horse a coin, it aims its tail at you with considerable force. Legend has it that the original intent of the horse was to scare away the Danes and other invaders. The festivities begin on the eve of May Day and continue for three days, with a number of ceremonies associated at various times and venues.

Welford-on-Avon—Maypole Dancing

The ancient, striped Maypole erected on the village green is one of a long line of poles dating back two centuries. It's decked with colored ribbons, and children dance and skip around it in the age-old custom.

ENGLAND

Brighton—Brighton Festival

This international festival brings artists from Britain and around the world to perform in symphonic and chamber concerts, opera, ballet, jazz, pop, theater, and dance. Founded in 1967, a special character of the Brighton event is the locales chosen for the performances: the Royal Pavilion (once the seaside residence of the Prince of Wales), the Dome Concert Hall, Theatre Royal, and St. Peter's Church.

The Merrydown Jazz Festival, held with the main festival, features jazz events ranging from pub dates to concerts in the Dome.

For more information, contact Brighton International Festival, 111 Church St., Brighton BN1 1UD. (throughout May)

Newbury—Newbury Spring Festival

Concerts, exhibitions, jazz, and children's events comprise the Newbury fest, first celebrated in 1978. Special programs have included the Philharmonic Orchestra, Halle Orchestra, Bournemouth Symphony Orchestra, and a performance of Handel's *Messiah*. Beautiful churches and fine country houses in the Newbury area host many concerts. An important visual arts program coincides. For more information, contact Festival Administrator, Suite 4, Town Hall, Newbury, Berkshire. (mid-May for 10 days)

Moulton—Moulton Village Festival

The festival here grew out of the local village fête and old traditional May Queen ceremony. These customs continue as an important part of the events with the accompanying Morris dancing, music, arts, and crafts. Morris dancing has strong Maytime associations and those participating wear bells and hats bedecked with spring flowers. (mid-May)

Felixtowe—Felixtowe Folk Festival

The Suffolk District of the English Folk Dance and Song Society organizes this weekend fair, which promotes folk music, song, and dance in the area. (mid-May)

Malvern—Malvern Festival

In 1929, Sir Barry Jackson invited George Bernard Shaw to write a play for what would become an international festival. In 1977, the music of Edward Elgar, England's most famous musical son, was added to the format. In 1983, the committee decided to concentrate the musical content of the festival on British composers and, wherever possible, include drama complementary to this theme.

In conjunction with the main event, locals interested in music and the arts operate "the fringe." Since 1977, the fringe has added events yearly and now boasts over 120 performances, workshops, and exhibitions. It's said to be the largest in Britain outside Edinburgh.

For more information, contact Festival Administrator, The Winter

Gardens, Grange Road, Malvern, Worcestershire WR14 3HB. (last
two weeks in May)

Glydebourne—Glydebourne Opera Festival

Founded in 1934 by John Christie and his wife, singer Audrey Mild-
may, this renowned artistic endeavor showcases five or six operas
each season from the third week of May to the second week of August. It's located on the Christie's country estate 50 miles south of
London, and special trains leave London's Victoria Station for opera
performances. The London Philharmonic Orchestra has been in residence since 1964.

One of the delights of Glydebourne is its long intermission (about
75 minutes), during which dinner is served in restaurants or patrons
picnic in the gardens. Another special quality is that evening dress,
"formal or informal," is advised. Performances begin at 5:30pm.
For more information, contact Festival Box Office, Lewes, East Sussex BN8 5UU. (mid-May to mid-August)

Chester—Chester Folk Festival

Based on traditional English song and dance, this week-long festival
is one of the largest and most established folk fests in northwest England. A large crafts market and music and dance workshops provide added interest to the charming walled city of Chester. Founded
by a Roman legion on the Dee River in the First Century A.D., the
city reached its pinnacle as a bustling port in the 13th and 14th centuries. It still boasts two miles of fortified walls intact. (late May)

Bath—Bath International Festival

A candlelight serenade opens this prestigious festival, an event perfectly matched to the graceful Georgian architecture and Roman
baths for which the city is famous. Beginning with the concert at dusk
in Victoria Park, the festival continues through 17 days of concerts,
recitals, and (usually) two operas. Conceived in 1947 as a children's
musical affair, the festival now includes theater, film, jazz, dance,
chamber music, and orchestral events as well. For more information,
contact Festival Office, Linley House, 1 Pierrepont Place, Bath, Avon
BA1 1JY. (late May-June)

Nottingham—Nottingham Festival

This general arts festival offers an opportunity for top-class artists
to appear in the popular tourist area made famous by Robin Hood
and his Merry Men. The whole spectrum of the arts is covered, but
part of the event is geared toward children.

Nottingham offers the visitor a wide range of attractions in addition to the festival, including Nottingham Castle, dating from 1068;
the Brewhouse Yard Museum, which houses the city's folk art; the
Robin Hood Statue and the Nottingham Story; and nearby Newstead
Abbey, the home of Lord Byron. (late May-June)

Grantham—Belvoir Castle Jousting Tournament

Located only a short distance from Nottingham, Belvoir Castle is the ancestral home of the Duke and Duchess of Ruland and provides a magnificent backdrop for a variety of functions. The most important event is the Jousting Tournament, held on several summer weekends including the May Bank Holiday, the last Sundays in July, and the August Bank Holiday weekend. Mounted knights dressed in authentic medieval costume provide a taste of Olde England, as well as free entertainment for visitors to the scenic Lincolnshire area. For more information, contact Jimmy Durrands, Belvoir Castle Estate Office, Grantham, Lincolnshire NG31 6BR.

Rochester—Dickens Festival

Begun in 1978, this event celebrates Charles Dickens' connections with Rochester and pays tribute to the man, his work, and his affection for the Medway Towns. Festival events include recitals, plays, music hall entertainment, and street fairs. Thousands of people dress in Victorian costumes to provide local color to the festivities and heighten the Dickensian spirit. For those interested in the literary aspects of the festival, several groups conduct Dickens readings and lectures. Costumed Dickens characters wandering the streets include Fagin ("always popular, but watch your pockets"); Miss Haversham in her bridal gown, searching for her husband-who-never-was; and Mr. Pickwick. A great day-trip from London, Rochester's Dickens Festival makes for fine weekend entertainment. (late May)

June

Aldeburgh—Aldeburgh Festival of Music and Arts

This festival, founded in 1948 by the English composer Benjamin Britten, attracts artists of the highest international standard to the concert hall at Snape. The festival includes a wide variety of events—chamber and symphonic concerts, recitals, lectures, and exhibitions—covering works from the 15th century to the present. Indeed, the *Financial Times* said the Aldeburgh "possesses almost every conceivable virtue to make a successful British festival—the finest concert hall in the country (and) an acute sense of place and tradition." Venues include Snape Maltings Concert Hall, Jubilee Hall, Oxford Church, and Blythburgh Church. For more information, contact Aldeburgh Foundation, High Street, Aldeburgh, Suffolk IP15 5AX. (mid-June, for two weeks)

Truro—Three Spires Festival

The Three Spires Festival developed from a festival held in a little creek-side church between 1964 and 1980. Now held in Truro Cathedral, the baroque and early classical music event brings music and other arts of the highest quality to Cornwall. (mid-June, for two weeks)

Sidmouth—Sidmouth Arts Festival

The Sidmouth Arts Festival starts the summer season of events in this area. All the performing arts are represented by both national and international professional artists, with orchestral works, drama, dance, and poetry. There's also a large arts and crafts exhibition displaying works typical of this area. (mid-June)

Exeter—Exeter Festival

Exeter is surrounded by some of the most beautiful countryside in Britain, including the wilderness of Dartmoor and Exmoor. Founded by the Romans almost 2,000 years ago, Exeter offers every period of major English architecture and provides a lovely backdrop for the two-week event. The magnificent Gothic cathedral is the setting for concerts featuring international artists and orchestras. For more information, contact Festival Office, Exeter, Devon EX1 1JN. (mid-June)

London—Beating Retreat of Massed Bands

Not a festival—but surely an event that represents what British pomp and ceremony are all about—the Beating Retreat is a fabulous display of over 500 musicians who assemble and perform as the Massed Bands of Queen Elizabeth. Held at Horse Guards, Whitehall, this assembly is really a warm-up for the more spectacular show that follows to celebrate Her Majesty's birthday. (mid-June)

London—Trooping the Colour

This military occasion of music and pageantry is held to celebrate the Queen's birthday officially, although her real birthday is April 21. The Queen, on horseback, leaves Buckingham Palace with a detachment of the Household Cavalry, rides down the Mall, then turns right into Horse Guards Parade. After a display of precision marching and riding by the five guard regiment, the Queen takes the salute as the colors of the First Battalion of the Irish Guards are paraded. If you want grandstand tickets, you must write between January and late February to The Brigade Major, Headquarters Household Division, Horse Guards, Whitehall, London SW1A 2AX. Enclose an international reply coupon. Names are drawn by lottery, and tickets cost about $10.

Greenwich—Greenwich Festival

Perhaps the most unique aspect of this 20-year-old arts festival is the fact that it is represented by three distinct groups: professional, including internationally known performing artists; local amateur artists and organizations affiliated with the Greenwich Arts Council; and community festivals centered around the various villages, housing estates, and churches within the borough. The Greenwich area, one of the highlights of tourist London, contains many wonderful venues to host a festival of uncommon variety. Each year's festival starts with an open-air concert in Cutty Sark Gardens and ends with a concert featuring an hour-long interval à la Glyndebourne. For more information, contact Greenwich Festival, 151 Powis Street, London SE18 6JL. (early June)

Ascot—Royal Ascot

Attended by members of the Royal Family, this important weekend event in the racegoer's calendar is as popular for its grand show of fashion and outrageous hats as for its high standard of racing. For admission to the Royal Enclosure, overseas visitors should apply to their respective Ambassador or High Commission in London, or obtain information from The Secretary, Grand Stand Office, Ascot Racecourse, Ascot, Berkshire SL5 7JN. (mid-June)

York—York Festival and Mystery Plays

This is one of England's largest festivals, the central event being the internationally known York Mystery Plays, a community event equalled only by Oberammergau. Like its German counterpart, it is performed in the open, within the ruins of St. Mary's Abbey. The event includes a cast of hundreds of York villagers. Dating from 1350, the Mystery Plays were staged by medieval guilds of York. Now in revival, they are presented much as they were then—from pageant wagons that move through the streets in locations near the River Ouse and from the ruins of the 11th-century Abbey.

In addition to the plays (performed only every four years, next in 1992), the music festival held concurrently offers outstanding orchestral, choral, dramatic, poetic, and cinematic performances. Venues are, typically, the Cathedral York Minster—the largest and grandest Gothic cathedral in England—and the city's many medieval churches, guild halls, country houses, and hospitals.

The ancient walled city of York, 200 miles north of London, is a remarkably complete example of a fort-town of the Middle Ages, with its half-timbered houses, early castle, interesting museums, and, for the non-medievalist, fine Georgian mansions.

For more information, contact York Festival, 1 Newgate, York YO1 2LA. (mid-June, for two weeks)

Dorchester—Dorchester Abbey Festival

Founded in 1959, this festival reflects the special qualities of the Abbey and its relationship with the village and surrounding countryside. Accordingly, the two-week event concentrates on professional music inspired by the Abbey's fine acoustics, while it retains a local character through exhibitions and traditional arts. (late June)

Lincoln—Water Festival and Wine Festival

Lincolnites celebrate the first week of June with both water and wine festivals, the latter honoring Lincoln's sister city in Germany, Neustadt ander Weinstrasse, with abundant wine sampling. The Water Festival celebrates with boat parades and a carnival atmosphere.

The city of Lincoln boasts a strong historical tradition, dating to the Roman occupation. The tower of its cathedral, which dates to 1072, houses one of the heaviest church bells in England, "Great Tom of Lincoln," a five-ton behemoth that rings every hour on the hour. The classical cloisters, designed by Christopher Wren, complement the Cathedral. Also, its library contains one of the four remaining copies of the Magna Carta. (early June)

Glastonbury—Fair and Pilgrimage
Originally a religious celebration, the fair has become somewhat of a pop festival with singing, dancing, and assorted mystical happenings. Because of the legends that surround Glastonbury (the town is the birthplace of Christianity in England, and supposedly King Arthur's bones rest beneath Glastonbury Cathedral), it has always attracted a sub-culture of mystics who keep the fair going each year. Glastonbury is five miles southwest of Wells, 20 miles northeast of Taunton. The pilgrimage is held at the Abbey ruins. (late June)

Ludlow—Ludlow Festival
Concerts, theater, exhibitions, films, jazz, children's events, historical tours, and fringe events mark this two-week festival set in the wooded hills and pastures of the English-Welsh borders. A charming market town, Ludlow provides an ideal setting for a festival and offers a fine center for touring Shropshire. The centerpiece of each festival is a Shakespeare play performed in the Inner Bailey of Ludlow Castle, which recently celebrated its 900th anniversary. In addition to the Castle, there is a series of concerts held in the 15th-century parish church. For more information, contact Festival Office, Castle Square, Ludlow, Shropshire SY8 1AY. (late June-July)

London—All-England Lawn Tennis Championships
Commonly known as Wimbledon, the two weeks of tennis here are far more than just the ultimate tennis spectacle. Like so many sporting events in England (Ascot and Henley among them), Wimbledon means tons of strawberries, gallons of champagne, and thousands of fans from around the globe, including the Royal Family. For more information, contact All-England Lawn Tennis and Croquet Club, Church Road, Wimbledon, London SW19 5AE. (late June/early July)

July
Ambleside—Rush-Bearing Festival
This traditional festival, unique to the Lake District area, is thought to have its origins in a Roman harvest ceremony. It's a simple, colorful event in which flowers and rushes are carried through the streets to St. Mary's Church. Traditionally held on the first Saturday of July.

Chichester—Chichester "900" Festivities

In 1975, to celebrate the 900th anniversary of the founding of its cathedral, Chichester held a birthday party. It was so successful, the party has become an annual two-week affair, with each festival being numbered 901, 902, etc. to correspond with the age of the cathedral, the city's breathtaking Norman landmark. The festivities include two weeks of concerts (many held in the cathedral), recitals, exhibitions, and outdoor spectacles. Impressive venues throughout the lovely city host the events. (early July)

Chichester—Chichester Festival Theatre Season

Chichester is pleasant anytime in summer, but it's even more delightful when combined with a night at the theater. The Chichester Festival Theatre Season, which runs May-Sept., is famous for its variety of presentations—from Robert Bolt's *A Man for All Seasons* to Oscar Wilde's *An Ideal Husband*. According to critic Felix Barker, "A summer evening in Sussex calls for a special kind of entertainment; that is, after all, a festival theatre playing to people, some of whom have left damp bathing costumes in their cars and can still feel the sand between their toes. This has very little to do with the art of the Theatre. It has everything to do with the Theatre of Enjoyment." For more information, contact Box Office, Oaklands Park, Chichester, West Sussex PO19 4AP.

Birmingham—Jazz Festival

Actually a huge, open-air jam session, the Birmingham event offers jazz as accessible as it gets—mostly free and on the streets. Parades, a jazz band ball, and the MRB Jam Session are all included in the week-long festival. (early July)

Henley-On-Thames—Royal Regatta

Rowing fans watch this international regatta from grandstands or from boats moored to the riverbank. Like Royal Ascot, this is both a popular weekend social event and a sporting competition. The regatta enclosure is open to the public. Immediately following the races, the town continues in the spirit with a Festival of Music and the Arts. For more information, contact The Secretary, Henley Royal Regatta Headquarters, Regatta House, Henley-on-Thames, Oxfordshire RG9 2LY. (early July)

Warwick—Warwick Arts Festival

Started as the Warwick Arts Week and built mostly around St. Mary's Church and its choir, the 10-day festival has expanded considerably in recent years. Located in a beautiful tourist area near Stratford-Upon-Avon, the town presents a variety of events not offered by neighboring festivals—namely, all forms of music, dance, and drama. (early July)

Cheltenham—Cheltenham Festival of Music

This international festival of music began in 1945 as a festival of contemporary British music. From its small beginnings encompassing a long weekend of orchestral concerts, it has expanded to a full fortnight, including three weekends. With chamber music every morning, orchestral concerts or recitals every evening, opera, jazz, ballet, and a range of fringe events, the Cheltenham festival presents something for every taste. For more information, contact Box Office, Town Hall, Imperial Square, Cheltenham, Gloucestershire GL50 1QA. (mid-July)

London—City of London Festival

The square mile of the City contains a rich array of buildings of historical and architectural interest—and a perfect festival setting. St. Paul's Cathedral, the Tower of London, Mansion House, the Barbican Centre, a host of fine churches, and the City's magnificent open spaces provide venues for two weeks of concerts, opera performances, poetry, drama, dance, and street events. (mid-July)

Lichfield—Lichfield Festival

Lichfield is world-famous for the three spires of its cathedral, The Ladies of the Vale, and for being the birthplace of Dr. Samuel Johnson. During Lichfield's festival, concerts with international artists, orchestras, and ensembles occur daily in the cathedral and Lady Chapel, as well as the church of St. Chads and the Civic and Guild Halls. Visitors to the city will find interesting shops, historic buildings, and charming villages nearby. (early July)

Chester—Summer Music Festival

Chester has had periodic music festivals since 1972 and currently offers a nine-day music fest, in which its bustling historic streets are complemented by an active and exciting musical program. The festival presents music from all periods, in venues ranging from Chester's ancient cathedral to smaller churches and civic buildings. In addition to the major festival, there is also a fringe to provide a "mini-Edinburgh." Set between the Welsh mountains and the Cheshire plain, this old Roman city is an exceptional festival center. (mid-July)

Cambridge—Cambridge Festival

Established to encourage performances of opera, drama, ballet, folk, and classical dancing, this two-week festival draws artists of international fame to perform with groups from the colleges. All events take place in some of Britain's most beautiful buildings, including Ely Cathedral, FitzWilliam Museum, the Corn Exchange, and the College Chapels of King's, St. John's, and Jesus. For more information, contact Festival Office, Mandela House, 4 Regent Street, Cambridge CB2 1BY. (mid-July)

King's Lynn—King's Lynn Festival

For the last 40 years, the ancient borough of King's Lynn has been attracting visitors to its annual festival to hear artists of international renown, to enjoy the historic buildings of the area, and to savor the friendly atmosphere. The multi-media, multi-musical event also includes the now-familiar "fringe." For more information, contact Festival Office, 27 King Street, King's Lynn, Norfolk PE30 IHA. (late July)

August

Buxton—Buxton Festival

The beautiful Georgian spa town of Buxton in Derbyshire possesses an exquisitely restored opera house, providing the centerpiece for the only arts festival in Britain with its own opera company. Each year, the three-week festival includes a range of events relating to a central theme and presents new productions of rarely seen operas. Past festivals included Thomas' *Hamlet*, Purcell's *King Arthur*, and Rossini's *L'occasione fa il ladro*. As the London *Sunday Times* once said, "In its aims and achievements, the Buxton Festival is what a festival should be." For more information, contact Box Office, 1 Crescent View, Hall Bank, Buxton, Derbyshire SK17 6EN. (mid-August)

Grasmere—Rush-Bearing Ceremony

Like its neighboring village of Ambleside, Grasmere also holds a rush-bearing ceremony on the Saturday nearest St. Oswald's Day (August 5). An added attraction is the gingerbread, a local specialty, which is distributed to the bearers.

Sidmouth—International Folk Festival

This well-known and popular week-long event aims to promote and preserve folk dance, song, and music. It's one of several fests sponsored by the English Folk Dance and Song Society. (early August)

Broadstairs—Broadstairs Folk Week

This week-long festival also seeks to preserve English folk song, dance, and music. Though designed to promote local knowledge and appreciation of folk traditions, all visitors will be entertained by the performances. (mid-August)

Worcester, Hereford, Gloucester—Three Choirs Festival

The oldest continuous music festival in Europe, with a history spanning more than 260 years, the Three Choirs Festival rotates each year between the cathedrals of Worcester, Hereford, and Gloucester. It has long been regarded as one of the friendliest of festivals, with its unique feature being a chorus of over 300 choir members and locals from the three counties. The cathedrals remain the center for all the major concerts, while important performances are held in several other locations. The festival offers a rich fare of traditional and contemporary masterpieces, and the chorus is supported by the City of Birmingham Orchestra, the Royal Liverpool Philharmonic, and the English String Orchestra. There is also an enterprising fringe festival. For more information, contact Festival Society, 132 Henwick Road, Worcester WR2 5PB. (late August)

Rochester—Norman Rochester

For a remarkable experience of "living history," visit Rochester Castle for its Norman weekend. Archery, falconry, trial by combat, war horses, tournaments, music, and dance all combine to capture the spirit of Norman England. (late August)

Winchester—Southern Cathedrals Festival

The venues for this event are the three cathedrals of Winchester, Salisbury, and Chichester. The performances are given mainly by the choirs of the three cathedrals and include a variety of church music, organ recitals, and services. Of course, all three cathedrals are splendid to visit, but when combined with the music of the festival, they are truly a rare delight.

Winchester's cathedral stands spiritually and physically in the center of the city. Its massive transepts are Norman, but the long nave was the work of a 14th-century bishop. It also houses a memorial to British author Jane Austen. Salisbury's elegant cathedral is crowned with the highest spire and oldest clock (circa 1386) in the country. Plus, Salisbury is only 10 miles from Stonehenge. The Chichester Cathedral is largely Norman, built between 1091 and 1199. Its 15th-century bell tower is the only example of a detached belfry in England. (mid-August)

Ely—Ely Folk Weekend

This festival aims to present the best in English folksong and -dance in an area that was once the stronghold of traditional music. English country and ceilidh, Cotswold, Border, and Northwest Morris dancing are featured, as well as Irish, Scottish, Welsh, and East Anglican music and arts. (mid-August)

Canterbury—Chaucer Festival

This series of festivals was organized to contribute to the enjoyment of Geoffrey Chaucer and his work. In 1987, a huge celebration marked the 600th anniversary of The Canterbury Tales. (late August)

Grantham—Belvoir Castle Jousting

Belvoir Castle is the setting for this authentic medieval jousting tournament. (see May for details)

Arundel—Arundel Festival

Held for nine days each August, this festival takes place in a charming South Downs resort dominated by Arundel Castle. Its magnificent Tilting Yard is used as an open-air theater to stage Shakespeare plays, dances, and opera events. Many other events are held in connection with the festival, including many for children. (late August)

September

Salisbury—Salisbury Festival

Each day of this two-week festival, Salisbury hosts events throughout the city. Venues include the cathedral, City Hall, St. Martin's Church, and the Guildhall. An interesting aspect of the Salisbury event is its four-year cycle celebrating the four elements: earth, fire, water, and air. A recent festival, for example, lavishly expressed the fire theme and included a rare performance of *Prometheus, Poem of Fire* by the Royal Philharmonic Orchestra. When water was celebrated in 1989, the fest was headed by *Noye's Fludde* by Britten, *La Mer* by Debussy, and both Handel's and Telemann's *Water Music*. For more information, contact King's House, 65 The Close, Salisbury, Wiltshire SP1 2EN. (early Sept.)

Tewkesbury—Tewkesbury Festival of the Arts

This 10-day festival endeavors to include all the arts—theater, dance, music, visual arts—and its concluding event is truly a tourist delight. On the last Saturday of the festival, the entire town dresses in Victorian costume for Dickens' Day and pays homage to the English novelist. For tourists interested in recapturing a spirit of old England, Tewkesbury is an excellent choice. (late Sept.)

Windsor—Windsor Festival

This event presents a balanced program of orchestral, choral, and chamber music performed by top national and international musicians. The beautiful Windsor Castle State Rooms, St. George's Chapel, Eton College, the Theater Royal, and Windsor's Parish Church are venues during the two-week festival. For more information, contact Windsor Festival, Dial House, Englefield Green, Surrey TW20 0DU. (mid-Sept.)

October

Canterbury—Canterbury Festival

This international mixed arts festival was founded in 1984 to utilize the geographic and cultural links between Kent and mainland Europe. Each year, the event takes a European country as its theme, reverting to the arts of Great Britain every third year. The three-week festival enhances the cultural life of East Kent considerably and encourages tourists to visit the area in the autumn. As you might expect, the cathedral plays a major role in the festival.

The Canterbury Festival also has its own fringe events, which try to balance and counterpoint the main festival by presenting work new to the town. The fringe usually chooses to use the main event's theme indirectly to create its own statement. (early Oct.)

Nottingham—Goose Fair

According to Nottingham Borough Records, the Goose Fair was first mentioned in 1541. But centuries before, the Charter of King Edward I referred to city fairs on the Feast of St. Matthew, September 21, and Nottingham folks believe this is the origin of today's Goose Fair, now celebrated on the first Thursday, Friday, and Saturday in October on the Forest Recreation Ground. Promotional literature describes the fair as "acres and acres of colour and delight, mushy peas and Grantham gingerbread, gentle Edwardian roundabouts and Space Age stomach-turners, strong men and small mice—a Nottingham extravaganza." In essence, it's an enormous carnival, Nottingham-style, and it should delight any visitor.

Stratford-Upon-Avon—Mop Fair

Stratford's Mop Fair is a survivor of the ancient Hiring Fair, held in the town as early as the 14th century, when laborers and domestic servants would line up in rows wearing or carrying some symbol of their trade (shepherds with tufts of white wool, maids with mops, etc.). After a period of "sizing up," the domestics would then offer their services to the local gentry. Today's mop fairs last a day rather than a week and are purely an occasion for revelry, with a huge funfair and side shows. Venues for side shows in Stratford are along Wood, High, Bridge, and Rother Streets. One of the classic ingredients of the old English fair is a large brick fireplace, in which a whole ox is roasted. Fair-goers can buy slices and maintain this ancient tradition. (mid-Oct.)

Later in October (usually the third weekend), the Runaway Mop is held. Traditionally, the event gave any dissatisfied employers or employees an opportunity to break their working contracts and make alternative arrangements. Stratford's version is a scaled-down interpretation of this English folk custom.

Additional Mop and Runaway Mop Fairs are held in Tewkesbury (Gloucestershire), Cirencester (Gloucestershire), and Warwick (Warwickshire).

Norwich—Norfolk and Norwich Festival

This 10-day festival recently changed from a triennial to an annual event. Traditionally a music festival, it has begun to incorporate other art forms, especially dance. The fine Norman cathedral, the medieval St. Andrew's concert hall, and the Castle Museum head a variety of interesting venues. For more information, contact Director, St. Andrew's Hall, Norwich NR3 1AU. (mid-Oct.)

Perranporth—Perranporth-Lowender Festival

Each Celtic nation holds its own festival to promote its native culture.

This week-long festival, billed as "Cornwall's Festival," presents a grand opportunity to see the Cornish people in action. (mid-Oct.)

Maypoles & Mop Fairs: English Heritage Keeps Traditions Alive

As one would expect in the heart of a country rich in tradition, intriguing customs and festivities have been preserved through the years. While many of England's unique customs probably originated in pagan times, others are more modern.

Two organizations dedicated to preserving and promoting English traditions are the English Folk Dance and Song Society, founded in 1932, and English Heritage, a group that brings history alive by recreating battles and staging events in period costumes at historic settings. Both groups provide classes and demonstrations, hold fairs and festivals, and publish pamphlets on a number of folk traditions.

One such event that starts the summer calendar in Great Britain is the Hobby Horse tradition of May Day celebrated in a number of Cornwall and Devon towns. May Day celebrations also include the Crowning of the May Queen, Maypole dancing, and garland-making. In many places, chiefly Buckinghamshire and Bedfordshire, the Mayers go door-to-door carrying the May Garland made from leaves and flowers gathered in the early morning.

Well Dressing is another folk custom practiced especially in Staffordshire and the Peak, where, in a special ceremony, wells are decorated with flowers as a thanksgiving for supplies of fresh water. Endon (near Leek) and Newborough (near Burton) provide good examples of this custom. Also, Cheese Rolling, Woolsack Races, Horndances, and Sword Dances provide additional entertainment, as do the Mop Fairs, still celebrated in October to commemorate the time when domestic and agricultural labor was hired for the year.

For those with an interest in history, English Heritage provides an array of historical, dramatic, and theatrical entertainment, including battle displays and tournaments with mounted knights. The society uses a number of the 350 ancient and historic properties throughout Great Britain for its events.

Falconry has an ancient heritage, and English Heritage gives demonstrations at Middleham Castle, North Yorkshire, Kenilworth Castle (Warwickshire), and elsewhere, with lectures on how falcons and hawks were used for hunting and discussions on breeds and equipment.

Music buffs should make a point to hear medieval and renaissance music played on authentic copies of the period instruments. Check Kirby Hall, Northamptonshire, and Castle Acre Priory, Norfolk. Shakespeare fans should check Pendennis Castle, Cornwall and Bayham Abbey, East Sussex. Also, Roman legionnaires parade at Richborough Castle, Kent, and the Bishop's Waltham Palace in Hampshire.

In all, the English Heritage events diary lists over 200 theatrical and historical events, surely enough to satisfy a wide range of tastes. For more information and a diary for the coming year, write English Heritage, Special Events Unit, 429 Oxford Street, London W1R 2HD. For information or material on English music and folk events, contact the English Folk Dance and Song Society, Cecil Sharp House, 2 Regent's Park Road, London NW1 7AY.

Shakespeare & Stratford-Upon-Avon

The 1564 parish register of Stratford-Upon-Avon notes the birth of "Gulielmus filius Johannes Shakespeare"—better known as William—and the village has become nearly synonymous with its favorite son. Even without the celebrity air the playwright lends, Stratford-Upon-Avon is a charming, lively market town in the midst of the English countryside.

The Shakespeare Birthplace Trust is the official body that, on behalf of the nation, owns the five most important buildings connected with Shakespeare: his birthplace on Henley Street; his wife Anne Hathaway's Cottage at Shottery; his mother Mary Arden's House and the Shakespeare Countryside Museum at Wilcote; Hall's Croft in Old Town, the home of his daughter Susanna; and New Place on Chapel Street. All of the sites are open 9:00am-6:00pm weekdays and Saturday, and 10:00am-6:00pm Sunday. Hours change slightly Nov.-March.

In addition to its summer festivals, the town celebrates the Bard's birthday on the Saturday closest to April 23 with an event of international renown, featuring a procession during which flags of all nations are unfurled. Dignitaries and ambassadors from around the world walk from his birthplace to Holy Trinity Church to lay floral tributes on his grave.

In June, the Boat Club at Stratford-Upon-Avon holds a colorful Regatta on the River Avon, and in October, the town upholds an ancient tradition known as "The Mop Fair" (discussed above).

The Royal Shakespeare Company

If you tried to stage one of Shakespeare's plays in Stratford in 1616, the year he died, you would have been breaking the law. Even 150 years later, in 1769, there were no plays performed in his hometown during the first recorded festival there—a sprawling feast of food, drink, and fireworks in celebration of the Bard, organized by David Garrick, the leading Shakespearian actor of the day.

In fact, another century would pass before the idea took root that this country lad could write a pretty good play. It also took a century for all the talk of building a permanent theater in Stratford to be turned into action. In 1879, the Shakespeare Memorial Theater opened. A fire destroyed the building in 1926, but seven years later the present building opened with a production of *Henry IV, Part I* in the afternoon and *Part II* in the evening.

The festival struggled during World War II and readily embraced the sweeping changes introduced by Sir Barry Jackson in 1946. He stressed youth and teamwork, extended the workshop facilities, and hired relatively unknown actors like Paul Scofield, Peggy Ashcroft, John Gielgud, Ralph Richardson, Vivien Leigh, and Laurence Olivier.

The festival season continued to grow and change, becoming the Royal Shakespeare Company in 1961. In 1982, the RSC moved its London operation to the Barbican Centre, and in 1986 the Swan Theater opened in Stratford, built within the shell of the original Shakespeare Memorial Theater that escaped the 1926 fire. Today, the Swan has a London counterpart at the Mermaid Theater, neighbor to the Barbican.

Both theaters now have two seasons: in London from March to early July, and in Stratford from March to mid-January. For more information, contact Barbican Centre, Barbican, London EC2Y 8DS, or Royal Shakespeare Theater, Box Office, Stratford-Upon-Avon, Warwickshire CV37 6BB.

London Pageants & Ceremonies

Pageantry is part of London's daily life. Perhaps no other city is characterized so much by pomp and ceremony, probably because no other city has such a cherished royal heritage. And the best thing: most ceremonies are free. Below are a few of the best. For more information, you may wish to consult *London for Free* by Brian Butler (Mustang Publishing, $7.95).

The Changing of the Guard occurs daily in front of Buckingham Palace. At 11:30am, a band leads the new guard, in full dress, from Chelsea or Wellington Barracks to the palace and, after the replacement of the old with the new, leads the old guard back to their barracks. The event takes place every other day in winter.

The Changing of the Queen's Life Guard occurs at 11:00am (Sundays at 10:00am) at the Horse Guards Arch in Whitehall. The new guard rides daily from Knightsbridge Barracks.

Mounting the Guard is the cavalry version of the Changing of the Guard. It occurs daily at 11:00am (Sunday at 10:00am) at the Horse Guards Parade, the great square facing Whitehall. Units of the Household Cavalry form the guard. When the Queen is in London, additional troopers and a trumpeter on a gray horse also participate. As with all of the ceremonies involving the guards, arrive early for the best view.

One of the most unusual ceremonies, and certainly the briefest, is the Ceremony of the Keys, which occurs every night between 9:53pm and 10:00pm, when the Chief Warder of the Yeoman Warders, with his escort, locks up the Tower of London. At the Bloody Tower, a sentry challenges them, and the traditional conversation ensues: "Halt!" "Detail halt." "Who goes there?" "Keys." "Whose keys?" "Queen Elizabeth's Keys. God preserve Queen Elizabeth." The sentry replies, "Amen."

While thousands of visitors pass through the Tower of London each day, very few witness this 700-year-old ceremony. (It was interrupted once during 1679 and several times during World War II.) Visitors wishing to attend this eerie spectacle should write in advance for free tickets to Resident Governor, H.M. Tower of London, London EC3N 4AB. Include your name, number attending, date (with alternates), self-addressed envelope, and International Postage Reply Coupon.

Other events involving British royalty are Trooping the Colour, the Queen's Birthday (observed on a selected Saturday in mid-June—see June calendar), and the State Opening of Parliament, held in late October or early November, one of the most colorful events of the ceremonial year. The Queen, arriving at the Palace of Westminster in the Irish State Coach, is met by the robed and wigged Law Lords and other Officers of State. In the House of Lords, she presents a prepared speech outlining the government's activities for the coming session.

Lastly, though only marginally "royal," the Lord Mayor's Show offers a huge procession through the City of London (the square mile of the London financial district), when the Mayor rides in a golden coach to present himself to the Queen. In a tradition that dates back 800 years, the Lord Mayor, the head of a council older than Parliament, takes every advantage of his office during this enormous, colorful parade. Dressed in ermine robes and wearing his chains of office, he rides in a 4.5-ton coach built in 1757. The procession route runs from Guildhall to St. Paul's Cathedral, where the new Lord Mayor is blessed by the Dean; then to the Law Courts, to perform his duties; and finally to Mansion House, where he is greeted by the City Aldermen. The procession includes an array of bands, battalions, and floats, and ends with the Lord Mayor's coach. (November)

Scotland

May

Glasgow—Glasgow Mayfest

A three-week international festival that invites participation from professional companies all over the world, Mayfest encompasses almost all art forms—opera, dance, cabaret, and street entertainment. A visit to Glasgow, the third most-visited city in Britain (after London and Edinburgh), is enhanced greatly by the Mayfest activities.

Pitlochry—Pitlochry Festival Theater

Custom-built to provide a repertoire of six plays in six days, the splendid Pitlochry Theater was opened in 1981 by Prince Charles. The original Festival Theater was founded in 1951, in a tent, by the late John Stewart. Much of the money required to re-house his vision of a summer theater in the Scottish hills was raised by patrons, whose generosity reflects the special place the theater has in their hearts.

Stewart's great dream was to create a Scottish Malvern or Stratford in a theater away from the bustle and pressure of Scotland's big cities, and he dedicated his money and his life into making that dream come true. Promoters suggest that a visitor can "stay six days and see six plays" from a range of comedies, classics, and modern drama performed by a large company of professionals. Pitlochry, 28 miles from Perth and adjacent to the River Tay, is generally considered to be the midpoint of Scotland. For more information, contact Festival Theatre Box Office, Pitlochry PH16. (early May-Oct.)

Perth—Perth Festival of the Arts

Established in 1972 to bring high quality performances to the city, this event has grown into one of the brightest and liveliest interludes in the Scottish calendar, showcasing both established talent and youthful promise. (late May)

Edinburgh—Edinburgh Spring Fling

This late weekend event, a fun-filled prelude to summer, includes parties, open-air galas, arts, and entertainment. (late May)

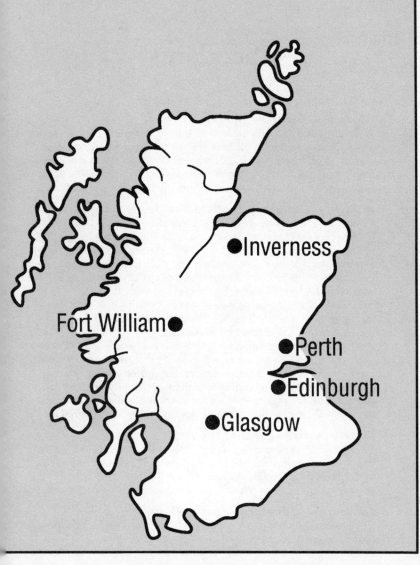

SCOTLAND

●Inverness

Fort William●

●Perth

●Edinburgh

●Glasgow

June

Lanark—Lanark Lanimer Days

The Burgh Standard Bearer Celebrations of the Royal Burgh of Lanark, held since the 12th century, include a vast procession of children, tableaux, over 1,000 bandsman, the Riding of Marches, horse races, and professional athletics. It's a lovely introduction to Scottish folk traditions. (early June)

Ayr—Ayrshire Arts Festival & Robert Burns Festival

This festival was conceived by the Ayr Arts Guild to encourage local talent and to present professional performers from the UK and abroad. The two festivals, which run concurrently for 10 days, seek to celebrate all the arts as well as the life and works of Robert Burns (1759-1796), Scotland's national poet. The festival includes ballet, opera, jazz, drama, poetry, suppers, and folk nights. The Land O' Burns Centre and Burns Cottage Museum at Alloway, two miles south of Ayr, provide related Burns material for the festival. For more information, contact Festival Office, Wallace Tower, High Street, Ayr; or Land O' Burns Centre, Alloway, Ayr. (early June)

Dingwall—Dingwall Highland Music Festival

This weekend event was first held in 1981 to present musicians from the north of Scotland or those performing in the Highland tradition. The festival highlights the traditional music of the area, and many performers are locals. Guests from other Celtic countries are also invited. (mid-June)

Aberdeen—Aberdeen Bon-Accord Week

Officially marking the beginning of summer, this festival features indoor and outdoor events, dance, classical and popular music, street entertainment, and a spectacular parade down Union Street to start things off. A pipe band, mime workshop, beer garden, and jazz sessions all contribute to the week-long event. (late June)

July

Glasgow—Glasgow Folk Festival

Held to promote international understanding and cultural exchange through the medium of traditional folklore, music, and dance, the Glasgow Folk Festival is also an opportunity for Scottish visitors to see Glasgow as a center of traditional culture throughout the UK. (early July)

Stirling—Stirling Tartan Week

This week-long program features traditional Scottish events including pipe bands, Highland dancing, ceilidhs, and fiddling. (mid-July)

Edinburgh—Old Town Arts Festival

This festival celebrates popular Scottish culture with both modern and traditional events in the arts and entertainment. (mid-July)

Aberdeen—Aberdeen French Week

Aberdeen and its French sister-city Clermont-Ferrand sponsor this week-long event, a unique, multi-cultural attempt to promote absolutely anything that's French—music, dance, food, exhibitions, and, of course, wine. The sudden explosion of Francophilia in the midst of Scotland comes as quite a surprise for the unsuspecting tourist— a nice vacation bonus! (late July)

August

Aberdeen—German Beer Festival

Surprise again! Aberdeen continues its international festivities, this time celebrating its German twin, Regensburg in Bavaria. German beer, food, music, and dance all contribute to Aberdeen's cultural exchange and provide another bonus for the traveler to this lovely city. (early August)

St. Andrew's—Lammas Fair

Like its Irish counterparts in Killorglin, Ballinasloe, and Ballycastle, the five-day St. Andrew's Lammas Fair encompasses traditional market days with social activities, local food, and spirits. It is reputed to be Scotland's oldest medieval market. Long recognized as *the* place for golfing aficionados, St. Andrew's is home to the renowned Old Course, the frequent site of the British Open held in late June/early July. (early August)

Auchtermuchty—Auchtermuchty Festival

This two week-plus community festival offers events for all ages and interests, from traditional to popular, including street entertainment, Scottish food, and drink. There is also a massive pageant during the second weekend. (mid-August)

Irvine—Marymass Festival

Much of the Marymass celebration hinges on Irvine's connection with Mary, Queen of Scots, and one of the main features of the festival is the crowning of the Marymass Queen and her Marys. Another feature is the annual Marymass races, held to commemorate the Battle of Langside. Americans will recognize the huge Budweiser Clydesdales in these races, which are possibly the oldest example of horse racing in Europe. (mid-August)

Fort William—Fort William Extravaganza

Caber tossing, pipe band performances, Highland dance, shinty, and hill races are all part of this festival, which provides a multifaceted image of Scottish Highland life—including the Scottish Open Haggis-Eating Championship. (mid-August)

Fairlie—The Viking Games
The strongest and most athletic sportsmen from Scandinavia and Britain compete in a series of spectacular games of skill and strength, including wrestling, battering ram races, hauling the longboat, and hurling the McGlashen Stones. Scottish and Scandinavian dancing provide an interesting taste of both cultures in one location. (last weekend in August)

September
New Lanark—Victoria Fair
Like a number of British communities that strive to present a bit of Victoriana, the village of New Lanark holds a weekend market and fair in its center square. Villagers dress in appropriate costume and relive Victorian days with period entertainment as well. (early Sept.)

October
Stirling—National Mod
Instituted in 1891, this is Scotland's equivalent of Wales' National Eisteddfod. The Mod is mainly a competitive festival of music, dance, and poetry, with a strong choral element. It attempts to bring together Gaels from throughout Scotland and beyond to promote Gaelic language and music. (mid-Oct.)

Edinburgh: Festival City

Edinburgh's reputation as one of the fairest cities in Europe is most evident in the last three weeks of August, when it hosts the ever-growing International Festival, the Festival Fringe, its Film Festival, and the McEwan's Jazz Festival. During festival time, Edinburgh emerges as the cultural capital of Great Britain, perhaps even all of Europe.

Since 1947, the International Festival has brought artists and companies of the highest standard in all fields to the city. It's said to be the largest and most comprehensive such endeavor in the world, with performances in music, opera, dance, theater, and poetry throughout the capital. One of the most exciting spectacles of the festival is the Military Tattoo on the floodlit esplanade in front of Edinburgh Castle. The Tattoo showcases precision military marching, maneuvers by the Scottish regiment, bagpipes, and colorful kilts.

As if this three-week event wasn't enough, the Edinburgh Festival Fringe, established in 1947, involves professional and amateur groups from around the world. It recently sold 500,000 tickets for one year's shows, with 494 companies performing 960 shows. Categories include theater, cabaret, ballet, revue, folk, opera, and orchestral music. The Fringe gives everyone free rein to perform wherever they can find an empty stage or street corner.

The Film Festival, also founded in 1947, originally was intended as a forum for documentary films and filmmakers. Since then, the fest has grown to cover all aspects of filmmaking—feature films, documentaries, shorts, experimental films, and student work. The Film Festival is a public event, with almost all screenings open to anyone who wishes to purchase a ticket.

Finally, from its start in 1978 with just two or three bands, the Jazz Festival has become one of the biggest jazz festivals in Europe, with over 40 bands playing 20 venues. It's an exciting complement to an almost overwhelming event!

For more information, contact the following:

International Festival, 21 Market St., Edinburgh EH1 1BW.
Festival Fringe, 170 High Street, Edinburgh EH1 1QS.
Film Festival, Filmhouse, 88 Lothian, Edinburgh EH3 9BZ.
Jazz Festival, 116 Canongate, Edinburgh EH8 8DD.

Highland Games & Gatherings

Shimmering lochs. Fjords, rivers, and streams, teeming with trout and salmon. Craggy peaks snow-capped year-round. Verdant glens carpeted in wildflowers. Games and clan gatherings. Kilts, bagpipes, and traditional cuisine, plus some of the most surprising exhibitions of physical strength known anywhere.

In two words, the Highlands.

Throughout the northern third of Scotland, hundreds of men compete in tests of strength, young girls dance and leap between crossed swords, and bagpipes fill the air with stirring melodies. The Highland Games celebrate the pride and fervor of Scotland's romantic past. They also yield a marvelous crop of anecdotes and legends.

One legend has the Games originating in the 11th century, during the reign of King Malcolm Canmore. Clan chiefs would hold competitions to pick the strongest men as bodyguards and the fastest as couriers. The King needed a fleet-footed *gille-ruith*, or running footman, to carry his messages, so he organized a race to the summit of Craig Choinnich, overlooking Braemar. King Malcolm is also said to have introduced the variation of the sword dance that's now popular at the gatherings.

However, the villagers of Ceres, in Fife, claim their Highland Gathering is the oldest in Scotland. They note that their village is named for Ceres, the Roman goddess of agriculture, in whose name great sports were instituted. More important, however, is the fact that after the Battle of Bannockburn, the people of Ceres cheered the return of the 600 bowmen from their district with contests and feasts, and they say the celebration has been held annually ever since, without any break except for the Great Wars.

Another legend relating to the games evolves from Bonnie Prince Charlie and his Highland hosts, who watched their men compete in athletics while passing time between skirmishes. The battle of Culloden in 1746 brought a drastic end to the fun. In fact, the brutal fight virtually denuded the Highlands of its male population. "The Act of Proscription" followed, which banned carrying arms, wearing a kilt, playing bagpipes, and local gatherings. By one Act of Parliament, many of the cultural traditions of Scotland were destroyed.

By the 1780's, the Highland Societies began to encourage the rejuvenation of Scottish culture and heritage. The first Society Gathering took place in 1781, and they led to the gatherings as we know them today. Records of the societies make it clear that the prime function was to arrange social gatherings of the nobility and gentry, but as dancing, piping, and Scottish arts competitions were featured from the beginning, it seems likely that this main aim was added to prevent accusations of nationalistic activities.

In 1818, the St. Fillans Society promoted a full-scale event with piping, dancing, and athletics. For the first time, the sword dance, previously considered a war dance, was included in a competition. By the 1820's, there were Highland gatherings, almost identical to those today, throughout the country.

Modern gatherings and games include the same agricultural implements originally used in everyday work around the farm: a blacksmith's hammer for throwing, a well-rounded stone from a river bed for putting (shot-putting), and tree trunks for "caber tossing."

The most celebrated of the games are the Braemar Royal Highland Games held annually on the first Saturday in September, with the Royal Family in attendance. The gathering, held in the same place in some form for almost 1,000 years, attracts over 25,000 visitors annually. Perhaps it's the chance to catch a glimpse of some of the Royals (whose summer residence, Balmoral Castle, lies down the road), or perhaps it's the opportunity to see the perpetuation of an extraordinary Scottish tradition. Whatever the motive, the games are always a fascinating and colorful aspect of Scottish life and legend.

In addition to the Braemar Royal Highland Gathering held at Memorial Park, other important gatherings include Atholl Gathering at Blair Castle, Pitlochry (late May); Aberdeen Games, Aberdeen (mid-June); Cupar Games, Cupar (early July); Balloch Games, Moss O'Ballock Park, Balloch (mid-July); Inveraray Games, Games Field, Inveraray (mid-July); Isle of Skye Games, Portree, (early August); the Cowal Gathering, Dunoon, and the Argyllshire Games, Games Field, Oban (both late August).

In May, games and gatherings are held in Gourock, Bathgate,

Blackford, and Garnock. In June, they're at Strathmiglo, Markinch, Ardossan, Forfar, Lesmahgow, Burghead, Granton-on-Spey, and Ceres (reportedly the oldest event).

In July, games are held at Thurso, Elgen, Shotts, Kilmore, Thornton, Alva, Dingwall, Forres, Dundee, Arbroath, Rosneath and Ckynder, Stonehaven, Kinochard, Kenmore, Morvern, Burntisland, Luss, Airth, Balquhidder, Lochearnhead, Iroine, Tobermory, Arisaig, Dufftown, Halkirk, Fort William, Resneath, Tayhuilt, and the Aviemore Games at St. Andrew's.

In August, gatherings are held at Morar, Dornach, Aberlour, Aboyne, Brodick, Strathpeffer, Stirlingshire, Ballater, Nairn, Perth, Rotheday, Helmsdale, Rannoch, Whitebridge, Drumnadrochit, Invergordon, Strathardle, and Dunkeld.

In September, following the Braemar Games, two more gatherings occur at Blaigowrie and Ardgay, where the Invercharron Games take place at Bonar Bridge.

Wales

May

Cardiff—Mayday Celebration

An afternoon of entertainment and a celebration of springtime is an apt description of this annual May 1 event. Music, Maypole dancing, clowns, carnivals, food, and drink are essential elements of Mayday in Wales.

Llantrisant—Llantrisant Festival

This weekend festival aims to provide cultural experiences that might not otherwise be available within the mid-Glamorgan area. Like so many other festivals in Britain in early May, this event is based on Mayday traditions and celebrates historical connections dating to the Middle Ages. (early May)

Llandudno—Victorian Extravaganza

This colorful weekend event is set in the streets of Llandudno, amid the town's lovely Victorian buildings. Theater groups perform, steam vehicles are displayed, and carriage rides, buskers, and parades enliven the celebration. (early May)

Holywell—Victorian Fayre

This major annual fair adds a touch of nostalgia to present-day Wales with its street games, boar roast, side stalls, singing, and games for all ages. The "fayre" is also a costumed event, and many of the locals wear 19th-century dress. (early May)

Caernarfon—Medieval Combat

The excitement of knights in combat comes to life with this reenactment sponsored by the Escafield Medieval Society. The event also includes displays of dancing. The Caernarfon Castle event is one of several such fests throughout Wales at historic properties. (late May)

Beaumaris—Weekend of Song and Dance

Lovely Beaumaris Castle presents a romantic venue for a weekend of traditional Welsh, Cotswold, clog, and folk dance performances. (late May)

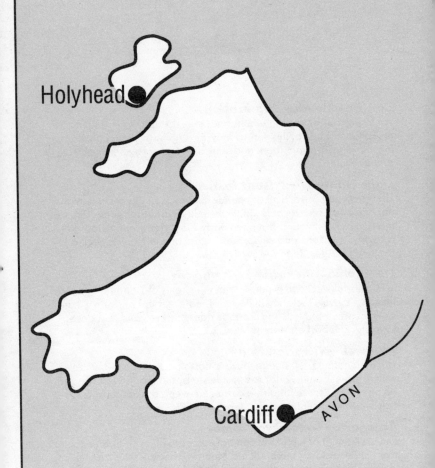

Newton—Eisteddfod

The largest youth festival of its kind in Europe, involving over 12,000 competitors from throughout Wales, this event is a joy for music lovers. The venue is the Eisteddfod Field, Newtown. (late May/early June)

June

Llangefin—Eisteddfod

Anglesey's annual weekend music festival, like countless others held throughout the country, is a highlight of the North Wales cultural calendar. (early June)

Saundersfood—Edwardian Week

During this week of events with an Edwardian theme, both visitors and residents are encouraged to dress in period costume. The festival encourages visitors to partake in Welsh folk customs and events. (early June)

Harlech—Medieval Fayre

Like its counterpart at Caernarfon Castle, this event is part of a series of dancing displays and historical reenactments organized by the Harlech Medieval Society. (mid-June)

Swansea—Mumbles Victorian Weekend

Theater and music of the Victorian era, costumed cricket matches, vintage vehicles, and a genuine country fair atmosphere are all part of the weekend event throughout the Mumbles area of West Glamorgan. (mid-June)

July

Margam—Margam Festival

This delightful music festival, described as "a feast of music for summer," offers a varied program set in the idyllic Orangery in Margam County Park. (throughout July)

Avergavenny—Avergavenny Summer Festival

This month-long summer event, held at various venues throughout Avergavenny, offers a variety of attractions: a medieval market, music, drama, exhibitions, and native crafts. Many of the festival's offerings are based on both the past and present of this historic border town in the Usk Valley. (throughout July)

Llangollen—International Music Eisteddfod

Each year, the small town of Llangollen (population 3,000) in North Wales holds an international music festival in the traditional style of a Welsh eisteddfod (pronounced eye-steth-fud), "a cultural gathering at which singers, dancers, poets, and musicians compete in friendly pursuit of artistic excellence." Thousands of performers from all over the world take part in this cosmopolitan event, held amid the splendid Welsh scenery.

In terms of scale and standards, the Llangollen event, founded in 1947, is the most ambitious of its kind anywhere in the world. A recent addition to the musical program is the "Choir of the World" competition, where one choir from the three major choral categories—female, male, and mixed choirs—is designated "Choir of the World" by a panel of international judges.

The six-day event is a great opportunity to hear spectacular music from around the world—perhaps even a future star or two. (In 1968, the concert program featured a little-known Mexican tenor: Placido Domingo.) For more information, contact International Eisteddfod Office, Llangollen, Clwyd, North Wales LL20 8NG. (early July)

Fishguard—Fishguard Music Festival
Fishguard is on the 170-mile coastal path skirting the Pembrokeshire National Park, only a short boat trip from Ireland. The Music Festival attracts enthusiasts from Britain and abroad with its offerings of orchestral, recital, and choral music. Plus, an expanding visual arts section reflects the talent in the country. Venues include local churches and St. David's Cathedral. For more information, contact Festival Office, Fishguard, Dyfed, SA65 9BJ. (late July)

Aberystwyth—Aberystwyth Summer Festival
From mid-morning to late evening, there's always something to do, hear, or see during the 16 days of this summer event. Musical and cultural events of all types are available throughout this charming Welsh community. (late July-August)

August
various locales—Royal National Eisteddfod
Held at a different location every year in the north and south of Wales, this festival aims to give Welsh people in every area a chance to host and enjoy the delightful nine-day event. The main purpose of the festival is to help preserve Welsh cultural traditions and one of the world's oldest languages (all events are conducted in Welsh). The Eisteddfod has been called a "celebration of all things Welsh," where everyone is invited to join, including all visitors. Poetry and pageant, concerts and drama, arts and crafts, dance and music—all form a rich backdrop to the fun. For more information, contact Royal National Eisteddfod of Wales, 10 Park Grove, Caerdydd, Cardiff CF1 3BN. (first week of August)

Brecon—Brecon Jazz
Jazz is truly an international musical form, and even in this area of Wales it is highly regarded. Brecon Jazz, a unique three-day event, includes over 80 concerts held throughout the town in indoor and outdoor venues. (mid-August)

Llandrindod Wells—Victorian Festival

At the turn of the century, Llandrindod Wells was the premier Welsh spa town, hosting thousands of Victorian gentlefolk in search of a cure for the ailments of the era. Time has been kind to the town's architecture, and the village takes full advantage of this backdrop to stage an event of merriment in the Victorian style. Daytime street theater, Gilbert and Sullivan in the music halls, and bandstand concerts contribute to the nine-day program. (mid-August)

Caernarfon—Castle Fire and Fantasy

A nightly pageant of music and magic, held within the castle, culminates in a son et lumière of legends and history with floodlights and fireworks. The program provides a charming interlude for visitors to the historic castle, built in 1283 by Edward I and considered the center of Welsh nationalism. (late August)

September

St. Asaph—North Wales Music Festival

The ancient Celtic city of St. Asaph, with its acoustically superb cathedral, hosts this event. Visitors will discover that the festival has an atmosphere all its own, achieving an extraordinary rapport between renowned musicians and an enthusiastic audience. For more information, contact North Wales Music Festival Office, High Street, St. Asaph, Clwyd LL17 0RD. (late Sept.)

Swansea—Festival of Music and the Arts

Created in 1948, Swansea is the largest arts festival in Wales. With the Princess of Wales as the Royal Patron, Swansea includes theater, opera, dance, jazz, and literary events. The Young Welsh Singers Competition also occurs during the three-week program, and a number of symphony orchestras from around the UK and Europe perform. Concerts take place in the Brangwy Hall and other venues in Swansea, and there's a festival "fringe." For more information, contact Civic Information Centre, P.O. Box 59, Singleton Street, Swansea SH1 3QG. (late Sept.-Nov.)

Holidays in Great Britain

New Year's Day, Good Friday, Easter Monday, May Day Bank Holiday, Spring Bank Holiday, Summer Bank Holiday, Christmas, Boxing Day (Dec. 26).

For further information, contact the **British Tourist Authority**. In the U.S., the addresses are 40 West 57th Street, New York, NY 10019-4001 (212-581-4700); 625 N. Michigan Ave., Suite 1510, Chicago, IL 60611-1977 (312-787-0490); and 350 S. Figueroa St., Suite 450, Los Angeles, CA 90071-1203 (213-628-3525).

For information on Scotland, contact the **Scottish Tourist Board**. In the U.S., the address is P.O. Box 18686, Washington, DC 20036 (202-872-0782).

THE BENELUX COUNTRIES

4

The Benelux Countries: Belgium, The Netherlands, & Luxembourg

A visit to any of the Benelux countries provides a delightful combination of cultures and customs. Splendid in history and aesthetics, the three countries also excel in fine cuisine and vintage wines and beers served amid convivial sidewalk pubs and intimate "brown cafes."

From the battlefields that dot the plains of Flanders in southern Belgium to the canals of Utrecht, Bruges, and Amsterdam, Belgium and the Netherlands are amply endowed with both natural and man-made attractions. The Dutch somehow maintain balance and order out of considerable contradiction. Both Rembrandt and contemporary jazz, for example, are among the most revered art forms, particularly in Amsterdam. In Belgium, where over 90% of the population is Catholic, public religious ceremonies, outdoor processions, and celebrations of saints' days occur frequently. The non-religious visitor should not shy from these events, however. The *ommegangs* and processions of holy relics are both religious rites and colorful examples of historic Belgian pageantry.

Always closely linked with neighboring Belgium and Holland, the Grand Duchy of Luxembourg is the smallest of the Benelux group (999 square miles), but it's full of treasures and diversity. Encompassing two distinct regions—the richly forested hills of the Ardennes and the vineyard-laden Valley of the Moselle—citizens take full advantage of their present surroundings while cherishing their unique past. For example, they honor a 7th-century Christian, St. Willibrod, in Echternach with a unique skipping procession on Whit Tuesday, as well as General George Patton in Ettlebruck, with a festival celebrating his 1944 liberation of the town.

In general, from May to early June, folk fairs and celebrations are almost a national pastime in the Benelux countries. Plus, there are festive wine-tasting days and harvest festivals throughout the wine-growing regions in spring and fall.

BELGIUM

Ostend

Bruges

Ghent

SCHELDE

Antwerp

BRUSSELS ★

Louvain

MEUSE

Liege

Neufchateau

Belgium

May

throughout Flanders—Festival of Flanders

This regional festival, which takes place from April-November in several cities throughout the four Flemish provinces of Belgium, has been called "ubiquitous, diverse, and lengthy." Staged in a number of major cities in Flanders, it presents a range of musical performances and lasts almost six months!

The Festival was born in 1958 as a direct result of the Brussels World's Fair. The cities of Brussels, Bruges, Ghent, Kortrijk, Limburg, Antwerp, Leuven, Mechelen, and others decided to form a consortium to create a regional event, and each city would have a special musical offering.

Kortrijk opens the festival in the spring with choral music. In June, Limburg offers chamber, symphonic, and choral music. Bruges, in late July, emphasizes historical music and musical competitions. Ghent holds its festival from August-October with symphonic and chamber music, solo performances, jazz, and dance concerts. Brussels and Leuven follow in September with a variety of musical offerings. And Antwerp and Mechelen offer the finale in autumn with a wide variety as well.

The festival often plans its concerts thematically, so for the latest information, contact Festival of Flanders, Eugene Flageyplein 18, 1050 Brussels.

Ypres—Kattenwoensdog

Over 2,000 people participate in the "Cat Festival," one of the most colorful events in Europe. Decorated floats representing famous felines like Puss-in-Boots and Cieper the King of the Cats pass through the streets of Ypres. The festival culminates with the "casting down of cats," a rather bizarre segment when the town jester tosses woolen cats to the waiting crowd from the top of the Belfry. (Until 1817, live cats were used!) The custom originated centuries ago when the great Cloth Hall, filled with cloth stored until sold, attracted thousands of mice. The town imported hundreds of cats to eliminate them, but soon the cats became the problem. Eventually, the solution was to fling them from the Belfry, thus inaugurating the feline frenzy now held every even-numbered year. The throwing of velvet cats takes place each year, however, so the citizens of Ypres are never without their beloved cat festival in some degree. (second Sunday of May)

Zottegem—Giants Ommegang
In typical Belgian fashion, this parade of giants, both local and foreign, parade through the streets of Zottegem. Bands and local folklore groups accompany the huge, stilted giants. (mid-May)

Mechelen—Hanswyk Procession
This colorful religious event pays homage to "Our Lady of Hanswyk." Over 2,000 residents participate in this annual ritual, held the Sunday before Ascension Day.

Bruges—Holy Blood Procession
This major traditional religious event is among the most important on Bruges' calendar. The shrine containing the Holy Blood, brought from the Second Crusade by the Count of Flanders in 1150, is carried by the Bishop in a solemn procession. Beautifully costumed residents follow, reenacting scenes from the Old and New Testament in mime, song, and speech. The procession is held at 3:00pm annually on Ascension Day, and a Pontifical High Mass is celebrated earlier at 11:00am. (On the Christian calendar, Ascension Thursday is the 40th day after Easter.)

Mons—Ducasse de la Trinité
Mons, the capital of the province of Hainault, hosts this annual religious and historic event on Trinity Sunday (the first Sunday after Pentecost) to commemorate the city's delivery from the Plague in 1349. The relics of St. Waudru parade through the streets in the *Car d'Or*, an 18th-century golden carriage drawn by white horses. The sumptuous procession includes girls richly dressed in brocades and Belgian laces and solemn clerics carrying the silver reliquary with the saint's skull. When the procession is over, a boisterous, rollicking battle between St. George and the Dragon (called the *Lumeçon*) breaks out, witnessed by thousands of spectators singing the ancient *Song of the Doudou*, accompanied by the carillons of the Belfry. This battle, an evocation of a ritual unchanged since 1490, inaugurates a three-day folk festival which includes the "Pageant of Mons," a performance of several thousand musicians, singers, and actors.

June
throughout Wallonia—Festival of Wallonia
This internationally-known festival takes place in several cities through-

out Wallonia, the French-speaking region of southern Belgium. Processions, carnivals, feasts, and festivals are enormously popular, and the area loves to use its historic venues to showcase all types of music. Like the Festival of Flanders, musical programs are spread among the cities of Chimay, Hainaut, Liège, Huy, Mons, Namur, and Saint-Hubert. Chimay usually opens the festival with concerts and recitals, while other cities focus on orchestral, vocal, choral, and solo performances. For more information, contact Festival of Wallonia, Rue Sur-les-Foulons 11, 4000 Liège. (June-Oct.)

Tournai—Day of the Four Processions
Four folklore processions take place on this day: a traditional procession led by the Knight of the Tower, a carnival procession, a floral procession, and an advertising float. One of the most colorful aspects of the processions is the parade of historical giants including Childeric, the 5th-century Merovingian King who chose Tournai for his capital; Lethalde and Engelbert, two heroes of the First Crusade; and Christine de Lalaing, Tournai's version of Joan of Arc. (second Sunday in June)

Waterloo—Recreation of the Battle
Ever since armies clashed in Waterloo, tourists from all over the world have come to the battlefield, seeking the ghosts of those who fought. To bring the Napoleonic era to life, parades are organized consisting of marchers from the Empire, English, French, and Swiss Napoleon Societies, all of whom wear the uniforms of 1815. These remarkable reconstitutions immerse the observer in a thrilling show, leaving unique memories of a page from history. A light and sound show is held on the properties, which include several museums and a vast building called the Panorama of the Battle at the foot of the Lions' Mount. (mid-June)

Oostduinkerke—Shrimp Festival
On the final weekend of June, Oostduinkerke celebrates its *pecheurs de crevettes a cheval* (horse-mounted shrimp fishers), the last in the world to practice the ancient profession. The event begins on Saturday afternoon with a fishing competition. Immediately after, the shrimp is cooked and sold to the flocks of visitors. At 9:00pm, there's a public ball; folk dancing and concerts begin on Sunday. At 4:00pm, a folklore procession goes through the streets, using the sea, fishermen, and shrimp as its theme. (late June)

July
Brussels—Bruzzle Festival
Popular, classical, jazz, and even New Wave concerts are held at landmarks such as the Grand 'Place, Place de la Monnie, and the Ancienne Belgique Theater. (early July)

Brussels—The Ommegang

This historical pageant evokes the celebration staged by the magistrate of Brussels in 1549, in honor of Charles-Quint and his son Don Philippe, Infant of Spain and Duke of Brabant, and of his sisters Elenore of Austria, Queen of France, and Mary of Hungary. It takes place annually on the first Thursday in July, and recently it has also been held on the first Monday to accommodate more spectators.

Ommegang—from the Flemish *om* (around) and *gang* (march)—means a walk around the town or main square and usually refers to the processions around monuments or outside city walls. These parades used to describe a large circle—in the pattern of a magic ring—with the hope that marchers would be saved from a particular danger, like Plague. During the Middle Ages, *ommegangs* were held in Antwerp, Bruges, Ghent, Veurne, and Mechelen.

The first procession was mainly religious, with Princes honoring it with their presence. Magistrates, archery guilds, and corporations later joined and began to compete for splendor. Every year, the people of Brussels looked forward to the event, which presented an opportunity to display both faith and wealth. As time went by, the Ommegang incorporated allegorical floats, banners, trumpets, and horseback riders—elements more profane than religious.

The present Ommegang, held regularly since 1930, maintains the historic splendor and pageantry. Before the event begins at 9:00pm, the Grand-Place has been cleared by strolling musicians and costumed, dancing "peasants." It is, indeed, a strikingly beautiful event, unequalled in Belgian folklore. For more information, contact Tourist Information Board, Hôtel de Ville, Grand-Place, B-1000 Brussels. (first Monday and Thursday in July)

Furnes—Procession of the Penitents

The Procession of the Penitents, firmly based on historical and religious facts, attracts both spectators and true pilgrims. The event dates back to the 12th century, when Robert, Count of Flanders, was spared from a storm at sea. He promised that, should he escape the peril, he would give his relic of the True Cross to the first church he saw. The storm abated, and the Church of St. Walburge at Furnes appeared on the horizon.

To commemorate the gift, it was decided that a procession would be held every year, and the modern ritual preserves the austere and penitential aspect. Beginning at the Church, the members of the procession put on rough serge robes and hoods, and they carry a cross throughout the two-hour march. There's no music, singing, or dancing—only six Theban trumpets at the head and a few men with wooden rattles. The naive and picturesque aspect of the procession has impressed thousands of spectators throughout the centuries. (last Sunday in July)

August

Brussels—The Meyboom
The traditional Meyboom is held on August 9, the day before the Feast of St. Lawrence. A folklore procession takes place in the center of Brussels, and the event reaches its climax at 5:00pm with the planting of a tree called "Meyboom" at the intersection of the rue des Sables and rue du Marais. According to legend, the ceremony is patterned after a rite from 1213.

Liège—Outremeuse Folklore Festival
The Outremeuse district, an area of Liège on the right bank of the Meuse, is the site of an interesting harvest and folklore festival highlighting city customs. The festivities include a procession that stops at various *potales* (shrines of stone or wood hooked into the fronts of houses and containing a small statue of the Virgin), constructed to thank Mary for a favor or to obtain her protection. (mid-August)

Bruges—Pageant of the Golden Tree
This beautiful event is held every five years (next in 1995), making it highly anticipated by the residents of Bruges and visitors to the area. The colorful procession recalls the history of Flanders and Bruges until the marriage of Charles the Bold in 1468. (late August)

Ath—Giants Festival
The Gouyasse Wedding and folklore procession, held on the fourth Saturday of August, both feature the giant Gouyasse (Goliath) and his wife, whose marriage was first celebrated in 1715 and is remembered each year on the day before the Ducasse (Festival of Ath). The ceremonies on Saturday are the wedding and the *Jeu Parti* (the challenge between David and Goliath). Several floats of giants also participate in the festivities, which are genuine classics on the Belgian calendar. (late August weekend)

Bruges—Reiefeest
The Festival of the Canals, held every three years (next in 1995) on the illuminated canals of Bruges and in Vurg Square, is a captivating pageant, with scenes that take spectators into the Middle Ages, the Renaissance, and the Baroque period. All scenes, involving over 600 participants who sing and dance, are performed without intermission, each independent of the others, so you can wander from one to the other and spend as much time as you desire. Tickets were recently 250 bf, but may increase for the next pageant. For more information, contact Tourist Office, Burg 11, B-8000, Bruges. (late August weekends)

September

St. Hubert—International Hunting Day
The small town of St. Hubert, which stands on a plateau in the heart

of the Ardennes forest, developed around the Basilica and the 7th-century Abbey. This religious event begins with High Mass in the Basilica at 11:00am and is followed by a historical pageant at 2:30pm. (first Sunday in Sept.)

Tournai—Procession of the Plague

This religious event, held in the second-oldest town in Belgium, commemorates the end of the plague that swept through the area in the 11th century. On September 14, 1090, a grateful bishop led a procession through the Notre Dame Cathedral to honor the Virgin Mary, who was credited with several miraculous cures. Held annually since that day (except once in 1559, when Calvinists forced its cancellation), the procession includes splendid pageantry and a display of the cathedral's priceless art treasures. Notre Dame, considered one of the finest examples of Romanesque architecture in Western Europe, houses a collection of paintings by such masters as Reubens, Metsys, and Jordaans; murals 700 years old; and statues, tapestries, and religious objects dating from the 6th and 7th centuries. (second Sunday in Sept.)

Wingene—Breughel Festival

The Breughel Festival seeks to recreate the festive atmosphere that really stems from the people, by means of scenes of everyday life. To do this, 52 paintings are represented, grouped into four sections: Flanders in the 16th century; Proverbs and Children's Games; Paintings of Pieter Breughel; and The Village Festival. Over 1,000 inhabitants, all dressed in 16th-century fashions, mime scenes in the style of Breughel's pictures. Following the 3:00pm parade, a feast à la Breughel is held at 6:00pm, complete with sausages, boiled rice, pancakes, and beer, plus singing and dancing. (second Sunday in Sept.)

October

Ghent—International Film Festival of Flanders

This film festival was organized in 1974 by members of the university film club and the owners of Studio Skoop, Ghent's most important art cinema. By 1988, the Ghent festival presented 100 films—for an estimated 45,000 spectators—and special events like concerts, silent films, and live musical accompaniment. Music is the festival's theme, with a competition section on "The Impact of Music on Film," an event which emphasizes the creative role of music in the general concept and effect of a film. For more information, contact International Film Festival of Flanders—Ghent, Kortrijksesteenweg 1104, Ghent 9820.

Belgian Folklore:
On- & Off-Season

Although pre-Lenten carnivals like the Gilles de Binche (a 430-year tradition) and the Brussels Ommegang are the best-known, almost every Belgian city and town offers manifestations of a people enjoying their traditions on a year-round basis.

Belgium's curious folklore celebrations keep haunting memories of old raptures and terrors alive. Varying proportions of the solemn and the bizarre, the fervently Christian and the devoutly pagan combine—sometimes incomprehensibly—to make Belgian folklore pageants among the most unusual in the world. The Old Testament and the New, harvest time and planting time, barely remembered rites of pre-Christian cults—all are cause for carnivals and tableaux in cities and villages throughout the country.

The most famous and most solemn of all traditional festivals is the annual Procession of the Holy Blood in Bruges on Ascension Day. Magnificent and dramatic, the procession celebrates the return of the Thierry d'Alsace, Count of Flanders, from the Second Crusade in 1150. At the other extreme, the annual pre-Lenten carnivals draw thousands to enjoy the rousing fun, feasting, and fireworks. White-winged angels descend on Rutten every May—at least they have for 1,000 years! Giants loom and spin in parades and dances in Niveles, Ath, Aalst, Lier, Tournai, Ghent, and Arlon. Good St. George slays the evil dragon to the terror and joy of Mons. Pagan bonfires burn at Wallerode, Trois-Ponts, Gouvy, Saint Vith, and Geraardsbergen.

In November, the whole country seems to honor St. Hubert and St. Martin with markets, parades, and *ommegangs*. In Eupen, for example, St. Martin and his legendary goose are escorted by Roman soldiers and hundreds of light-bearing children in a procession through town. The event culminates in a large bonfire. On November 3, the Feast of St. Hubert is observed in the historic town of the same name, with a Mass for huntsmen and the Blessing of Animals.

By weaving the past into the present, the Belgians both in Flanders and Wallonia have managed to preserve their yesterdays. This land of two cultures, Flemings and Walloons, each with its own character, offers great opportunities to discover folklore through traditional celebrations. Festivals there also offer "admission-free" pageantry for an extra value for the traveler.

Belgian Holidays

New Year's Day, Easter Monday, Labor Day (May 1), Ascension Day, Whitmonday, National Day (July 21), Assumption (Aug. 15), All Saints Day (Nov. 1), Armistice Day (Nov. 11), Christmas.

For further information, contact the **Belgian Tourist Office**. The U.S. address is 745 Fifth Ave., New York, NY 10151 (212-758-8130).

NETHERLANDS

The Netherlands

May

Alkmaar—Kaasmarkt

Every Friday morning in late spring and summer, a fascinating cheese market is held in the Waagplein (town square) adjoining the ancient Weigh House. The colorful tradition includes teams of cheese porters dressed in white with straw hats of red, blue, yellow, or green (the colors represent the four sections of their guilds), trotting from the auction ring to the Weigh House, pulling sleds piled high with cheese to be weighed. A handshake seals bids in the ring before the sleds are loaded, and the bill is tallied by each guild's scales. Carriers are so proud of their guild's standards that every week they post the name of any carrier who has indulged in profanity or been late to the auction. Barrel organs, old world crafts exhibitions, and the friendly Dutch make the Kaasmarkt a delightful way to spend a Friday morning—with plenty of time left to stroll Alkmaar's 12th-century streets. This cheese market is one of several in Holland in the summer (see *Windmills & Market Days* below).

Lisse—Lelietuin

Keukenhof Gardens offers a gorgeous display of lilies during 10 days in May. (late May)

Scheveningen—Vlaggetjesdag

The Dutch herring fleet leaves each year with a colorful Flag Day celebration and returns with the first herring catch amid much fanfare and fun. The first fish of the catch is sent to the Queen, and a lively auction follows, as local restauranteurs bid for the honor of serving the first herring of the season. (early May)

June

Amsterdam—Holland Festival

The Holland Festival, established after World War II to restore the great traditions of European culture, has been held every June since 1948. Now the premier event on the Dutch cultural calendar, it has spotlighted musicians like Leonard Bernstein, Maria Callas, Leopold Stokowski, and Otto Klemperer, as well as orchestras, ballet companies, and theater troupes from around the world. Performances are held throughout Amsterdam, especially in the Royal Concertgebouw, and prices remain reasonable at about $25. Important annual events get added recognition at the Festival—like the Van Gogh Centenary of 1990, which included a series of films related to the artist's life and works. For more information, contact The Holland Festival, 21 Kleine-Gartmanplantsoen, 1017 RP Amsterdam.

Den Haag—North Sea Jazz Festival
This jazz fest runs in conjunction with the Holland Festival for one weekend in mid-June and offers three days of performances by top artists like Dizzy Gillespie and Miles Davis. Over 1,000 artists perform on 14 stages under one roof in the Congress Hall of the Hague. For more information, contact North Sea Jazz Festival, P.O. Box 87840, 2508, DE, The Hague.

Gouda—Kaasmarkt
From 9:30am-noon every Thursday morning in the summer, a lively cheese market is held in this historic town, world-famous for its orange-skinned cheese (pronounced "how-dah" locally). Quite different from its Alkmaar counterpart, the Gouda market lures farmers in their work clothes to town, driving brightly painted wagons piled high with cheese. Following the market, visitors can walk behind Town Hall, where samples of cheese and a video explaining its production are available. A crafts market runs with the Kaasmarkt.

Warfum—Op Roakeldais
This week-long folklore dance festival, held in Warfum annually since 1966, combines dance groups from all over the world with a big fair, an art exhibition, and a famous market. Both the dancing and the music are extraordinary in originality and variety. Though held in an area north of Groningen, it attracts thousands. (mid-June)

Zwolle—Midzommerfestival
This mid-summer festival boasts over 120 performances, including concerts on 15 stages; pop, blues, jazz, folk, and brass music; and folk and modern dance. Plus, all kinds of theater runs in the old town center—indeed, the entire town becomes one big theater! (late June)

Schagen—Westfrisian Folk Market
A lively folk market held every Thursday throughout the summer has made the old city of Schagen well-known. At 10:15am, the Schagenese, in original Westfrisian folkdress, assemble near the train

station to prepare for the pageant. They are preceded by a peasants' band called *De Uienhoop* accompanied by antique carts. At 11:30am, the procession reaches the Grote Kerk (Great Church) on the Marktplein (Market Square), and the festival begins, with performances by children dancers and the Westfrisian wooden shoe troupe. An afternoon program, starting at 1:00pm, includes crafts displays and exhibitions.

On the ten "Westfrisian Thursdays," the city's 17th-century farmhouse, Vreeburg, serves as a museum of the region and provides demonstrations of local crafts and trades. The additional nine Westfrisian Thursdays offer a variety of special events, including a "Day of the Old Trades," when tradespeople show how work was once done; a "Day of the Animal," with sheep-shearing and woolspinning; and a "Day of the Child," with ancient games like stiltwalking, trundle, and potato sack races, plus a "Punch and Judy" show. If possible, don't miss the day called "Tilting the Ring," when the most beautiful horses in Holland compete to be "Best Ringsteker." It's the real highlight of the Schagen folk days and a classic example of country life in Holland. "Final Day" marks the end of summer, and costumed residents spend the entire day with music, dancing, and eating.

Hoorn—Romantische Markt

This summer-long regional market, where all the produce is brought on barges, is a unique Dutch folk event. The former Zuider Zee port bulges with historic buildings, cafes, and pubs, and a stroll around the harbor is an lovely treat. During the ten Wednesdays of the summer, you can see even more at the "Heart of Hoorn" market.

July

Nieuw Lekkerland—Windmill Days

National Windmill Days are held at Kinderdijk, where 18 windmills stand in perfect working condition. This area of southern Holland has the largest concentration of windmills in the country, most of which are in full operation on summer Saturdays from 1:30pm-5:30pm. (throughout July)

Purmerend—Kaasmarkt

Like Alkmaar, Gouda, and many other cheese-producing towns, Purmerend also holds a market on Thursdays in July and August. A market town for 500 years, Purmerend's cheese market is held at the foot of the Town Hall, with its carillon and new *kooepel* (church). The porters with their straw hats make the market a historic event even today. On summer Thursdays, they show tourists how they carry the cheese to the weigh-house, taste it, weigh it, and buy it.

Middleburg—Tilting at the Ring

Middleburg, on Holland's west coast in the Zeeland area, holds a colorful market every Thursday when Zeelanders, many in native dress, mingle in the market square with friends and visitors alike. The ritual perpetuates a long-standing, popular custom of this region of Holland. (throughout the summer)

Bruinisse—Fishery Days

The opening of the mussel season is cause for much celebration in this area and is welcomed annually with festivities. Of course, there's lots of food and drink! (mid-July)

Zwolle—Blauwvinger-Dagen

A summer festival, crafts market, and folk entertainment keep residents and visitors entertained during this annual round of festivities. (mid-July/early August)

Nijmegen—International Zomerfeesten

A popular, week-long festival of music, fireworks, and general merrymaking runs here with emphasis on the international—heavy doses of American Dixieland, jazz, and Latin music prevail. Though Nijmegen is one of the oldest towns in Holland, it's quite cosmopolitan during the Zomerfeesten. You can hear innumerable languages in the squares, and music is, literally, everywhere! (mid- to late July)

Scheveningen—Swinging Scheveningen

For two weeks in July, this popular seaside resort is host to a number of cultural activities, including street parades, jazz concerts, and performances. (mid- to late July)

August

Gouda—Goveka

A bit like an Irish country fair, the Goveka combines cattle and cheese in an exhibition on the Market Square from 9:00am-2:00pm, usually on the second Wednesday of the month. A Potter's Festival, also held in Gouda on a Wednesday (usually between August 16th and 31st), brings potters from all over the country to demonstrate their skills and craft. Like most events in Gouda, the Market Square is the setting. It's backdrop, the Town Hall, is the oldest Gothic building of its kind in the Netherlands.

Yerseke—Mussel Day

This celebration features the harvesting and cooking of mussels, a dietary staple in all of the Low Countries. Everyone turns out to celebrate the new harvest with a free, "all-you-can-eat" feast from steaming vats in the town square. (Saturday in mid-August)

Breda—Breda National Tattoo
Billed as "A Feast of Sight and Sound," the Breda spectacle is a color-ful show of sound, color, and movements perfectly timed from be-ginning to end. The band performance, which includes military ensembles from around Europe, begins with the ringing of the 45 bells of the carillon of the Grote Kerk, a 13th-century Brabantine Gothic edifice. Only the top of the church is lighted at this time, and thousands wait breathlessly for the first sounds and the simultane-ous lighting of the entire church. This spectacle, repeated nine times more, has presented show bands and trumpet bands, in addition to the Royal Military and Marine Band. (late August/early September)

Maastricht—Preuvenemint Burgundian
This food festival, held on a late August weekend in this city in the Limburg region, offers all the pleasures of Dutch food and drink. Maastricht is Holland's oldest fortified city, with origins dating to a Roman settlement circa 50 B.C.

Raalte—Stoppelhaene
A "harvest home" weekend, this event includes a parade and a tradi-tional butter market on Friday. The procession of floats is prepared using the produce being harvested at that time. (late August)

Utrecht—Holland Festival of Early Music
Billed as "ten days of music from the Middle Ages, Renaissance, Ba-roque, Classical, and Early Romantic period," this event is a cornuco-pia that will satisfy any classical music lover. Besides the performances scheduled each day (concerts, chamber music, dance productions), there's an Early Music Fair during the two weekends, with instrument makers and workshops, antiquaries, records, and books; carillon con-certs and an organ *estafetta*; and lectures and workshops. Events occur in historic settings like churches, monuments, and museums.

Utrecht is often called the "Venice of the North," and since Venice is one of the festival's main themes, a special project involving the canals is called "Boat Trip a la Venice" and includes a three-hour boat ride with a concert.

For more information, contact Central Festival Box Office, P.O. Box 734, 3500 AS Utrecht. (late August)

September
Gouda—Jazz Festival
Held in the town center usually during the first weekend, the Jazz Festival includes concerts, a street parade, and a series of small band performances in cafes and pubs throughout the city.

Zwolle—Nederlandse Jazzdagen
Utilizing both indoor and outdoor facilities, this festival offers over

40 concerts by the most important Dutch jazz artists. All styles are presented—blues, pop, Dixieland, and swing—in the concert halls of Schouwburg Odeon and the Papenstraattheater and in large festival tents. (usually the first weekend)

The Hague—Prinsjesdag
The Palace Noordeinde is considered the "working palace" of Queen Beatrix (her official residence is the Palace Huis ten Bosch in Haagse Bos). Every year on the third Tuesday of September, the Queen and Prince Claus depart Noordeinde in a golden coach drawn by eight horses to open Parliament at the Binnenhof. The coach is escorted by military bands and officials and brilliant pageantry, and thousands of Dutch citizens turn out to watch. Queen Beatrix later addresses the States General and Parliament in the Ridderzaal.

Enkhuizen—Brandaris Balkoppenrace
A huge tug-of-war between fishing vessels is held on the Ijsselmeer Lake, usually on the last weekend of the month.

October
Zuidlaren—Zuidlaardermarkt
Billed as "the biggest horse market in Western Europe," this event is both colorful and entertaining, and it emphasizes the variety of activities the Dutch offer visitors to their country. (mid-Oct.)

Flowers:
Holland's National Passion

Flowers are Holland's national pride. No other country displays such magnificent color in the spring. The most important bulb-growing areas are just behind the dunes of the provinces of North and South Holland from Den Helder down to Haarlem and Leiden, and in the extreme northeast of North Holland Province.

The Dutch take every opportunity to show off their pride with flower parades and flower barges. In late April, the parades from Haarlem to Noordwijk, and the one from Amsterdam to Aalsmeer to Rijnsburg, are viewed by thousands. Aalsmeer is also the site of the biggest flower auction in the world, with a daily turnover of nine million cut flowers. Whatever season, there are numerous flower markets in the towns, on barges in Amsterdam, Haarlem, and Utrecht, and by the canals in Leiden and Delft.

Every decade, an international horticultural exposition called *Floriade* becomes the ultimate homage to the flower. The show recognizes Holland's role as a world leader among flower-growing nations and showcases industry achievements worldwide. Floriade next runs April 10-Oct. 11, 1992 at Zoetermeer, near The Hague, on a site with 175 acres of park and 70 acres of indoor exhibition space. Admission will cost about $11.

Windmills & Market Days

No image of Holland is complete without windmills, which continue to stand proudly atop the flat land. While over 9,000 windmills once operated around the country, about 1,000 remain today.

Supposedly, the windmill blades "speak" sentiments when they're at rest. When the blade is rising to the top, set just before 12:00, it's celebrating. If it's just after 12:00, it's mourning. The miller is taking a brief break when the blades are at 3:00, 6:00, and 12:00, and for a long time when they're at 1:30, 4:30, 7:30, and 10:30.

Many windmills were used to drain the flat terrain, while other processed corn, timber, paper, and oil. The most famous drainage windmills, 19 in all, are located at Kinderdijk, near Rotterdam, and are illuminated during Windmill Days in September. Others located near Zaanse Schans, an open-air museum, and at Valk, Falcon, and Leiden, also can be viewed during Windmill Days in May.

A beautifully restored example is "The Red Lion," a traditional corn mill originally shaped in 1771 and restored in 1986. Visitors can see the owners practice the old craft of milling, transforming corn into products used by bakeries around Gouda, where the mill is located. On April 30, the official Queen's birthday, the mill's sails are decorated with flags. Other festivities involving the mill include National Milling Day (second Saturday in May), harvest feasts in September, "The Week of Bread" in early October.

If windmills are the spectacle of the polders and canals of The Netherlands, then folk markets are the cause célèbre of the villages and towns. Romanticism, nostalgia, tradition, and conviviality are abundant throughout the summer in the large weekly markets at Schagen and Hoorn. Cheese markets are colorful attractions at Alkmaar, Purmerend, and Gouda. Traditional costumes and folk events enliven these markets, as inhabitants dress for the occasion and offer demonstrations of native crafts and skills.

Dutch Holidays

New Year's Day, Good Friday (most shops open), Easter Sunday and Monday, Queen's Birthday (April 30), Liberation Day (May 5), Ascension Day, Whitsunday, Whitmonday, Christmas, and Dec. 26.

For further information, contact **The Netherlands Board of Tourism**. In the U.S., addresses are 355 Lexington Ave., New York, NY 10017 (212-370-7367); 225 N. Michigan Ave., Suite 326, Chicago, IL 60601 (312-819-0300); and 90 New Montgomery St., Suite 305, San Francisco, CA 94105 (415-543-6772).

LUXEMBOURG

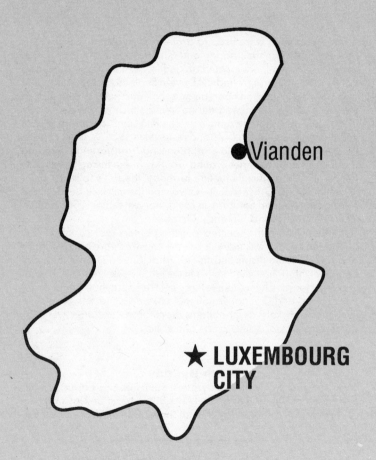

●Vianden

★ **LUXEMBOURG CITY**

Luxembourg

May

throughout—Spring Festival
On the morning of May 1, members of local clubs and bands assemble in the forest to make wreaths of the first green branches to symbolize the rebirth of nature. The wreaths are carried to the village, preceded by the local brass band, and are used to decorate cafe entrances and the homes of local officials. Like "May Days" in other countries, the Luxembourg festival is colorful, with deep roots in folk traditions.

Remerschen—Moselle Wine Tasting Day
This event speaks for itself. The land east of the capital lies on the Moselle River, and towns celebrate the light, dry wines grown in the vineyards on its steep bank. Many of the vineyards date from the Roman era. (May 1)

Luxembourg City—Octave
Since 1628, Catholics of the Grand Duchy and nearby regions have made an annual pilgrimage to worship Our Lady of Luxembourg in the Cathedral. Opposite the Cathedral is the "octave market," with food stands and souvenir shops. The "octave" runs from the third to the fifth Sunday after Easter.

Luxembourg City—Closing of the Octave
This closing ceremony, a solemn procession, expresses the religious tradition of the country. The Grand Ducal family and other Catholic dignitaries attend this major event. (fifth Sunday after Easter)

Echternach—Festival International Echternach
This classical music festival includes performances by an array of international artists, including past shows by the Jerusalem Chamber Orchestra, the Cleveland Choir, the Sorbonne University Choir, and the Berlin Philharmonic. The Church of Saints Peter and Paul and the

11th-century Basilica host the events. Echternach, a lovely town on the banks of the Sure, is also the location of the unusual skipping procession held on Whitsun Tuesday. For more information, contact Festival International Echternach, P.O. Box 30, L-6401, Echternach. (throughout May)

June

Wiltz—Genzefest

This "Broom and Gorse Festival" is held when the slopes of the Ardennes are covered with the golden blossoms of the gorse. To celebrate, the people hold a parade with folklore groups, bands, and floats decorated with broom flowers. The festival is traditionally held on Whitmonday.

Echternach—Springprozession

This unique dancing parade honors St. Willibrod, a Northumberland missionary who established an abbey here in 658 A.D.—one of the continent's earliest centers of Christianity. The procession forms at 9:00am, and participants dance and sometimes skip through the narrow streets to a haunting tune played over and over by various bands, before entering the Basilica. Pilgrims from all over Europe march and chant to the ancient melodies, in an odd combination of religious solemnity and native gaiety. One writer called it "an unspoiled survival of ancient, sanctified merry-making." The procession is held on Whitsun Tuesday. (Whitsunday is also known as Pentecost, the 7th Sunday after Easter. Many European countries hold special events on the Monday and Tuesday following Pentecost.)

Wormeldange—Wine Fair

Within the tiny borders of Luxembourg, miles of vineyards produce delightful wines like Riesling, Pinot, Elbling, and Gewurtztraminer. Many towns pay homage to the harvest with fairs like the one at Wormeldange. Lots of fun and wine-tasting! (early June)

Wellenstein—Sampling Day

Another fun wine-tasting fair. One of the prettiest and most productive of the region's wine villages, Wellenstein is easy to visit on a tour of the Moselle area. Other charming wine villages are Wasserbillig, Ehnen, Remich, Schengen, and Grevenmacher, capital of the Luxembourg Moselle and endowed with cooperative cellars and striking medieval fortifications. (late June)

throughout—National Holiday

Traditional festivities, parades, concerts, receptions, and dancing fill all the towns and villages on this national holiday. In the evening preceding the National Day, Luxembourg City hosts torchlight parades and fireworks and illuminates public buildings. (June 23)

Grevenmacher—Sampling Day
More wine-tasting in the cooperative cellars. (late June)

Wormeldange—Folklore Fair
More fun, folk dancing, and wine-tasting are on tap at this country fair. (late June)

Ettelbruck—Remembrance Day
Unique on the European calendar of events, this day honors American Gen. George Patton, liberator of the Grand Duchy in 1944. Patton is buried at the American Cemetery at Hamm, with 5,100 soldiers of his famous Third Army. "Remembrance Day" includes a military parade, air show, and exhibitions of military equipment. (early June)

Wiltz—Open-Air Theater & Music Festival
Top international artists in opera, drama, classical music, and jazz perform in the open-air theater of the Castle of Wiltz. For more information, contact Festival European du Théâter, Castle of Wiltz, Wiltz. (throughout July)

August

Rosport—Procession to Our Lady of Girsterklaus
In the very Catholic country of Luxembourg, the Procession to Our Lady, held since 1328, is unique in that it winds through fields and orchards in a delightfully spiritual manner. (mid-August)

Luxembourg City—Schueberfouer
This ancient Shepherd's Market has become the capital's amusement fair. Founded in 1340 by John the Blind, Count of Luxembourg and King of Bohemia, the Schueberfouer is a delightful example of Luxembourg folk culture. On Sunday, sheep festooned with ribbons march through several city districts, accompanied by shepherds dressed in folklore costumes. A band plays a gay old tune, the Hammelsmarsch (the Sheeps' March), to the delight of hundreds of participants and on-lookers. (late August/early Sept.)

September

Schwebsingen—Wine Festival
Yet another wine day, with concerts and dancing in the public square. And best of all, wine flows from a fountain in the center of town! (early Sept.)

Luxembourg City—Braderie Sidewalk Sale
The busy capital takes the day off for the Braderie Sidewalk Sale, when the avenues and streets of the city center are closed to traffic. The entire city adopts a festive look in an atmosphere of mingling crowds, music, the smell of grilled sausages, and, of course, more wine! (early Sept.)

Grevenmacher—Grape and Wine Festival
Over 10,000 people visit Grevenmacher this weekend for the most famous of Luxembourg's many wine festivals. This tiny town of 3,000 becomes the center of attention in the Moselle Valley, with fireworks, a folklore parade, wine sales, and dancing in the evening. (early Sept.)

Luxembourg Off-Season
In mid-November, the town of Viandem celebrates *Miertchen* (St. Martin's Fire), an ancient custom marking the end of the harvest and the payment of the levy to the feudal lord. Two large bonfires blaze, and a torchlight procession winds through the streets.

Throughout December, from the smallest village to Luxembourg City, shops, homes, and streets glow with Christmas lights and decorations. On the 6th, St. Nicholas arrives to reward the children who have been good through the year. The Sunday before the 6th, the saint and his gloomy companion, Pere Fouettard (dressed in black and carrying a whip to chastise naughty children), are welcomed throughout the country. After a procession, St. Nicholas gives sweets to the children.

Carnival season is observed in Luxembourg on the days before Lent. On *Fetten Thursday* (Fat Thursday), children disguise themselves and go house to house singing a carnival song. A village family prepares a reception for them consisting of carnival pastry donated by adults and called *pensees brouilles* (mixed thoughts).

Also during Carnival season, a Carnival Prince reigns supreme. Afternoons are reserved for parades, evenings for masked balls. Five localities are especially known as the places to really celebrate before the six weeks of fasting: Vianden, Weiswampach, Wormeldange, Echternach, and Steinsel.

Luxembourg Holidays
New Year's Day, Shrove Monday, Labor Day (May 1), Ascension Day, Whitmonday, National Day (June 23), Assumption (Aug. 15), All Saints Day (Nov. 1), Christmas, and Dec. 26.

For further information, contact the **Luxembourg National Tourist Office**. In the U.S., the address is 801 Second Ave., New York, NY 10017 (212-370-9850).

5

France

"There is no French race. There is a French people made up mostly of invaders and immigrants who have become one through several thousand years of living together, fighting together, and creating together a culture, a way of life, a civilization on the same land."
—Claire Huchet Bishop, *Here Is France*

While there may not be a French race, fortunately there is a France, a country with as much diversity of landscape and climate as of people. United now by a modern government and a common language, France remains a nation whose people cling steadfastly to their many cultural distinctions.

From its earliest days, France has been inhabited by "foreigners." Celtic tribes, Gauls, Cretans, Phoenicians, Greeks, Romans, Druids, Franks, Vandals, Visigoths, Huns, Britons, Arabs, Vikings, Normans, Saxons—all invaded the land at one time. After the 15th century, people came from Italy, Portugal, and Spain as well, adding new pieces to the cultural mosaic that had been forming for centuries.

Other factors which could cause more chaos than harmony are the political divisions created by the Revolution in 1793. Instead of the traditional fiefdoms like Aquitaine, Burgundy, and Toulouse, France was divided into 96 *départements* and countless *arrondissements*, cantons, and communes. Further division came in the establishment of 24 provinces. Recently, these provinces have been grouped economically and geographically into six regions which, according to one source, are "too distinct to compare, and far too magnificent to miss."

Painfully aware of the vastness and variety of France, Charles de Gaulle, who served as President from 1958-1968, once asked, "How could you expect to govern a country that has more than 400 kinds of cheese?"

Four hundred cheeses (actually around 348), probably as many types of wines, 20 *arrondissements* in Paris alone, 96 *départements*,

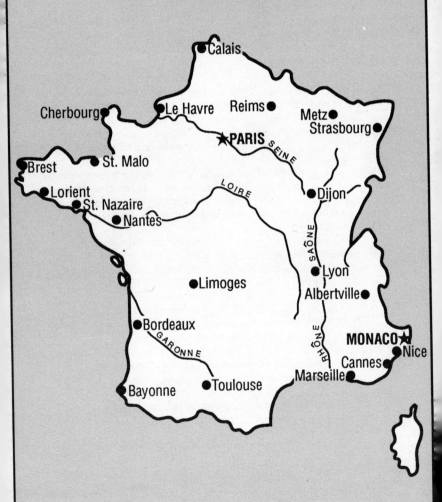

six regions, 212,000 square miles, and at least three temperature zones—a rich source for delightful cultural contributions from all its corners. Sophisticated opera and theater festivals play at ornate theaters in Orange and Avignon; a peasant wedding or cherry festival highlight the weekends in Alsace or Lorraine; a gypsy pilgrimage or bullfight in Provence recalls ties to Roman days; Celtic celebrations in Brittany or Normandy evoke French links to neighbors across the English Channel. France has it all!

Paris and the Region

May

Paris—French Open Tennis

The French Open lures all the big names in the game to the Roland Garros Stadium. Tennis has become enormously popular throughout France since the early 1970's, and with the Open being the world's premier red clay court tournament, as well as the first of the four Grand Slam events, it is a very big draw. France hosts another international tournament for men (also a big clay court event), the Monte Carlo Open, in April. Tickets for early matches in Paris are fairly easy to obtain by mail or in person, but you'll need to request seats for the semi-finals and finals well in advance. For more information, contact Fédération-Française de Tennis (FFT), 2 Av. Gordon-Bennet, 75016 Paris. (late May/early June, for two weeks)

Paris—Festival de l'Ile St.-Louis

A melange of theatrical events takes place for a month on the smaller of the two islands in the Seine. Just across the footbridge behind Notre Dame (on l'Ile de la Cité), this lovely neighborhood is quite provincial in nature and charm, and the setting greatly enhances the performances. Be sure to leave time to explore the area before or after the events. Check locally for current details. (throughout May)

Versailles—Festival de Versailles

Located close enough to Paris (only 13 miles southwest) to be a "city sight," Versailles offers both a spectacular tour and terrific entertainment. *Grandes Eaux Musicales* (illuminated fountain shows) run Sunday evenings through the summer, and the Festival itself presents ballet, opera, concerts, and theatrical events at venues throughout the city. (late May through late June)

June

Paris—Festival du Marais

Once considered the neighborhood of high fashion, Le Marais now offers over 100 magnificently restored old mansions, making it one of the most charming areas of Paris. Many of the events of the festival—classical and jazz music, theater, exhibitions—are held in the courtyards of the renovated Renaissance buildings. For more information, contact Festival du Marais, 68 rue François-Miron, 74004 Paris. (mid-June to mid-July)

July

Paris—Festival de l'Ile de France
Primarily musical, this event consists of free concerts in the châteaux and parks throughout the city. Check locally for current details. (throughout the summer)

Paris—Festival de l'Orangerie de Sceaux
With the orangerie of the Château de Sceaux as its setting, this festival offers a mix of chamber music, popular music, and piano recitals. Concerts begin at 5:30pm Saturday and Sunday. (mid-July to mid-Sept.)

Paris—Bastille Day
This national holiday is celebrated throughout France, but Paris offers the greatest panache, with a huge parade, fireworks, dancing in the street, and a youthful propensity for tossing firecrackers into Metro stops! It's a day of great fun. (See also below.) (July 14)

Paris—Festival Estival
The Paris Summer Festival bridges the cultural gap (though you'd hardly notice one exists) between the Marais event and the Festival d'Automne (late Sept.-Dec.). Founded by Bernard Bonaldi, a young entrepreneur who wanted to create an active summer cultural life during the deserted months of July and August (deserted by natives, not tourists), the festival focuses on symphonic, chamber, vocal, and contemporary music, and solo recitals. Concerts run throughout the city in places like Saint-Chapelle church, the church at Saint-Germain-des-Prés, the Conciergerie, and the Salle Pleyel. For more information, contact Estival de Paris, 20 rue Geoffroy L'Asnier, 75004 Paris. (mid-July to mid-Sept.)

Paris—Tour de France Finish
This three-week bicycle race across 2,112 miles—from the Valleys of the Loire to the passes of the Alps—finishes its final stretch from Bretigny-sur-Orge to Paris (113.5 miles) in grand style. Thousands line the Champs-Elysées to cheer the winner of this most famous of all cycling events. The finish in Paris is truly a grand finale! (mid-July)

August

Since August is the vacation month for Parisians, tourists pretty much have the city to themselves. The Festival Estival and Versailles Grandes Eaux Musicales continue.

September

Paris—Festival d'Automne

The city resumes its normal cultural pace in September, and the new season begins with the Festival d'Automne, which usually focuses on two themes or composers. Its moving spirit, Pierre Boulez, arranges drama, ballet, expositions, and chamber music in the Pompidou Center and other museums throughout the city. For more information, contact Festival d'Automne, 156 rue de Rivoli, 75001 Paris. (late Sept.-Dec.)

Paris—Festival d'Art Sacré

Those fortunate enough to enjoy Paris without the summer crowds should attend at least one of the sacred music concerts. With Notre-Dame and St.-Séverin serving as concert venues, this festival (like Marais) is doubly enjoyable. The Radio France Philharmonic Choir and Orchestra and the Societé de Musique Contemporaine are among the featured performers. For more information, contact Bureau de Festival, 4 rue Jules Cousin, 75004 Paris. (Sept.-Dec.)

Montmarte—Fêtes des Vendanges

Imagine a vineyard in the heart of Paris! The last vineyard in the city, just minutes from the Basilica of Sacré-Coeur in the hill area of Montmarte, produces enough of a harvest to be a cause for a celebration. Most visitors to Paris see the sites of Montmarte, so a visit on the first Saturday of October is a delightful bonus.

Bastille Day

July 14th, France's national holiday, marks the anniversary of the storming of the Bastille prison in 1789 and the start of the French Revolution. In Paris, the day starts with a military parade down the Champs-Elysées and ends with fireworks at Montmarte, the Parc Montsouris, and the Palais de Chaillot. Traditional street dances on the eve of Bastille Day occur at places like the I'lle de St. Louis, the Hôtel de Ville, Place de la Contrescarpe, and, of course, the Bastille. Firecrackers tossed into Metro stops are de rigueur, so beware! The fun of the 14th can be, well, explosive.

Paris doesn't corner the market on celebrating. In the medieval citadel of Carcassonne, for example, the whole town is set on fire! Actually, the fireworks spectacle there is called L'Embrasement de la Cité, which translates as ''the setting on fire of the ancient fortress-town.'' The effect is made by illuminating the 50 towers of the walled city as a reminder of revolutionary tactics. And since Carcassone has much less traffic than Paris, dancing in the streets is much easier.

In addition, Bastille Day events in Nancy at the Place Stanislaus are said to be a close second to the festivities in Paris. And many places on the Côte d'Azur hold national balls to commemorate the event, and fireworks displays are everywhere.

Northwestern France
(Normandy, Brittany, Loire Valley, Western Loire, Poitou-Charentes)

May

Mont-St.-Michel—St-Michel de Printemps
Night is spectacular at Mont-St.-Michel, the tiny island on the west coast of Normandy, home of the Benedictine monastery and abbey buildings dedicated to the archangel St-Michel. At the spring folklore festival in early May, the island comes alive with singing and dancing groups. During the festival, the Mont is illuminated to make it even more memorable. (It's also lit at all church feasts and on high tide nights.)

Orléans/Rouen—Festival Jeanne d'Arc
The most beloved of French saints, Joan of Arc is honored in many regions on days that mark her courageous accomplishments. Three major events in her life are most commonly commemorated, the first of which is associated with the town of Orléans. On May 7 and 8, 1429, Joan liberated this city from the English. Today, Orléans celebrates with a series of pageants and ceremonies.

In Rouen, on the weekend nearest May 30, pageants mark the day she was burned at the stake in 1431. Held prisoner in Rouen by the English after her campaign across France, she was later tried for heresy by the French clergy. After standing resolute for over three months, she finally weakened, disavowed her faith, and was sentenced to life imprisonment. But the English sought a heavier punishment, and Joan was killed in Rouen's Place du Vieux Marche.

The third major event occurs in Reims (see Northeastern France).

Sees—Son et Lumière at the Cathedral
For a description of son et lumière, see below.

Colleville-sur-Mer/Arromanches—D-Day Commemorations
The 50 miles of Normandy shore that played such a vital role in the events of D-Day (June 6, 1944) are best known as the Invasion Beaches. Technically, Sword, Juno, Gold, Omaha, and Utah were part of Operation Overlord, with U.S. Gen. Dwight D. Eisenhower in command. When the D-Day invasion ended, nearly 25,000 men and 17,000 vehicles had come ashore to liberate Europe. This momentous event, recalled annually in military and civic celebrations, is testimony to the valor of thousands from the Allied forces.

Le Lude—Son et Lumière

Le Puy du Fou—Son et Lumière

Chenonceaux—Son et Lumière

Amboise—Son et Lumière

Noirlac—Eté de Noirlac
The Cistercian Abbey of Noirlac is the setting for a two-month event of classical, sacred, and medieval music and exhibitions. Performers of international standing participate along with secular and religious choirs and orchestras. For more information, contact Amis de l'Abbaye de Noirlac, 5 rue de Seraucourt, 18000 Bourges. (through mid-August)

July

Blois—Son et Lumière at Château de Cheverny

Chambord—Son et Lumière

Ste-Anne d'Auray—Sainte-Anne's Day Pardon
See below.

Valencay—Son et Lumière

Montguyon—International Folk Festival
This annual music and dance festival features over 1,000 performers from at least 20 nations. One year, Spain alone boasted 350 dancers and 120 musicians. Montguyon is located in Cognac Country, about 60 km. north of Bordeaux. For more information, contact Bureau de Festival, 6 Place du Champ de Foire, 17270 Montguyon. (late July)

Rennes—Les Tombées de la Nuit
Dance, theater, mime, cabaret, puppetry, and song—over 180 performances—are presented throughout Rennes, which becomes a huge, multi-faceted stage with more than 16 prestigious venues featured, including Places Royales, cloisters, medieval squares, and gardens. One year saw more than 120,000 spectators. For more information, contact Office of Tourisme de Rennes, 8 Place du Marichal Juin, 35000 Rennes. (early July)

Quimper—Festival de Cornouaille
Each year between the third and fourth Sundays of July, Quimper presents Breton culture of yesterday and today. Historically the capital of La Cornouaille, the oldest and most traditional region of Brittany, Quimper's festival is another attempt to preserve the heritage of this beautiful region so closely linked to its Celtic past. (Unlike most

French, Bretons are a Celtic people whose ancestors came from Britain to escape Anglo-Saxon invaders in the 5th and 6th centuries).

The seven days of the festival offer dancing, music, costumes, songs, exhibitions, and native food and crafts. During the festival, which draws over 4,000 participants and 100,000 visitors, Breton traditions abound, including the "Gathering of the Bagpipes of Europe." Games, bell-ringing competition, band concerts, fireworks, street players, folklore performers, pottery workshops (Quimper pottery is world-renowned)—all contribute to a week of unique regional culture. For more information, contact Festival de Cornouaille, BP77, 2 Place de la Tour d'Auvergne, 29103 Quimper Cedex.

August

Lorient—Festival Interceltique de Lorient

This festival is the major annual get-together of artists, musicians, writers, and speakers from the Celtic areas of Scotland, Ireland, Wales, and the Isle of Man. On each day of the 10-day event, some type of concert, pipe band competition, symphonic creation, or parade occurs to honor the Celtic traditions that remain so important in the Breton community.

An average year attracts over 4,500 traditional and classical musicians, singers, dancers, and artists. A huge arts and crafts fair runs concurrently, along with language workshops, symposiums, and regional culture and cuisine lectures. For more information, contact Festival Interceltique de Lorient, Place de l'Hôtel de Ville, 56100 Lorient. (first fortnight in August)

Perros-Guirec—Pardon of Notre-Dame de la Clarté

See below.

St-Guenolé Penmarch—Pardon of Notre-Dame de la Joie

See below.

Le Son et Lumière

Spectacular, breathtaking, moving—these are some of the adjectives used to describe the unique form of entertainment known in France as *son et lumière* (sound and light shows). Modern musical and lighting technology notwithstanding, the château setting is what really gives these spectacles their uniqueness, their *je ne sais quoi*.

The shows are highly theatrical events which bring to life aspects of French history and culture. Occasionally, performances include actors who revive historic personalities. In fact, the docudrama *Cinescenie du Pay du Fou* in Pay du Fou used 650 actors, 1,550 spotlights, and countless floats and pyrotechnics to recall the story of

France through the eyes of one peasant.

Son et Lumière first became popular in the Loire region, and other areas have adapted the idea to fit their unique architecture, often with a church or cathedral as the setting. These events, scattered throughout the country, generally run in the summer—but not on a daily basis, however, so check the area you'll be visiting for specific days and times.

Days of Wine and Saints

While Joan of Arc might be France's most beloved saint, countless other religious figures have feast days with events ranging from processions to bullfights.

In Brittany, for example, annual festivals to honor local saints, called *pardons*, date to the days when penitents received indulgences on saints' days and Ascension Thursday. While *pardons* honor the saints on a religious basis, they also give residents an excuse to don traditional Breton costumes and to display Breton heritage in food, song, and dance. The best known and most frequently visited *pardons* take place in Tréguier in May, Ste-Anne-d'Auray in late July, Locronan on the 2nd Sunday in July, Perros-Guirec and Ste-Anne-La-Palud on August 15, and at Josselin in September.

Most towns with St-Jean in their names celebrate the feast day of St. John the Baptist on or near June 24. The Feast of the Assumption (August 15) is also a day for festivities in many communities.

Like other wine-growing countries, France celebrates its wine harvest with great ceremony, with entire weekends dedicated to the glorious grape. *Fête de Vin Nouveau, Fête des Vendanges, Fête des Vignerons, Fête des Caves, Fête du Vin*—all amount to a great deal of sampling the local variety. Some villages, in the Alsace region for instance, combine wine fests with tribute to local foods. *Choucroute, oignons, tartes aux quetsches*, raisins, *fois gras, cerises, griottes*, even *bière*—all have their time for a French celebration. They're too numerous to list individually, but travelers need only to look for the word *fête* to be assured of a great time.

North/Northeastern France
(Nord-Pas-de-Calais, Picardy, Champagne-Ardennes, Alsace, Lorraine, Franche-Comté, Burgundy)

May
Strasbourg—International Music Festival
The magnificent rose-colored cathedral of Strasbourg is just one of the concert sites during this two-week event. Founded in 1932, the

festival presents works by well-known composers like Bach, Beethoven, Mozart, and Haydn, and great composers are honored on major anniversaries. Some contemporary music is also on the program, and new works are premiered. For more information, contact Festival International de Musique de Strasbourg, 24 rue de la Mesange, 67081 Strasbourg. (early May)

Reims—Festival Jeanne d'Arc

The third city associated with St. Joan is Reims, where she returned the Dauphin for his coronation as Charles VII. Processions and other ceremonies mark this victorious occasion. (early May)

Belfort—Son et Lumière at the Castle

(early May through late July)

Nancy—Son et Lumière at Place Stanislaus

(mid-May to mid-Sept.)

Wissembourg—Vent d'Est/Fêtes de Pentecote

A long-standing Pentecost tradition, the Wissembourg event is part sacred and part profane. The weekend festivities include a costume display, folk dancing, exhibitions, and tributes to the music of countries other than France, especially Eastern European nations. A spectacular equestrian display and folklore parade takes place Sunday afternoon. (early May)

Sarré-Union—La Fête Medievale

This weekend event features everything you would expect in a medieval pageant—oriflammes, trumpets, costumes, knights in armor, and even a joust! A special attraction is the re-creation of the 1463 marriage of Nicolas de Sarréwerden and Barbe de Fenetrange amid 15th-century splendor. A historical cortege with 800 costumed participants is held before the mock marriage. Appropriate food and drink accompany the festivities. (mid-May)

Vandoeuvre-Les-Nancy—Contemporary Music Festival

Everything's up-to-date in Nancy, at least where music is concerned. For a week in mid-May, the town hosts a contemporary music fest that highlights modern innovations like multi-channel sound, digital systems, electrophones, and video systems. The event draws an international audience and performers of world-renown. For more information, contact Centre Culturel Andre Malraux, 1 Place de l'Hôtel de Ville, 54504 Vandoeuvre-Les-Nancy Cedex.

Reims—Cathedral of Light Festival

The Gothic Cathedral of Notre Dame is the setting for this son et lumière that lasts through the summer. (late May-Sept.)

June

Champagne—Champagne Summer Festival

Dedicated to a different composer each year, this festival is produced with the winners of the Advanced Cycle of the National Higher Conservatories of Paris and Lyon. Concerts begin every Saturday at 9:00pm, and special exhibitions run in conjunction with the musical offerings. For more information, contact Château de Braux-Sainte-Cohiere, 51800 Sainte-Menehould. (late June-Sept.)

July

Beaune—International Music Festival

This event, set in the winery region of Burgundy, offers a classical music program at the Hospices de Beaune and the Basilica of Notre-Dame. A number of tours to wine-producing villages in the countryside complement the musical offerings. Beaune is 20 minutes by train from Dijon. For more information, contact Office of Tourisme, Place de la Halle, 21000 Beaune 6. (early to mid-July)

Douai—Gayant à Douai

One of the essential folklore elements of the northern regions of Picardy and Nord Pas de Calais involves the *gayants* (giants), enormous mannequins revered by residents and featured in parades and carnivals. The Gayant à Douai, the oldest and most famous of these processions, features a venerable giant who first made his appearance in 1530. He was a given a wife and two children several years later, and today the family participates in a grand procession followed by folklore groups and appropriate music.

There are about 100 giants in the festival, but some are much more important than others. Most represent legendary or historic figures—like saints or Biblical heroes—and are the creations of local guilds who take great pride in their construction. Originally constructed for religious pageants, the *gayant* gradually dropped their exclusively Christian connections and now appear at civil functions, as well as at pre-Lenten carnivals in Dunkirk, Cassel, Hazebrouck, Lille, Avesnois, Valenciennes, and elsewhere.

A typical giant, like the venerable father in the Douai family, is 8.5 meters tall, weighs 370 kg., and requires six men to carry him. Certainly among the most unusual folk figures of France, they should not be missed. For more information, contact Comité Regional de Tourisme du Nord Pas de Calais, Place Rihour, 59800 Lille; or Comité Regional du Tourisme de Picardy, 3 rue Vincent Auriol, B.P. 2616, 80026 Amiens Cedex. (early to mid-July)

Autun—Pageant of Antiquity

The only Gallo-Roman theatrical show in France involves 600 costumed residents in the fabulous Roman Theater of Autun. Vercingetorix, the Triumph of Caesar, the Legions, chariot races, music, and dance are all presented. At one time, Autun was the largest city in Roman Gaul and boasted a circus, theater, and amphitheater. Pageant performances run weekends through late August. For more information, contact Office of Tourisme, 3 Avenue Charles de Gaulle, 74100 Autun.

Troyes—Son et Lumière
At the Cathédral (through Sept.).

Château-Chalon—Son et Lumière
Through August.

Mutzig—Cortege des Sans Culottes
This traditional parade recalls the events of July 13, 1789 by telling the story of the night before the storming of the Bastille. This patriotic, historic procession combines music and drama. Colorful and spirited, it's a great way to get ready for *quartorze Juillet*. (July 13)

August

Schiltigheim—Beer Festival
Plenty of eating and quaffing beer from "the beer capital of Alsace" occurs during this mid-August *bièrfescht*. This festival has been going strong since 1979, though history hints at a similar event as early as 1738. *Beaucoup de bière, beaucoup de musique* aptly describes this week of homage to the hops in Schiltigheim.

Colmar—Wine Fair
Drawing over 160,000 visitors in the last 10 years, the Colmar Wine Fair is one of the biggest and most versatile fests in the Alsace region. Local foods, folk music, and dance groups add to the fun. (early August, for 10 days)

Marlenheim—Friend Fritz's Wedding
This festival celebrates the wedding of Fritz Kobus and the charming Suzel, characters made famous in the writing of Erckmann and Chatrian. Each year, both actors and audience re-enact the storybook event. Like a real wedding, the festivities begin the evening of the 14th with traditional music and dancing. On the morning of the 15th, a huge procession presents Fritz and Suzel to their friends. The mock ceremony at City Hall is followed, naturally, by a banquet, with music, dancing, and Alsacian cuisine. A country fair runs concurrently, with regional crafts demonstrated and sold. (August 14-15)

Lille—Braderie de Lille
Someone once remarked that in northern France, "the whole year is spent having a good time." (I think someone once said the same thing about the south—and the west and east!) Those looking for

fun will always find a food fair, a beer *kermesses*, a religious fête, a carnival, or a *braderie* (an open-air jumble-sale) in the area.

But perhaps no *braderie* is more famous than the one in Lille, a thriving commercial center. In keeping with the popular traditions of the Middle Ages in this area, Lille's fairs and markets feature not only antiques and crafts but also food—tons of food. In one year, visitors consumed over 500 tons of *moules* (mussels) alone, not to mention the tons of french fries and grilled fish, so popular in this area on the English Channel. The Lille *braderie* runs from August 15 to mid-Sept.

September

Strasbourg—MUSICA: Festival of Today's Music
This two-week event features the finest in contemporary music, often with innovative, high-tech additions. The internationally acclaimed festival draws modern musicians from throughout the world to this lovely city on the Rhine. For more information, contact MUSICA, 9 rue du General Frere, 67000 Strasbourg. (early Sept.)

Besançon—International Music Festival
For two weeks in one of Franche-Compté's major cities, this festival emphasizes symphonic concerts and recitals ranging from works by Bach to George Enesco. Many major symphonies perform in historic venues like the 12th-century St-Jean Cathédral, the Palais de Justice, the Abbaye de Montbenoit, and the Théâter de Belfort. For more information, contact Festival of Besançon, 2d, rue Isenbart, 2500 Besançon. (early Sept.)

Dijon and Côte d'Or—Folklore Festival
Over 20 folksong and dance groups from places like Sri Lanka and Turkey join an equal number of French groups to perform for a week in early September. To complement the music, a wine exposition— *Fête de la Vigne*—and countless tastings take place in many towns throughout the region. Great fun! For more information, contact Office of Tourisme, Pl. Darcy, 21000 Dijon. (early Sept.)

Picardie—Cathédrals Festival
Seventeen prestigious concerts are held in the exquisite cathedrals of these northern towns: Amiens, Beauvais, Noyon, Laon, Senlis, and Soissons. Others are held in venues like the Abbey Chapels of St. Leu d'Esserent, Corbie, and Ham. Various renowned performers, such as the Orchestra and Choir of La Scala of Milan, are invited to perform during the three weekends from mid-September to the end of the month. For more information, contact Bureau du Festival, Conseil Regionale de Picardie, 11 Mall Albert 1er, 80000 Amiens.

Off-Season: Les Trois Glorieuses
France's "three glorious days" take place in three Burgundy towns on the third weekend of November. Beaune, Clos-de-Vougeot, and Meursault (Côte d'Or) offer wine tastings, wine auctions, and a fabulous banquet for international *bon vivants* and wine merchants. Though much of the activity is reserved for professional wine merchants, there's plenty of sampling, dancing, and general merrymaking to accommodate all visitors. For more information, contact Comité Regional Bourgogne, 1 rue Nicolas Berthot, 21000 Dijon.

Southwestern France
(Aquitaine, Midi-Pyrenees, Languedoc-Rousillon)

May

Bordeaux—Mai Musical de Bordeaux
Set in the delightful wine-growing area of Aquitaine (Medoc, St-Emilion, Château Lafite, and Château Mouton-Rothschild are some local vineyards), Bordeaux is an active, sophisticated city with a marvelous 16-day musical event. The symphonic and chamber music concerts, operas, recitals, ballet, and theater presentations alternate between town and country settings—theaters, churches and châteaux. Venues include the 18th-century pride of Bordeaux, the Grand Théâter; the best-known wine castle in the region, Château d'Yquem; the Château de la Brede; and the Cathédral St-Andre.

Like many European music festivals, the setting is a great complement to the production. Add some wine-tasting, and it's truly a perfect event. National orchestras from throughout Europe perform along with internationally recognized soloists and pianists. For more information, contact Mai Musical de Bordeaux, Grand-Théâter, Pl. de la Comedie, 33074 Bordeaux. (early May)

June

Carcassonne—Troubadours in Carcassone
As do so many festivals in France, this two-week celebration of medieval music and theater has a perfect and complementary setting—the double-walled, fortified city that dates to the first century A.D. The Cité, as it's called, is the pride of the Languedoc region. (mid- to late June)

July

Vigan—Festival du Vigan
This event, which even has a "fringe," includes a wide range of musical offerings—jazz, ballet, chamber music, regional and national

orchestras, choir performances, and piano recitals. Two or three concerts run weekly from mid-July to late August. For more information, contact Festival du Vigan, Cap de Breau, 30120 Le Vigan.

Nimes—Mosaiques Gitans

Gypsy groups from all over Europe perform at various outdoor venues throughout Nimes (Place du Palmier, Scene de l'Esplanade, and Scene de la Placette) at 7:00pm, 8:00pm, and 9:00pm each night for one week in mid-July. Though not what you might expect in a *French* city, the event is very popular in this area.

What you might expect, though, is a jazz festival, and Nimes provides it in the third week of July. Prominent American jazz musicians on the European summer circuit perform in the spectacular Roman arena, the city's focal point. (At one time, the city was Augustus' gift to his troops.) For more information, contact Office du Tourisme, 6 rue Auguste, 30000 Nimes.

Carcassonne—Festival de Carcassonne

Everyone from Ray Charles to the Ballet of Monte Carlo has performed at this event, which usually runs throughout the month. The Grand Théâter, Château Comtal, or the Basilique Saint-Nazare host most performances. For more information, contact Théâter Municipale, BP 236, 11005 Carcassonne.

Sète—Sète Festival

This dance, theater, and music festival features Broadway companies, national orchestras, and solo performers. It follows the Sète Jazz Festival, held for five days in early July. The main festival runs for three weeks, from mid-July to early August. For more information, contact Théâter Municipale, Avenue Victor Hugo, 34200 Sète.

Montignac—Festival of Montignac

The popularity of folk festivals is evident throughout France, and Montignac is no exception. Guest countries often include the U.S., Russia, and several Asian and European nations. Five evening shows, two matinee ''panoramas,'' and daily street entertainment make this week-long event in the Perigord-Noir region a worthwhile stop. For more information, contact Amicale Laique de Montignac, 57 Rue de 4 Septembre, 242290 Montignac. (mid-July)

St. Céré—St. Céré Festival

Over 40 concerts in the Midi-Pyrenees region—operas, symphonies, chamber music—are offered at St. Céré, which began the festivals in 1960 and added opera in 1980. Selections are wide-ranging—from *The Tales of Hoffman* to *Bolero* and *Don Quixote*—and dinner shows feature regional specialties like *foie gras, confit,* and Cahors wine. For more information, contact Festival of St. Céré, 64 Rue Saint Honoré, 75001 Paris. (mid-July to mid-August)

Souillac—Jazz Festival

For a touch of New Orleans in France, visit the "Sim Copans" Jazz Festival, where jazz quartets and New Orleans bands perform in concert halls and in the streets for a long weekend of traditional American music. For more information, contact Bureau de Festival, B.P. 16, 46200 Souillac. (mid-July)

Salers—Festival Renaissance

Somewhat like the event in Puy-en-Velay, this *Grand Fête Historique* recalls a period in French history quite distant to modern travelers. A "total Renaissance immersion" for three weeks (late July to mid-August) is available to visitors to this lovely area of the Massif Central. For more information, contact Syndicat d'Initiative, Place Tyssandier-D'Escous, 15410 Salers.

Montignac—Perigord-Noir Music Festival

Each year, this festival takes a different theme for one week and presents a variety of musical offerings within that topic. Thereafter, you can hear classical music of all types in churches and abbeys throughout the city. For more information, contact Bureau du Festival du Perigord-Noir, 49 Rue du General Foy, 24290 Montignac. (mid-July to late August)

Prades—Pablo Casals Festival

The great cellist honored by this event spent the last 23 years of his life in Prades. Though several performances feature Casals, the festival is not restricted to his works. Performances are wide-ranging, including Beethoven, Brahms, and Schubert, with groups like Festival Strings Lucerne, the Slovak Chamber Orchestra, and the Scottish Chamber Orchestra. The Abbey of Saint Michel de Cuxa is the venue. For more information, contact Bureau du Festival Pablo Casals, Rue Victor Hugo, 66500 Prades. (late July to mid-August)

Oloron Sainte Marie—Festival of the Pyrenees

In a single year, this festival brought together over 1,000 dancers and musicians from five continents, plus 45 folklore ensembles from 25 countries, for a "celebration of friendship between peoples." Some of the representatives were from as far away as Papua New Guinea and South Korea, and as close as Spain and Belgium. Quite a few folklore groups from the nearby Basque, Bearnais, and Bigourdan areas contribute as well. For more information, contact Bureau du Festival, 11 Place de la Marie, B.P. 95, 64403 Oloron Sainte-Marie Cedex 03. (late July to early August)

Côte Vermeille—Eté Musical en Côte Vermeille

Beethoven, Mozart, Vivaldi, and Bach all appear on the musical menu of this regional event, which uses several venues on the Côte Vermeille: Banyuls, Port-Vendres, and Collioure. There are several performances a week from early July through early September. For more information, contact Château Royale, B.P. 33, 66190 Collioure.

Perpignan-Roussillon—Festival Mediterranean

From early July to mid-August, all varieties of music are performed throughout the Languedoc-Roussillon area: Puccini's *Tosca* in Estagel by the Camerata de France; Mozart's *Requiem* in Montpellier and Perpignan by the Ensemble Vocal and Instrumental de Lausanne; and classical music in venues like Narbonne, Baixas, and Amelie les Bains. For more information, contact Festival Mediterranean, B.P. 4, 13129 Salin de Giraud.

August

Marciac—Jazz in Marciac

Marciac lies in the ''Deep South'' of France, in the heart of Gascony about 100 km. from Toulouse and 30 km. from Lourdes. Jazz greats rendezvous in Marciac for a week of nightly concerts—a week jazz fans should not miss. For more information, contact Jazz in Marciac, 4 Place du Chevalier d'Autras, 32230 Marciac. (early August)

Carcassonne—Medievales

Throughout August, the ancient Cité reverts to life of the Middle Ages, as townspeople don period costumes and practice traditional crafts. Epoch music and theater are offered daily, and at night a *son et lumière* is staged at La Cité.

Rhône-Alps & Central France
(Rhône Valley, Dauphine, Savoie Mont Blanc, Limousin, Auvergne)

May

Vichy—Théâter Opéra de Vichy

The Théâter Opéra of Vichy, a permanent opera festival, runs from April-October. Begun in 1902, the productions are always first-rate. Recent shows included Mozart's *Idomeneo*, Rossini's *The Barber of Seville*, and Bellini's *Romeo and Juliet*. In addition to major opera performances, ballets and concerts give vast musical variety. The venue is the Théâter Opéra House in Vichy. For more information, contact Théâter Opéra de Vichy, rue du Parc, 03200 Vichy.

June

Lyon—Lyon International Festival

First held in 1946, the Lyon Festival has developed into a first-class music, dance, theater, and art showcase. The program includes symphonic, choral, and chamber concerts, recitals, opera, organ competitions, and jazz. The Théâter Romain de Fouvière, a large Roman arena that seats 3,000, hosts many of the symphonic productions. Considered the gastronomic capital of France, Lyon is an excellent festival venue. For more information, contact Festival International de Lyon, Hôtel de Ville, Place de la Comedie, 69268 Lyon. (mid-June to mid-July)

July
Vienne—Jazz Festival
With scores of renowned jazz musicians playing throughout Europe in the summer, you can expect almost every region to host at least one. This is Dauphine's offering, and patrons are rarely disappointed. (early July)

Tournon—Son et Lumière
At the Château (through mid-Sept.).

Grignan—Son et Lumière
At the Château (through mid-Sept.).

Vollore—The Concerts of Vollore
The Auvergne region hosts this classical and sacred music concert for two weeks mid-month. Vollore (Puy-de-Dôme) is about 50 km. from Clermont-Ferrand and Vichy. For more information, contact Concerts de Vollore, B.P.1, 63120 Volloreville.

Chamonix—Mont Blanc Music Weeks
The spectacular mountain town of Chamonix, bordered by the Mont-Blanc range and the Aiguilles Rouges chain, hosts this classical music fest each summer. Strauss Family waltzes, Chopin, and Bach are all included to underscore the splendid scenery and air. Concerts take place in the Salle du Majestic at 9:00pm. For more information, contact Office of Tourisme, 74000 Chamonix. (mid-July to mid-August)

Le Puy-en-Velay—International Folklore Festival
For 10 days in mid-July, 15 cities of the Haute-Loire region have the opportunity to view this folk dance and music fest. Since the mid-1960's, representatives of over 100 countries have performed at the event, held in Le Puy-en-Velay, Yssingeaux, Saint-Didier, Saint-Sigolene, Le Monastier, Craponne, Langeac, Barges, Saint-Genest-Malifaut, Le Chambon/Lignon, Rosieres, and Montfauçon. You may see folklore groups from as far away as Japan and Thailand, or as close as Holland and Portugal. For more information, contact Office de Tourisme du Puy-en-Velay, Place du Breuil, 43000 Le Puy-en-Velay.

Gannat—World Folklore Festival

To present as many aspects of traditional cultures as possible, this central France city hosts more than 400 dancers, musicians, singers, and craftsmen from four continents at its annual 10-day festival. One year alone saw groups from the U.S., Luxembourg, Spain, Africa, Paraguay, and Bulgaria. Gannat is 320 km. from Paris, 18 km. from Vichy. For more information, contact Bureau du Festival, 4 Avenue de la Republique, 03800 Gannat. (mid-July)

Hérrison/Chateloy—Bourbonnais Music Festival

Located in the area of the Aumance Valley and the Troncais Forest, the Roman Church of Chateloy dominates the landscape and serves as the serene venue for these Sunday evening concerts. For more information, contact Festival Office, Sohier, 03190 Hérisson. (late July through late August)

Bourbonnais—Nuits Musicales en Bourbonnais

This "itinerant" festival moves throughout the region of the Auvergne in an attempt to combine high-quality art and architecture with historic venues like châteaux and churches. The program, which has included performances by the Choir of Christ Church Cathedral, Oxford, often features the works of Beethoven, Schubert, Bach, and Debussy. For more information, contact Association Musiques Vivants, 3 rue Jean-Joures, 03200 Vichy. (late July)

August

Le-Puy-en-Velay—Fêtes Mariales

This traditional folk procession is generally held on the eve and again on the day of the Feast of the Assumption, August 15. It's a colorful example of Auvergne folk practices (*fêtes patronales*). The procession winds through the cobblestone streets which lead to the beautiful Cathédral Notre-Dame.

September

Dijon—Folkloriades and Vines Festival

Each year, the Folkloriades lures groups from nearly 30 countries for a folk music and dance competition. The final Grand Parade, viewed by over 100,000 on the cobbled streets of Dijon, is a spectacular display of costumes and cultures. The festival brings groups from Africa and South America to join Europeans. It's a colorful addition to the lovely Burgandy landscape. For more information, contact Festival de Musiques et Danses Populaires, Cellier de Clairvaux, 27 Boulevard de la Tremuille, 211025 Dijon Cedex. (early Sept., for 10 days)

Lyon/La Côte-Saint-André—Hector Berlioz Festival

The first Berlioz Festival was launched in 1979 to honor the French composer, a native son (of sorts) of Lyon. During early September, Berlioz's operas, symphonies, choral works, songs, and oratorios are performed, usually by the Lyon Orchestra, with a guest orchestra sitting in, too. Most performances are held at the Maurice Ravel Auditorium in Lyon, but there are concerts in La Côte-Saint-André, Berlioz's hometown, 40 miles southeast of Lyon. For more information, contact Festival Berlioz, 127 Rue Servient, 69003 Lyon.

Le Puy-en-Velay—Roi de l'Oiseau Festival

This festival is based on the ancient tradition of "shooting for the king," a 16th-century archery competition to determine the best bowman in the area. The Roi de l'Oiseau revives the tradition in a fabulous Renaissance fest. Events maintain an authentic 16th-century air, with jugglers, acrobats, fire-eaters, dancing bears, ancient crafts, and period costumes. You even need special coins to spend at events or in cafes, where drinks of the time are featured. In addition to the archery competition and the crowning of the winner as "King of the Bird," there's an exciting contest on horseback between the various quarters of the city. Le Puy-en-Velay is 134 km. from Lyon in the Auvergne. For more information, contact Office de Tourisme du Puy-en-Velay, Place du Breuil, 43000 Le Puy-en-Velay. (mid-Sept., for one week)

Southeastern France
(Provence, Côte d'Azure, Monaco, Corsica)

May

Arles—Fête des Gardians

This colorful rodeo-like event is an annual gathering and parade of the *gardians*, men of the Camargue who herd the wild horses unique to this region. An excellent introduction to the folklore of Provence, it's only one of many intriguing folk customs. (May 1) (Throughout the summer, in Arles' great Roman arena, *corridas* [bullfights] are held on Saturday and Sunday.)

Toulon—Toulon Music Festival

Until 1964, this classical music event was called "The Festival of the Royal Tower." Past performers have included the Moscow State Choir, the Ballet of Nancy, and the Orchestra of the Salzburg Mozarteum. Venues include the Toulon Opera House, the Church of St. Louis d'Hyères, the royal tower of Fort de Bregancon, and the Abbaye du Thoronet. For more information, contact Bureau de Festival de la Bourse, Ave. Jean Moulin, 83000 Toulon. (late May to mid-July)

Cannes—International Film Festival

Though this prestigious film festival is not for the average tourist, no calendar can overlook it. Some screenings are open to the public, but mostly you must be content to hang around and star-gaze as directors, producers, and film stars from around the world gather at the Palais des Festivals for the annual unveiling of the world's best films. (mid-May)

Monaco—Grand Prix

Like Cannes, this event is not for everyone. But the name is synonymous with Monaco, so how could we overlook it? If you like auto racing with a flair, Monaco's Grand Prix, which runs on the winding streets of this sumptuous principality, is something to behold. The best international drivers compete in this world-class event, which never lacks for thrills and excitement. (late May)

St. Tropez—Grande Bravade

This religious procession and folklore event honors St. Torpes, whose statue is paraded through the streets for two days. The tradition, dating to 1558, marks the arrival of the saint to this area. The parade is punctuated by the sounds of bugles, drums, and blunderbusses, and with some reverence as the *bravadeur's* antique firearms are blessed. Like other such events, it's not purely religious—fun, food, music, and wine accompany. (usually May 16-18)

Les Saintes-Maries-de-la-Mer—Gypsy Pilgrimage

The wild marshland at the western edge of Provence is known as the Camargue, an area that can seem more Spanish than French. Full of wildlife (from pink flamingos to black bulls), its main settlement, Les Stes-Maries, gets even wilder on May 23-25, when the annual *Pelerinage* goes into full swing. According to legend, the town was founded by two followers of Jesus, Mary Salome and Mary Jacobe, who were expelled from Judea and cast adrift with their servant Sarah. They miraculously washed ashore at this site that now bears their names.

Sarah became the patron saint of Egypt and of the gypsies, and nomadic people from all over Europe assemble here to honor her in a variety of festivities, including a candlelight vigil in the church crypt where the statue of Sarah is kept. The festival ends with an exuberant parade of her statue to the sea amid flowers and fanfare. Post-procession events include singing, dancing, and colorful displays of the gypsy life. For more information, contact Syndicat d'Initiative, Ave. Van-Gogh, 13460 Stes-Maries-de-la-Mer.

June

St. Tropez—The Bravade des Espagnoles

This event commemorates the French victory over the Spanish fleet in 1637 and is only slightly less frenetic than its May counterpart, the Grande Bravade. (usually June 16)

Luberon—Festival of Luberon

An international string quartet festival runs throughout the summer in the villages of the Luberon area (Roussilon, Goult, La Fontaine-de-Vaucluse, and Silvacane). Performers come from as far as Russia and Czechoslovakia. Several French quartets also perform, many of whom won national competitions. (early June through Sept.)

July

Arles—Fête de la Tradition

Usually celebrated July 2-4, this traditional folk event brings locals to the streets in native costume. Bonfires blaze as the ancient city recalls regional customs, history, and language in an exciting tribute to its past.

Nice—Grand Parade du Jazz

What jazz impresario George Wein did for Newport, Rhode Island, he also did for Nice. In 1974, Wein initiated this 11-day jazz event, which lures top performers to Nice for nightly (5:00pm-midnight) sessions in the ancient Romanesque Cimiez Gardens, a huge park with two stages and a large amphitheater. Once inside the Gardens, you may wander to any of the three stages to catch whoever is performing—from Count Basie's Band to Dizzy Gillespie and the Dave Brubeck Quartet.

Although Europe is bursting with jazz events throughout the summer, this is really the biggest. Plus, jam sessions run in hotel bars, on swimming pool terraces, and in jazz clubs throughout Nice to add to the marathon atmosphere. It's also a good chance for U.S. tourists to satisfy a craving for "a taste of home," as American music is abundant.

Other jazz festivals with similar high quality performers occur in Antibes-Juan-Les-Pins (which featured Ray Charles in 1990) and Salon-de-Provence (Miles Davis starred in 1990).

For more information, contact Grand Parade du Jazz, Opera de Nice, 4 Rue St-Francois-de-Paule, 06000 Nice. (mid-July)

Cannes—Nuits Musicales Du Suquet

Cannes' nights of classical music are held outdoors in the hill area of the city called Le Suquet, in the courtyard of the 17th-century Church of Notre Dame d'Espérance. The program includes performances by large orchestras like the Scottish Chamber Orchestra and the Orchestra da Camera del Festival of Brescia and Bergamo, plus piano concerts by international musicians like Gabriel Tacchino, Youri Bashmet, and Katia and Marielle Labeque. (mid- to late July)

Aix-en-Provence—Festival d'Aix-en-Provence

One of France's most popular festivals, this one combines beautiful music with a gorgeous setting and offers a wide range of productions. First held in 1948, Festival d'Aix emphasizes opera, with three staged each season. One is usually Mozart, while the others range from Purcell to Rameau (his opera-ballet, *Les Indes Galantes* was recently featured). Again, the venues enhance the productions, and some of Aix's most beautiful buildings are used: Saint-Sauveur Cathédral (Cezanne worshipped here); Cloître Saint-Louis; the courtyard of Hôtel de Ville; and the 1,200-seat outdoor Théâter de l'Archevêché. Other musical offerings include chamber and symphonic music, recitals, rock concerts, street dancing exhibitions, and solo concerts. For more information, contact Aix-en-Provence International Festival, Place de l'Ancien Archevêché, 13100 Aix-en-Provence. (mid-July to early August)

Avignon—Festival d'Avignon

Founded in 1947 as an "arts week," this event has grown to include theater, ballet, art, and music. While the official festival has at least 12 venues, virtually every possible space in the ancient walled city becomes a performing area. The "Off" fringe festival boasts an additional 35 locations!

Some consider the Avignon event to be France's theater festival *par excellence* for the level of performances as well as the variety of venues. Somewhat unusual is the festival's emphasis on experimental theater and innovative film and dance, all attempted in the 14th-century Pope's Palace. New art forms are always highlighted, while sacred music and organ recitals are performed simultaneously. Suffice to say that Festival d'Avignon is perhaps the most eclectic fest in France. For more information, contact Avignon Festival, Bureau de Festival, 84000 Avignon. (early July to early August)

Orange—Chorégies d'Orange

Although major works have been produced in Orange since 1869, it wasn't until 1971 that the Chorégies became a full-fledged festival. The city's ancient Théâter Antique, the best-preserved in France and the only one where the stage wall is still intact, hosts the opera, choral productions, and symphonic concerts. Recent spectacular productions included Wagner's *Der Ring Des Nibelungen* trilogy, Mozart's *Magic Flute*, and Verdi's *Don Carlos*. Other highlights have been Strauss's *Alpine Symphony*, Zubin Mehta's conducting the Israel Philharmonic, and a performance by the Gustav Mahler Youth Orchestra.

Though the festival remains small in terms of number of productions, every other aspect is grand—especially the ticket prices ($165 for opera performances and $70 for concerts!). For more information, contact Chorégies d'Orange, 18 Place Silvain, B.P. 205, 84107 Orange Cedex. (early July to early August)

Sisteron—Nuits de la Citadel

Sisteron, the main northern pass into Provence, hugs the Durance River and is the site of the 13th-century cloister of St-Dominique, where the musical evenings are held. Concerts feature classical music, theater, and dance. For more information, contact A.T.M. Place de la Cathédrale, 04200 Sisteron. (late July to early August)

August

Menton—Menton Music Festival

This classical music event has been going strong since 1948. The port of Menton, just over the Italian border near Nice, holds its concerts outdoors in the Parvis Saint Michael, the square of the old village between two baroque churches. A recent festival featured such luminaries as violinist Anne-Sophie Mutter and the Johann Strauss Orchestra of Vienna. Programs remain classical, with emphasis on chamber music and works by Beethoven, Mozart, Bach, Rachmaninoff, etc. For more information, contact Palais de l'Europe, B.P. 111, Avenue Boyer, 06503 Menton Cedex. (throughout August)

Corsica—Fête de l'Assomption & Napoleon's Birthday

As a Catholic country, France celebrates the Feast of the Assumption (August 15) with a variety of events, both sacred and profane. On the island of Corsica, the date also marks the birthday of Napoleon, and thus takes on additional festivities. Virtually every town uses the day as an excuse for a round of dancing in the streets, fireworks displays, and general merriment. In Ajaccio, where Bonaparte was born in 1769, there's an especially festive spirit before and after the 15th.

A Provençal Sampler

When a region like Provence publishes its own directory called *Terre des Festivals* (Land of Festivals), you know there's a lot more happening there than simple sun-bathing. Music-lovers won't be able to resist the "big three" events of Aix, Avignon, and Orange, but beyond the walled cities and antique theaters are countless folk events and markets that give new meaning to the phrase "local color."

Valréas celebrates the lavender harvest with the *Corso de la Lavande* in August. It's part carnival, part agricultural fair, part Rose Parade, but all French and lavender, with tractors pulling floats decorated with new crop. Other *Fête de la Lavandes* are held in Digne, Sault, and Mazan, often around August 15 to coincide with the Feast of the Assumption.

In late June, Valreas also stages *La Nuit du Petit St-Jean*. This charming, medieval-style event occurs in the evening, with only candles in the windows to light the procession honoring the saint. Youths in medieval jerkins stamp out their Gauloises and flank the great Romanesque gate of the 12th-century church. When the gates open to a fanfare of trumpets and fireworks, they reveal *Le Petit St-Jean*, a small boy riding a white horse to be crowned King of Valreas for a year. The ceremony, involving over 300 residents, is a beautiful example of a Provençal religious/folk tradition. It usually takes place around June 23-24. Other places that pay homage to St-Jean are L'Escarene, St-Paul, Belvedere, Le Broc, Châteauneuf de Contes, Fontan Guillaumes, Levens, Mouans Sartoux, St. Etienne de Tines, Auron, St. Laurent du Var, St. Vallier de Thiey, Villeneuve, Monaco, Sospel, St. Jean Cap Ferrat, and Vence.

Marseilles, once known as the Gateway to the Orient, stages a daily ''event'' to emphasizes the importance of seafood in the area, with its fish market on the Quai des Belges. On Tuesday, Thursday, and Saturday, an herb market is held at the Place des Pecheurs, while an annual event of equal gastronomic importance is the Garlic Fair on Cours Belsunce in June.

Other Provençal highlights are the summer wine fairs, held just about anywhere a grape has ever appeared; the *ferias* (bullfights/rodeos) held in Nimes in May and Stes-Maries-de-la-Mer in July; and the fabulous pre-Lenten bash, the Nice Carnival, beginning three weekends before Shrove Tuesday, with torchlight processions, costumed parades, regattas, masked balls, fireworks, flower battles, and non-stop revelry.

French Holidays

New Year's Day, Easter Sunday and Monday, Labor Day (May 8), Ascension Day, Whitsunday and Whitmonday, Bastille Day (July 14), Assumption Day (Aug. 15), All Saints Day (Nov. 1), and Christmas.

For further information, contact the **French Government Tourist Office**. In the U.S., the addresses are 610 Fifth Ave., New York, NY 10020; 645 N. Michigan Ave., Chicago, IL 60611; 2305 Cedar Springs Rd., Dallas, TX 75201; and 9454 Wilshire Blvd., Beverly Hills, CA 90212. The public information number for all French tourist offices is 900-420-2003 (50-cents a minute).

Holidays in Monaco

New Year's Day, St. Devote's Day (Jan. 27), Easter Monday, Labor Day (May 1), Ascension Day (May 9), Whitmonday, Assumption Day, All Saints Day, Monaco's National Day (Nov. 19), Immaculate Conception (Dec. 8), Christmas.

For further information, contact the **Monaco Government Tourist and Convention Bureau**. In the U.S., the address is 845 Third Ave., 19th Floor, New York, NY 10022 (212-759-5227 or 800-753-9696).

Italy

"On a spring morning of the year 753 B.C., Rome was founded by Romulus, who with his twin brother Remus—so runs the tale—had been abandoned as a child on the banks of the river Tiber and suckled by a she-wolf. . . Three thousand years ago the history of Italy was already in full swing!"
—*A Glimpse of Italy*

Few countries in Europe are so adept at blending the rich past with the vital present in such variety as Italy. Historically a land known for hospitality, Italy continues to welcome tourists by the millions to revel in its unique antiquity.

Rome—"the eternal city," the center of Christianity, the capital of the western world for centuries—offers over 2,000 years of history. Florence was the cradle of the Renaissance; Genoa, the birthplace of Columbus, has been a chief seaport for centuries. And there's Perugia, queen of the Tiber plain and seat of a 13th-century University; and Palermo and Sardinia, both bearers of Norman, Arab, Spanish, and French history and culture.

The people of Italy—who created opera in the 16th century—delight in sacred plays from medieval times, showing their faith and penitence at celebrated sanctuaries or with religious rites followed by jubilant feasting. The Feast of St. Nicholas at Bari is observed with a procession of fishermen's boats. The Explosion of the Cart in Florence on Easter Sunday commemorates the victorious return of the First Crusade. The Flower Festival at Genzano marks the path of honor for the Corpus Domini procession.

Many traditional festivals originate from local history or recall the glories of a secular past. Italians don costumes and arms from the Middle Ages and the Renaissance enthusiastically. The jousting tournament at Arezzo, the tilting tournament at Foligno, crossbow competitions at Gubbio and San Sepulcro, bareback horse races at Siena—all are splendid evocations of Italian history and tradition.

Antique theaters at Verona, Macerata, Ravenna, and Taormina, plus the Baths of Caracalla in Rome, host operatic and dramatic events throughout the summer. Everywhere, during every season, Italy is alive with history.

In 56 B.C., the Roman poet Catullus sang the joys of the return of spring: *"Iam veregelidos refert tepores. . ."* ("Now spring returns with renewed warmth. . ."). His message, though seasonal in words, is universal in spirit, for Italy is always renewing itself in splendid ways.

May

Florence—Maggio Musicale Fiorentino

Despite its name, this major music festival extends well beyond the month of May. Since its establishment in 1938, the festival has grown to encompass two months of musical events. Opera, concerts, ballet, and sacred music are all included, at a wide variety of locations. The Teatro Communale and the Teatro alla Pergola are used for operas, and the Basilica of Santa Croce and the Palazzo dei Congressi for concerts and recitals. Some performances are held outdoors at the Boboli Gardens.

Many feel the Maggio Musicale Fiorentino is Italy's answer to the king of European festivals, Salzburg, because of its diversity. In addition to its own orchestra, the festival hosts opera companies from all over the world, from the Leningrad Philharmonic to the London Philharmonic. A highlight of a recent season was Luciano Pavarotti's return to Florence in *Il Travatore*. Pavarotti gave five performances with Zubin Mehta conducting at the Teatro Communale.

For more information, contact Maggio Musicale Fiorentino, Teatro Comunale, Via Solferino 15, 50123 Florence. (late April-early July)

Caligari—Sagra di Sant'Efisio

One of the biggest and most colorful processions in the world, the Festival of St. Efisio is perhaps the most important Sardinian folk event in the capital. The festival, held since 1657 to commemorate the end of a plague, features thousands of pilgrims in medieval costumes, *tracas* (ox-carts decorated with flowers, fruit, embroideries, and lace), and horsemen from the Campidano plain—all following the statue of St. Efisio to Pula, where he was martyred. (early May)

Lula (Nuoro)—Feast of San Francesco

This festival is celebrated in the sanctuary of San Francesco in the countryside near Mount Albo. In keeping with ancient custom, the faithful fulfill their vows to the saint, reaching the sanctuary on foot and offering votive candles. The prior welcomes them with bowls of *filindeu*, a soup made with cheese and meat. (early May)

Asti—Palio San Secundo

This *palio*, one of countless such events throughout Italy, opens with the annual celebration of Asti's patron saint. Supposedly, this event has been repeated without interruption for seven centuries. Representatives of all the town's quarters participate dressed in historical costume. The ceremony recalls the end of a long conflict between civil and religious authority, a truce that was sealed by the offering of a banner, the *palio*, to the church named for St. Segundo. The flagtossers of the Palio of Asti perform in Piazza San Secundo. Asti, a province of Piedmont famous for its vineyards and its religious festivities, is the home of sparkling wines Asti Spumante and Asti Cinzano. (early May)

Cocullo (L'Aquila)—Procession of the Serpari

At a procession in honor of St. Dominic of Foligno, who is invoked against snakebite, the saint's statue is draped with snakes handled by the *serpari* (snake-handlers). This unusual religious event stems from rituals of the pagan cult of the goddess Angizia. (early May)

Rome—The Nation's Cup

An internationally acclaimed horse show, the Nation's Cup brings together the cream of foreign and Italian riders to the Piazza di Siena in the Borghese Gardens. It is followed by a historic tournament, a stylish spectacle provided by mounted *carabinieri*. (early May)

Bari—Sagra di San Nicola

Two days of festivities mark the event dedicated to the patron saint of Bari. They include a historic Pageant of the Caravel on Saturday evening, when over 300 people in Norman-era costumes parade from the Swabian castle to the church of San Nicola. There they re-enact the delivery of the saint's bones to the Dominican friars, recalling the events of 1087 when merchants of Bari stole the saint's relics from their resting place in Myra. On Sunday, the saint's statue has a place of honor in a procession to the sea, with hundreds of boats sailing along the coast. Bari, one of the Tremiti Islands, is the capital of Perugia and one of Italy's principal embarkation ports for ferries to Yugoslavia. (early May)

Camogli (Genoa)—Fish Festival

In honor of San Fortunato, patron saint of fishermen, great quantities of fish are fried in a gigantic pan at the port and offered to the public. The event makes dining in Genoa both inexpensive and festive! (mid-May)

Camerine (Macerata)—Sword Race and Palio

Both history and folklore are the basis of these festivities in 15th-century costume. Again, a *palio* enters into the Italian events calendar as an example of marvelous traditional regional entertainment. (mid-May)

Gubbio (Perugia)—Festa dei Ceri

Gubbio, nicknamed "the city of silence," seems to be untouched by the passage of time. One obvious exception to the epithet is the raucous "procession of the candles" on May 15th, when shrines are carried to the Church of St. Ubaldo atop Mount Ingio. In this breakneck race, 20 men called *ceraiolo* carry enormous wooden constructions called *ceri* to the Church. The three *ceri*, hourglass-shaped wooden towers, are brought to the Piazza della Signoria from the basilica and topped with colorful statues of San Ubaldo, San Giorgio, and Sant'Antonio Abate. After 12 hours of flag twirling and elaborate preparation, the husky *ceraioli* heft the weighty shrines onto their shoulders and head toward Monte Ingino at a dead run. They eventually reach the basilica, where the candles remain until the following May.

Acquapendente (Viterbo)—Exhibition of the Pugnaloni

The highlight of these festivities in honor of the Madonna del Fiore is the exhibition of the *pugnaloni*, large decorative panels made of flower petals, grass, and moss. They recall a miracle—the sudden flowering of a cherry tree—that was a good omen for the town's revolt against Frederick Barbarossa in 1176. (late May)

Bucchianico (Chiete)—Festival of the Banderesi

This historical pageant honors Sant'Urbano with the conferring of the rings, investiture of the *sergentiere*, and the awarding of prizes for the best floats. (late May)

Massa Maritima (Grosseto)—Balestro del Girifalco

An imposing parade in historical costume precedes a competition between crossbowmen representing the three *terzieri* (districts) of the town (Cittanova, Cittavecchia, and Borgo). Traditionally, the event takes place on the Sunday following May 20 and again on the second Sunday in August.

Sassari—Sardinian Cavalcade

This fantastic parade, the greatest folklore gathering in Sardinia, recalls a victory over the Saracens in the year 1000. Over 3,000 people wear the various costumes of the island, and the event includes dancing, music, and singing contests. Horsemen and acrobats join this extraordinary festival of Sardinian folklore. (late May)

Florence—Cricket Festival

This festival, held at the Cascine Park, undoubtedly has its origins in the extermination of crickets, which farmers considered harmful. As floats parade through the park, vendors sell crickets in pretty cages. Once purchased, the chirping creatures are customarily set free in the park. (late May)

Venice—Wedding of the Sea
The Feast of the Ascension is the occasion of the ceremony recalling the "Wedding of the Sea" performed by Venice's Doge, who cast his ring into the sea from the ship *Bucintoro* to symbolize eternal dominion. As you may expect, the festivities include regattas of small gondolas. (Ascension Thursday is the 40th day after Easter.)

Zuglio (Udine)—Cross-Kissing Ceremony
Crosses from all the churches of the valley are adorned with multi-colored ribbons and carried in a lengthy procession to the Church of St. Peter, where they are placed before his cross and kissed by the faithful in fervent devotion. This lovely ceremony, devout and typically Italian, offers a quiet alternative to some of the more boisterous events honoring patron saints. (late May)

Ferrara—Palio of San Giorgio
This *palio* dates from the 13th century and features nearly 800 participants in costume representing the eight city districts. After a parade, various contests occur in the afternoon, including a horse race, a donkey race, and a number of races for children. (late May)

Gubbio (Perugia)—Palio dei Balestieri
The Piazza della Signoria in the lovely town of Gubbio is the scene of yet another highly regarded May festival, the Palio of the Archers. Basically a medieval contest (there are references to the event dating from 1410) between the representatives of Gubbio and Sansepolcro, this crossbow competition is the return match of the contest held in Sansepolcro the previous September. The strained expressions of the participants and the hushed crowds attest to the importance of the occasion. If Gubbio wins, an animated parade follows. In addition to the main event, there's a flag-tossing exhibition and a historical pageant. (last Sunday in May)

Legnano (Milan)—Carroccio Festival
This festival recalls the victory of the Lombard League over Barbarossa's troops in 1176. In the afternoon, hundreds of people in medieval costumes lead a parade, followed by the Carroccio, a cart drawn by three teams of oxen. After the historical pageant, a horse race is held, and the winner receives the Cross of Ariberto. (late)

Querceta (Lucca)—Palio dei Micci
Combining elements of history and folklore, this event features a parade in period costume and an amusing donkey race. Before the race, members of the eight town districts act out the historical and legendary episodes of the Versilia area. (late May)

Potenza—Parade of the Turks
This Parade of the Turks, part of the festivities honoring San Geral-

do, recalls the saint's return from Turkey. A picturesque parade of figures in Saracen costumes wends its way through the town, and a huge float shaped like a ship carries the statue of the saint, a group of Saracen corsairs, and a platoon of crossbowmen. (late May)

June

Almalfi/Genoa/Pisa/Venice—Regatta of the Great Maritime Republics

These four former maritime republics "fight" annually for supremacy of the sea with a historic regatta in which longboats representing the republics race for a prize. The regatta is preceded by a parade of over 300 people in historical costume. During the week before the regatta, a culinary contest pits the best chefs of the four cities against each other—to the delight of visitors, who may sample the results. The rotation order for this extremely colorful event is Amalfi, 1993; Genoa, 1994; Pisa, 1995; Venice 1996. (first Sunday in June)

Monterubbiano (Ascoli Piceno)—Sagra dei Piceni

This historic festival, recalling the folk customs of the Piceno region's celebration of Pentecost, mingles elements of history and folklore and features participants in costume. (Another major festival, the Joust of the Quintana, runs here on the first Sunday of August.) (an early Sunday in June)

Orvieto (Terni)—Feast of the Palombella

Every year, Orvieto celebrates Pentecost in an original way. A white dove (*palombella*), symbolizing the Holy Spirit, is tied to a metal "halo machine." At noon, the dove runs from the roof of St. Francis Church to a temple-shaped structure in front of the cathedral. The dove's arrival sets off firecrackers, and red flames light the Madonna and Apostles' heads. The feast began in the 15th century by Giovanna Monaldeschi della Cervara, a noble of Orvieto. (Pentecost is celebrated on the 7th Sunday after Easter.)

Pisa—San Ranieri

The centerpiece of this event is the spectacular illumination of the buildings along the banks of the Arno in honor of the patron saint of the area. Torches and thousands of candles float downstream on corks. On June 17th, the historic "Regatta of San Ranieri" is held—a historic rowing contest with eight teams in 16th century costume in hot competition on the river. (mid-June)

Faenza (Ravenna)—The Oath of the Cavalieri and Flag-Tossing Contest

Each horseman (*cavaliere*) swears before a magistrate that he will take part in the Palio del Niballo (on June 24), according to the chivalric code of honor and loyalty. A contest between flag-tossers representing the town's five districts follows. (mid-June)

Assisi (Perugia)—Corpus Domini

A number of beautiful processions called *infiorate* take place through-out Italy on the feast of Corpus Domini. In Assisi, colorful designs of flower petals adorn the streets, over which the procession passes. (Corpus Domini or Corpus Christi is a festival celebrated in honor of the Eucharist on the first Thursday after Trinity Sunday.)

Bolsena (Viterbo)—Infiorata

Floral compositions line the streets of Bolsena leading to the church of St. Cristina, where the miracle of the Host took place in 1263. In the morning, a solemn parade proceeds along the decorated streets. (Corpus Domini)

Brindisi—Procession of the Caparisoned Horse

This traditional procession of the decked horse dates to the Crusades. According to legend, in 1252 Louis IX, King of France, returning from Jerusalem on a ship carrying the Eucharist, was driven to Brindisi by a violent storm. Peter III, Archbishop at the time, rode to the ship on a white horse to take the consecrated host to safety. Since then, to recall this event, the Archbishops of Brindisi carry the Eucharist in a solemn procession, riding on a white horse. (Corpus Domini)

Campobasso—Festival of the Mysteries

A procession accompanies the ''parade of the Misteri,'' which are 12 tableaux from the Old and New Testament, formed by actors on large platforms carried on the shoulders of 40 young men. The tradi-tional procession dates to 1300. The wonder of this event is that, thanks to a special mechanical device, the people on the platforms appear to be suspended in mid-air. (Corpus Domini)

Rome (Genzano)—Infiorata

For the feast of Corpus Christi, an elaborate street procession is held in this hilltown outside Rome, where the marchers walk over a floral carpet of elaborate motifs representing coats-of-arms and other de-signs. The flowers, laid in just hours, require weeks of painstaking preparation, as artisans sketch designs on the cobbled streets of Via Italo Bellardi. During the afternoon and early evening of Corpus Christi, fresh flower petals are placed on the designs, creating a carpet of flowers—a riot of color and breathtaking art. To view the deco-rated street intact, visitors should see it on the first day, since the route to the church of Santa Maria della Cima is trampled during the actu-al procession at sunset the following day.

Cava de' Tirreni—Challenge of the Tromboniere

This challenge with blunderbusses (heavy ancient firearms) is a historic re-creation of the bloody battle of July 7, 1460, in which the inhab-itants rushed to help Ferrante I, King of Aragon. The participants wear period costumes, and the challenge is a contest in marksmanship between various groups. More than 800 people take part. (late June)

Ossuccio (Como)—Feast of San Giovanni

This is the oldest of Lake Como's traditional events. In the evening, an island facing the town is illuminated and fireworks are set off to give the illusion of the destruction of the island in a burning lake. The next day, a procession of boats sails to the island of Comacina for a festival of folk music, band concerts, and flag-tossing exhibitions. (late June)

Faenza (Ravenna)—Palio del Niballo

The event begins with a cortege in historical costume from the main square to the city stadium, where five horsemen representing the town's districts gallop, two at a time, to strike a target in the hand of a dummy, called the *Niballo*. This event is the finale of an earlier swearing-in ceremony, in which the horsemen (*cavaliere*) promised to participate in the race. (late June)

Nola (Naples)—Festa del Giglio

This event recalls the homecoming of Bishop Paolino in 394 A.D. after a long imprisonment in Africa, when the people welcomed him waving large bunches of lilies. Today, the lilies are 25-meters tall, decorated, storied, and painted. Each is carried on the shoulders of 40 bearers who, after the Bishop's blessing, make the "lilies" perform a remarkable choreographed dance. (late June)

Florence—Festa di San Giovanni Battista

During the feast of St. John the Baptist, the patron saint of Florence, a number of festive events occur in this exciting city. The *Gioco del Calcio*—sporting matches that resemble wrestling, rugby, and soccer, with a round leather ball thrown more often than kicked—are perhaps the most colorful. Four teams of 27 players in period costumes recall the days of the 16th-century republic, when a match was played in 1530 as a dare to the troops of Charles V, who had laid siege to the city. A historical procession of Florentine guild officials, followed by the four teams led by their resident noblemen on horseback, precedes each game. One game is usually scheduled on June 24, with the others within the week or two before or after. The event, which draws up to 8,000 spectators, has been held on Piazza della Signoria and Piazza Santa Croce, as well as in the Boboli Gardens. (See also below.)

Pisa—Gioco del Ponte

Pisa is divided into halves by the river Arno—in both a geographical sense and a competitive sense. The two communities, the Tramontana and Mezzogiorno (North and South), tolerate each other for 364 days of the year, but on a late Sunday in June they give free reign to their animosities and vie for the Ponte di Mezzo, a bridge over the Arno. The teams try to conquer the "middle bridge" by pushing a heavy cart to the rivals' side. In the past, this tournament involved hand-to-hand combat and often became violent; the cart is a modern convention. More than 600 participate in a historic parade in medieval costumes.

Spoleto—Festival dei Due Mondi

This renowned music festival has become one of Italy's most important cultural events. "The Festival of Two Worlds," founded by Italian composer Gian Carlo Menotti in 1957, includes opera, concerts, dance, drama, ballet, and film. Its setting is equally notable: Spoleto, the capital of the dukes of Lombard from the 6th-8th centuries, is a picturesque Umbrian hilltown full of narrow passages and interesting crannies, quaint shops, and colorful markets. The final concert is traditionally held in front of the 12th-century cathedral, with the audience sitting on the majestic stairway in the shadow of handsome palaces and hanging gardens. A twin festival is held in the "other" world: Charleston, South Carolina, USA. For more information, contact Festival Dei Due Mondi, via Cesare Beccaria 18, 00196 Roma, or via Guistolo 10, Spoleto. (mid-June to mid-July)

Orta San Giulio, Pettenasco, Isola di San Giulio— Cusius Early Music Festival

Italy's tranquil and elegant lake region is the ideal setting for this festival, which regularly features Gregorian chants, madrigals, cantatas, and baroque and renaissance music, as well as the works of Monteverdi, Scarlatti, Vivaldi, and others. Attendants in the church and salon venues wear period costumes. For more information, contact Festival Cusiano di Musica Antica, c/o A.A.S.T., 28016 Orta S. Giulio. (late June)

July

Siena—Palio delle Contrade

This renowned horse race for the *palio* (the city's silk banner) pits the city's 10 *contrade* (districts) in an ancient dash around the town square, Piazza del Campo. On the morning of July 2, there's a trial run in the square, but the preliminary events take place as early as June 23, when the *palio* for the winner is displayed. A splendid costume parade precedes the race.

The pageantry of Il Palio is incomparable; the entire city comes alive with excitement. Tickets are expensive for the best seats, and most of the grandstand seats belong to residents by birthright. Those without tickets can stand in the center of the square. In general, it's advisable to order tickets from Agenzia Viaggi SETI, Piazza del Campo 56, Siena 53100, or through your hotel. (See also below.)

Matera—Sagra della Bruna
In this religious celebration, an allegorical float decorated with papier-mâché friezes and statues bears a representation of Our Lady of the Burned Cart. The main event recalls the stealing of the image by the Saracens and its eventual recapture by her faithful. But to prevent a recurrence, the people of Matera decided to burn the cart on which the image of Our Lady was placed. This act became a custom in the area, and the destruction of the cart has become an annual event. (early July)

Minturno (Latina)—Sagra delle Regne
A series of religious, cultural, folk, and sporting events are held in honor of Our Lady of the Graces. The festival, with roots in local folklore, marks the offering of the first wheat to the Madonna. The main event is a thanksgiving ceremony for the abundant harvest. Other minor events and festivities are held throughout the week. (early July)

Verona—Outdoor Opera Season
The Verona Outdoor Opera, a tradition since 1922, offers productions of the world's best-loved operas staged in a spectacular first-century amphitheater, which seats 20,000 and is only minutes from Juliet's house. During the Verdi centenary celebrations in 1913, Verdi's *Aïda* played here, and his works remain the centerpiece of the season. Three operas are staged each season, along with ballet and selected concerts. Everything is of the highest quality—from the acoustics to the actors—and the tickets are rather expensive, though well worth the price considering the magnificence of the performances. For more information, contact Ente Lirico Arena di Verona, 28 Piazza Bra, 37100 Verona. (early July to Sept.)

Macerata—Outdoor Opera and Ballet Season
The enormous amphitheater of the Arena Sferisterio, built in 1829 as a ball field for *pallone a bracciale* (a popular sport from the 15th-19th centuries), now caters to opera and ballet lovers and has become one of the most important cultural festivals in Italy. The Arena Sferisterio seats 6,000 spectators and is set amid the medieval splendor of Macerata, a charming town in the central Italy area called The Marches. A recent season included *Il Trovatore*, *La Boheme*, and Verdi's *Messa de Requiem*. For more information, contact Festival Office, Piazza Mazzini, Sferisterio-Casella Postale 92, 62100 Macerata. (mid-July to mid-August)

Sedino (Oristano)—S'Ardia
This daring horse race along a treacherous course recalls the victory of Constantine the Great over Maxentius at the Milivan Bridge in 312 A.D. Performed by daredevils who come from all over Sardinia to participate, it's really more of a ''cavalry charge'' than a contest.

The riders race from an old stone cross in a field to the church, rounding it seven times at breakneck speed. (early July)

Castel di Tora (Rieti)—Dance of the Fantasima
This typical fest of the Sabine Hills includes a procession and a folk festival. In the crowded square, a three-meter tall figure of the *fantasima* (ghost) appears, and the man inside it lunges around to frighten onlookers. The festivities end with the destruction of the effigy and a bonfire. (early July)

Palermo—U Fistinu
The U Fistinu is the most important Sicilian celebration in honor of Santa Rosalia, Palermo's patron saint. An enormous float carrying a huge band parades through the streets. On the last evening, a spectacular fireworks display follows the pilgrimage to the shrine of the saint atop Mount Pellegrino. (mid-July)

Lucca—Feast of San Paolino
The feast of the patron saint of Lucca is marked by a torchlight parade in period costume and the ritual of the offering of a votive candle to the saint, with the blessing of the *palio* (the banner) following. A crossbow competition is held in the evening. (early July)

Venice—Il Redentore
Held on the night between the third Saturday and Sunday in July, the Feast of the Redeemer is an enormous, not-to-be-missed procession of gondolas and other craft commemorating the end of the epidemic of 1575. The festival begins quietly at the church of the Redentore on the Giudecca, where pilgrims visit throughout the first day. At night, there's a lovely fireworks display and an impressive barge full of flowers floating down the Grand Canal. The next day, the procession from San Marco to the church takes place over a bridge of boats. The lagoon is filled with boats and the shore is jammed with on-lookers in a scene that could only occur in Venice. (late July)

Ravenna—Summer Music at the Rocca Brancaleone
The remains of the majestic Rocca di Brancaleone (Fortress of Brancaleone), built by the Venetians in 1457, hosts this festival of music and the arts. In addition to the opera and ballet at the arena, other musical events take place in the beautiful basilicas throughout the city: Santa Apollinare in Classe, Santa Apollinare Nuovo, and the Byzantine Basilica San Viatale. Ravenna, capital of Rome's western empire in 402 A.D., is famous for its Roman and Byzantine buildings and 5th- and 6th-century mosaics. For more information, contact Ravenna Festival, Teatro Alighieri, Via Mariani 2, Ravenna. (early July to mid-August)

Trastevere (Rome)—Festa de Noantri

This ancient and popular festival includes a procession for a parade of boats on the Tiber (the *Vergine del Carmine*), gastronomic evenings, band concerts, parades of floats, and fireworks displays. Though it honors Our Lady of Mt. Carmel, it may be just an excuse for merry-making and indulgence for the *noiantri* ("we others"), the people of Trastevere who consider themselves the only true Romans and choose to celebrate their neighborhood when others have fled the July heat. (late July)

Rome—Baths of Caracalla

For years, the stone Baths of Caracalla, built during the reign of Caesar Augustus in 216 A.D., lay in near-ruin, but in 1937 the site was selected as the place to stage open-air opera. Today, over 35 opera and ballet performances are produced by the Rome Opera Company and ballet companies from Italy and around the world. In recent years, the festival has featured Luciano Pavarotti, Plácido Domingo, José Carreras, and conductor Zubin Mehta.

The stage, said to be the largest in the world, measures 100-by-162 feet, and the arena can seat 10,000. It's an acoustical nightmare, but the extraordinary setting makes you overlook the problems. For more information, contact Box Office, Teatro dell'Opera, Piazza Beniamino Gigle, 00100 Rome. (early July to mid-August)

Torre del Lago Puccini—Puccini Festival

Torre del Lago Puccini (Lucca), on the shores of Lake Massaciuccoli in Tuscany, is where Puccini's operatic masterpieces are glamorously staged at the edge of the lake. A recent season included *Tosca*, *Madame Butterfly*, and *Balletto*, produced by the festival company. Located near Viareggio, the master composer's beautiful villa Museo Puccini is a shrine for music devotees. His home from 1891-1921, it's now a museum in his honor. Admirers can see the chapel where he and his family are buried, the Forster upright piano on which he composed, and the rifle collection he kept for hunting. After *Manon Lescault*, Puccini composed all of his operas except *Turandot* here. For more information, contact Festival Pucchiniano, Piazzale Bellvedere Puccini, 55048 Torre del Lago Puccini. (early July to mid-August)

Perugia—Umbria Jazz

The Umbria region of Italy, famous for its centers of art, is host to

Send a Postcard!

If you discover a new festival or celebration you think should be included in this book, please send me a postcard about it. Write me in care of Mustang Publishing, P.O. Box 3004, Memphis, TN 38173 U.S.A. Thanks!

the country's top jazz festival. Jazz musicians and blues singers from Europe and America have moved into this quiet town to create yet another Italian contradiction. During the ten-day event, over 100 concerts take place in the ancient buildings of Perugia and other Umbrian towns. For more information, contact Associazione Amici della Musica, Via San Prospero 23, 06100 Perugia. (mid-July for two weeks)

Barga (Lucca)—Opera Barga
Opera Barga, one of the oldest Italian festivals, is an experience of living musical theater that includes young artists and seasoned professionals. Opera Barga offers performances in the Villa Gherardi gardens and in the Piazza Angelico. (mid-to late July)

Levanto (La Spezia)—Festival of the Sea
To honor San Giacomo, patron of fishermen, this festival features parachute jumps, flag-tossers, swordplay, a nocturnal costume parade, colored lights, fireworks, and a procession of boats. (late July)

Pistoia—Giostra dell'Orso
This typically Italian event, rich in historical and folk elements, boasts some rigorous competition. Twelve horsemen, three from each quarter of town, represent their districts in a contest where they must lance two targets (stuffed bears) at a gallop. With origins from the 14th century, the Joust of the Bear includes a series of cultural, musical, and sporting events known as "July in Pistoia." (late July)

August

Assisi (Perugia)—August Festival
A month-long series of events, ranging from history and folklore pageants to religious feasts, is held in this town so closely associated with St. Francis. The events include the Feast of Pardon, the Feast of San Rufino, the Feast of Santa Chiara, the Feast of the Assumption (with a ceremony in the Basilica of Santa Maria degli Angeli), and the Palio of San Rufino (featuring a parade in historical costume, a flag-tossing exhibition, and a crossbow contest). The Festa Musica Pro Mundo Uno also features internationally known musicians and opera singers.

Feltre (Belluno)—Historical Palio
History comes to life in a parade in period costume through this old fortress town. The contest for the *palio* pits the four quarters of the town in an archery competition. The event commemorates Feltre's decision in 1404 to join the Venetian Republic. (early August)

Ascoli Piceno—Torneo della Quintana
This fabulous historical pageant recalls a 15th-century event. Over

800 participants in period costume, representing musicians, hand-maidens, soldiers, lords, and ladies parade through the medieval streets before the tournament of the Quintana. In what is basically a medieval jousting competition, the horsemen ride at a figure representing a Saracen in hope of winning the coveted *palio*. In the evening, the procession to Piazza del Popolo culminates the four-day festival of Sant'Emidio, the city's patron. (early August)

Martina Franca—Festival of Utria Valley

Unique Martina Franca, wth its white-washed houses and baroque palaces and churches, is the site of southern Italy's top performing arts festival. This August festival has been going on since 1974.

Massa Maritima (Grosseto)—Balestro del Girifalco

This event is basically the summer edition of the crossbow competition held on the Sunday following May 20. Colorful, traditional, and typically Italian. (mid-August)

Sant'Elpidio a Mare—Battle for the Pail

In this re-enactment of an old medieval festival, the four quarters of the town compete in an amusing contest, with each team trying to throw a ball into a well and keep its adversaries from doing the same. The team with the most points wins the symbolic right to be the first to draw water from the well throughout the year. The festival is linked to the frequent quarrels that broke out among the women of the parishes for supremacy to draw water from the central well. (mid-August)

Piazza Amerina (Enna)—Palio dei Normanni

Piazza Amerina, a beautiful hillside town situated on three hills among medieval remains, is the site of this costumed re-enactment of the Norman troops' entry into the ancient city of Plutia. There's an offering of the symbolic keys and a tournament in which the town's horsemen compete for the *palio*. (mid-August)

Lavagna (Genoa)—Torta dei Fieschi

This period costume event re-creates an important event in Lavagna's history, the wedding of Opizzo Fieschi and Countess Bianca de' Biancha. After a lovely procession and a flag-waving exhibition, pieces from a colossal wedding cake made by local pastry cooks are distributed to the public. (mid-August)

Sassari—Festival of the Candelabra

This religious celebration in costume commemorates a vow made in 1652 for the end of a plague. Nine tall wooden columns, representing ancient votive candles, are carried by robust young men who perform "dances" along the route. *Li Candereri* is usually celebrated on Assumption Day, August 15.

Curatone (Mantua)—Exhibition of the Madonnari
The *madonnari* are artists who reproduce religious artworks on the pavement using colored chalk. This is a traditional exhibition of their work, held in the square outside the Church of Santa Maria delle Grazie. (mid-August)

Fermo (Ascoli Piceno)—Palio dell'Assunta
The re-enactment of an event from 1182, this *palio* celebrates the time when Raniero, lord of the castle of Monterubbiano, pledged his loyalty to Fermo in the form of a *palio* in honor of the Assumption. Ten districts parade in period costume for the *palio*. (Assumption Day is usually celebrated on August 15.)

Garda (Verona)—Palio delle Contrade
Another *palio*, another setting—this time in lovely Verona, where a fishing boat regatta adds another dimension to this familiar event! (Assumption Day, August 15)

Siena—Palio dell'Assunta
A re-running of the July 2 race, this *palio* is no less important to the Sienese, who are said to "measure time and social life from one *palio* to another, between victories and defeats in the great drama of July 2 and August 16." The August race begins on the 13th, with the *tratta* at 1:00pm. At 7:15pm, the first trial is held. On the 15th, the second and third trials are held, and the jockey's Mass opens the big day on the 16th. At 4:00pm, the track is cleared and, finally, the race starts at 7:00pm. (See also below.)

Pesaro—Rossini Opera Festival
In honor of the city's favorite son, Gioacchino Antonio Rossini, the government of Pesaro inaugurated an opera festival in 1980. The composer, who lived from 1792-1868, produced a lot of music, writing nearly 40 operas, sacred and orchestral works, chamber music, cantatas, and countless songs and arias. He always felt a special kinship to Pesaro and bequeathed a large portion of his fortune to the city. Each season, three or four operas and some of his choral works are performed at the Teatro Rossini, a beautiful opera house built in 1637. For more information, contact Rossini Opera Festival, via Rossini 37, 61100 Pesaro. (mid-August to early Sept.)

Stresa—Stresa Musical Weeks
Begun in 1961 and considered by many the connoisseur's classical music festival of Italy, Stresa's Musical Weeks incorporate stunning musical performances, old-world charm, and the exceptional beauty of the area: Lake Maggiore, the Borromeo Palace with its Gobelin tapestries on Isola Bella, and the Theater du Palais des Congres. The concerts include the music of the masters—Beethoven, Brahms, Bach, and Mozart—as well as pieces by 20th-century composers.

Each year the festival attracts outstanding visiting orchestras, conductors, and soloists. Stresa is about an hour's drive northwest of Milan on the western shores of Lake Maggiore. For more information, contact Settimane Musicali de Stresa, Via R. Bonghi 4, 28049 Stresa. (mid-August to mid-Sept.)

September

Arezzo—Giostra del Saracino

Early in the morning, a herald proclaims the challenge. A procession of the city's dignitaries in traditional costume follows, and in the afternoon, the actual joust takes place. Eight horsemen representing the old districts of the town take part in the contest, which requires the riders to charge a wooden effigy of the Saracen, "Buratto, King of India." If the riders hit him, they win; if they miss, the figure spins around on its pivot and hits them in the back with a heavy object. The winner is awarded a golden lance. The Pizza Grande, surrounded by a tower and medieval houses, is the perfect setting for the Giostra del Saracino, usually performed on the first Sunday in September. Feasting and processions accompany the event. Arezzo, the site of a number of colorful summer festivals, is about an hour by train from Florence.

Cabaras (Oristano)—Feast of San Salvatore

Continuing an old tradition, a large number of people run barefoot for 12 kilometers, carrying the statue of San Salvatore. The event recalls an episode during the Saracen invasions, when a group of women hastened to conceal the statue from invaders. (early Sept.)

Foligno (Perugia)—Giostra della Quintana

This historic event, involving 600 costumed "knights," recalls a 17th-century joust and is held in two stages: on Saturday night before the joust, there's a historical procession, and on Sunday the spectacular tournament begins. The joust tests the ability of ten riders to lance a ring held in a dummy's hand—no easy feat, since the riders are galloping at top speed in typical medieval fashion. A second contest is held later in the month. (early Sept.)

Terra del Sole (Forli)—Palio di Santa Reparata

On the parade ground of the 16th-century Medici Castle, lots are drawn to determine the starting order for a crossbow contest between the town's two districts. In the afternoon, the contest is held, with the participants and many of the townspeople in period costume.

Venice—Historical Regatta

The most sumptuous gondola race of the year, this traditional competition is held annually on the first Sunday in September. Inspired by historical events, the regatta takes place on the Grand Canal with a procession of Venetian boats recalling the epoch of the Republic. This cortege of vessels, the *Bucintoro* and several *bissone*, includes people in period costume on board representing various historic figures. The regatta features a seven-kilometer race along the canal for two-man gondolas. About 300 people in costume take part in the pageant, and thousands watch from the canal banks.

Viterbo—Feast of Santa Rosa

At 9:00pm, the people of Viterbo honor Santa Rosa with a marvelous, breathtaking event. One hundred men bear the enormous *Machina di Santa Rosa* (a towering construction of iron, wood, and papiermâché about 100 feet high) through the illuminated streets of the city. The procession is spectacular both as an endurance feat and a religious observance. The monument, reputed to weigh almost four tons, must be carried around the entire city, the last portion of which is uphill to the saint's church. The *facchini* (bearers) must perform this last segment while running! (early Sept.)

Maraostica—Partita a Scacchi con Personaggi Viventi

This event, literally a "living chess match," recalls an event of 1454 when the daughter of the Lord of Maraostica had two suitors. Since the law forbade duelling, the two decided to settle their dispute with a chess match. Today, it's performed by townsmen dressed as chess pieces in a charming setting in this small town between Vicenza and Bassano. (early Sept.)

Lanciano (Chieti)—Procession of the Donativi

On the feast of the Madonna del Ponte, the women of the town's various quarters carry copper vessels on their heads. The vessels, colorfully decorated with ribbons and paper flowers, are filled with seasonal produce. (early Sept.)

Noli (Savona)—Historical Regatta

A large procession to the square in the center of town precedes this unique regatta. Actually a contest between the area's four rural districts, this one includes Ligurian boats called *gozzi*. (early Sept.)

Borgomanero (Novara)—Palio Degli Asini

By the time the events calendar has reached September, you may have thought all the *palio* events were over. Not so! The twist to this one: eight donkeys represent the four quarters of town. The traditional parade in period costume remains. (early Sept.)

Sansepolcro (Arezzo)—Palio Della Balestra

In this event, originally a dispute in medieval times between the crossbowmen of Sansepolcro and their counterparts in Gubbio, the participants wear period costume and use antique weapons. The match, which returns to Gubbio (Perugia) in May for similar festivities, is an important event in this region. (early Sept.)

Lucca—Feast of Santa Croce

This traditional weekend event, with a procession of marchers bearing candles, honors the Volto Santo (Holy Countenance), an 11th-century crucifix. It starts at the Basilica of San Frediano and goes to the Church of San Martino. The second day of the festival includes a colorful fair in the Piazza San Michele. (mid-Sept.)

Asti—Palio

Over 800 participants in period costume open these festivities with a cortege of 100 horses. The procession starts at the cathedral square and wends to the playing field, where the jockeys race bareback for the *palio*. The marchers wear the colors of their districts in a tradition that dates to 1275. During the month, the wine festival of the *douja d'or* (an antique wine vessel) makes the fun last a little longer. (mid-Sept.)

Naples—Feast of San Gennaro

The faithful gather in the cathedral to pray and await the miracle of the liquefaction of the saint's blood, preserved in an ampule in the chapel dedicated to him. The numerous San Gennaro Festivals throughout the U.S. have ties to this original feast day, though most American celebrations lack the religious fervor of this event. (Sept. 19)

Chambave (Aosta)—Grape Festival

This traditional event includes a parade in folk costume as well as the characteristic offering of grapes and wine to the public. As in other wine-growing countries of Europe, the harvest season is always a festive time. (late Sept.)

October

Assisi (Perugia)—Feast of San Francesco

Religious rites in honor of Italy's patron saint are held in the churches of San Francesco and Santa Maria degli Angeli. Regional and national officials take part in the ceremony, during which oil is offered for the votive lamp that burns at the saint's tomb. The town of Assisi is inspiring any time of year, but at this time it seems to have an even more uplifting atmosphere. (early Oct.)

Alba (Cuneo)—Tournament of the Hundred Towers

This event, with another donkey *palio* and historic parade, recalls an episode of the 13th-century war between Asti and Alba. The troops of Asti had staged a race under Alba's walls while they lay siege to the town. In reply, the people of Asti also organized a race, but instead of horses, which had been butchered to feed the townspeople, they used donkeys as mounts. Centuries later, the tradition lives on. (early Oct.)

Merano (Bolzano)—Grape Festival

Exhibitions and samples of all the local wines make this festival a popular event. Held in the charming town of Merano, which was the capital of Tyrol before it was ceded to Italy (there's still a distinct Austrian influence), the Grape Festival includes a parade in folk costume, folk music, and shows in the Kurhaus. According to legend, eating Merano grapes has a medicinal value, but true or not, Merano at this time offers a number of gustatory pleasures. (mid-Oct.)

Taormina—Festival Dell'Opera Siciliana

Opera and the ruins of the ancient theater at Taormina make a perfect combination, thanks to the site's extraordinary acoustics. The setting is nothing short of spectacular. The ancient theater commands one of the most beautiful views in the world, with Mt. Etna and the seacoast as its backdrop. Built by the Greeks in the third century B.C, it was rebuilt by the Romans on the slope of Mount Tauro. Today it hosts a variety of theater, music, and operatic events, with the Opera Festival among the most highly acclaimed. A recent season included *Cavalleria Rusticana, I Pagliacci,* and *I Vespri Siciliana.* For more information, contact Festival Dell'Opera Siciliana a Taormina, 117, Via Cavour, 1-90133 Palermo, Sicily. (mid-Oct.)

The Calcio Storico of Florence & the Palio of Siena

To say ''history repeats itself'' in the festivals of Italy is as obvious as saying Rome is the capital. Few Italian festivals are *not* steeped in ancient traditions and colorful pageantry, and it's an unfortunate visitor who passes through without a glimpse of at least one traditional fair. But how fortunate, indeed, to be in Tuscany in late June/early July, when two of the country's most famous historical events occur.

Calcio Storico

In Florence, the birthday of St. John the Baptist (June 24) is observed with ritual and pageantry—and a good game of soccer! *Calcio Storico Fiorentino* originates from the games of the ancient Greeks (*sferomachia*) and Romans (*arpasto*). In Florence itself, the game has been played for centuries, and there's no doubt it dates to the game played by legionnaires of the Roman *Florentia.*

The ''matches in livery,'' as they were called, were played until the end of the 18th century. In 1930, to commemorate the fourth centenary of the siege of Florence, the historic game was renewed, and today, three soccer matches are played in June. The final game is preceded by a magnificent cortege of Florentine officials, noble families, members of the city's four quarters, and leaders of the guilds—all in 16th-century costumes. The procession starts from the ancient Monastery of S. Maria Novella, accompanied by a blare of trumpets and a roll of drums. On the Piazza della Signoria, the bells of the Torre di Arnolfo toll fiercely, awaiting the event. Clarinets announce the arrival of the cortege.

The *Famiglia de Palazzo*, composed of mace-bearers with silver maces, escorts the Standard of Florence (a red lily on a white field). Sergeants, the Master of the Field, standard-bearers of political parties, the ball-bearer, field judges, referees, captain of the artilleries, oxen-drivers with the heifer (the coveted prize of the winning team), the noblemen of each quarter, the players, foot soldiers of the guilds—42 groups—all march in to the beat of their ancestors.

The four quarters playing in the game are named from the principal church in their district: Santo Spirito, Santa Croce, Santa Maria Novella, and San Giovanni. Each has its own color and flag with symbolic animals or legends, and each quarter must march in the order of its result from the last match—the losing quarter goes last.

The pageantry of the *Calcio Storico* is spectacular, and the game is World Cup caliber!

Il Palio

If soccer is not your sport, just one week later and 68 miles from Florence, Siena's horse race, *Il Palio*, also lures thousands.

The race was first held on the feast of the Madonna of Provenzano, July 2, 1656, and it's been held every year since without fail. In 1701, leaders decided to hold two races a year—the second on August 16, the Feast of the Assumption.

The word *palio* means a mantle or cloak, and the custom of offering a piece of precious fabric as a prize for a race was common in many towns in the Middle Ages. During the centuries, *Il Palio* assumed different meanings linked to the political affairs of the town and to its statement of independence. Today, it evokes the spirit of local pride in a contest among the town's 10 *contrades* who vie passionately for the coveted cloth. (There are 17 *contrade* in Siena, with ten participating each year.)

The field of the race is the Campo, the venerable town square, whose perimeter is covered with dirt; bleachers are built at certain locations. Otherwise, spectators must stand in the center or be among the privileged families who have balconies or windows overlooking the Campo. The whole town is covered with the flags of the *contrades*, whose members proudly wrap their colors around themselves.

June 29 sees the *tratta* of the horses and the first trial race. On June 30, the second and third trial races run, and July 1 has the fourth trial, the *Prova Generale*. The *palio* is then taken in procession to the Basilica de Provenzano for a blessing, where it remains until 1:00pm on July 2. Each *contrade* hosts a good-luck dinner before the race day. Tourists are welcome to participate in any of the pre-Palio events, including the dinner.

Like its Florentine counterpart, the actual race is somewhat anticlimactic, since it takes only a few minutes to run. It is preceded, however, by a magnificent procession of all the *contrades*, Sienese officials, and other trappings unique to this event. Like the colors of the four quarters of Florence, each *contrade* in Siena has its own flag, its own church, and its own museum. But if the *Calcio Storico* is a "rough and tumble" game of soccer, *Il Palio* borders on "death-defying." In fact, during the July 2, 1990 race, a spunky steed had a false start, delaying the start of the race. With an impatient crowd of thousands shouting (in as many languages) to get things underway, the excitement and tension mounted. Ten nervous jockeys waited behind the ancient rope on equally apprehensive mounts. Finally, with all ten ready to run, the rope dropped and the race began.

After only a half a lap, the course proved too narrow for much of the field, and the jockey and horse of the Torre *contrade* were knocked over and virtually trampled by the others. The jockey recovered and the horse was later destroyed, but not before a stampede of supporters and opponents alike turned the Campo into a wild, terrifying scene. For the jubilant Sienese, the party was just beginning. Frightened foreigners (myself included) headed to one of the narrow alleyways spiraling away from the Campo, to the safety of a waiting *trattoria*.

Il Palio is not your average summer festival, nor your standard derby. It is, however, a spectacle unparalleled in Italian history and medieval splendor.

Italian Holidays

New Year's Day, Epiphany (Jan. 6), Easter Monday, Liberation Day (April 25), Labor Day (May 1), Assumption (Aug. 15), All Saints Day (Nov. 1), Immaculate Conception (Dec. 8), Christmas, and Dec. 26.

For literature and further information, contact the **Italian Government Travel Office**. In the U.S., offices are at 630 Fifth Ave., New York, NY, 10111 (212-245-4822); 500 N. Michigan Ave., Chicago, IL, 60611 (312-644-0990); and 360 Post St., Suite 801, San Francisco, CA, 94108 (415-392-6206).

7

Malta

The Republic of Malta, five small islands (three of which are inhabited—Malta, Gozo, and Comino), lies at "the crossroads of the Mediterranean," about 60 miles south of Sicily. The Maltese claim "the sun shines from the heart," and weather-wise, this aphorism seems accurate. The temperature averages 57° November-April and 90° from May-October.

Malta has hosted numerous notables—from St. Paul, shipwrecked off the coast for three months in 60 A.D., to Napoleon and Lord Nelson, to George Bush and Mikhail Gorbachev. And according to Homer, Odysseus was an early visitor, spending seven years under the spell of Calypso on the island of Gozo.

While famous visitors come and go, historical and traditional events flow continuously from one century into the next, especially in a place like Malta, where the warm climate prompts colorful pageants year-round. The Maltese love festivals, and those that preserve ancient traditions are especially popular.

Between May and October, every town in Malta and Gozo celebrates the feast day (*festa*) of its patron saint—the most important event in each village's annual calendar, requiring considerable preparation. The church, the pride of every village, is draped with red damask and decorated with flowers. All of its treasures are displayed to create a setting for the statue of the patron saint, placed prominently in the church. Multicolored bulbs illuminate the church facade, as well as the streets, across which massive, colorful drapes hang. Hundreds of flags fly from rooftops and the balconies of Maltese traditional houses, and the houses on the main streets usually get a fresh coat of paint for the occasion!

The feast day is the culmination of three days of preparation and non-stop merriment. On the *festa*, the statue of the saint is carried shoulder-high along the streets of the village, accompanied by church bells and marching bands, while children throw confetti from balconies onto the procession. The crowd becomes quite impassioned as the statue reaches the church, and generally its re-entry is announced with fireworks. (The Maltese specialize in the manufacture of fireworks, a fact that often leads to inter-village rivalries for the best and noisiest displays.)

During the summer, there's a village *festa* almost every weekend. There are also national *festas* on June 29 and September 8.

May
throughout Malta—Feast of St. Joseph the Worker
This May 1st public holiday is celebrated nationwide with religious processions and general merry-making.

June
Mnarja—Feast of St. Peter and St. Paul
This important public holiday, also called the *Imnarja* (a corruption of Italian *luminaria* or illumination), is a traditional harvest festival characterized by an all-night picnic at Buskett Gardens near Malta's former capital, Mdina. Mnarja is one of the most popular feasts of the year—in fact, wedding tradition calls for the husband to promise to take his bride to Buskett on Mnarja-day every year. The festivities open in the evening with folk singing and music competitions. Maltese dishes, especially rabbit, are served with lots of local wine. On the second day, a donkey and horse race runs in the street leading to Rabat. Race winners receive *palji*, banners like Italian *palio*, which they donate to their village church. (traditonally held the weekend preceding June 29)

July
The entire month of July is *festa* season, with each town and village commemorating its saint's feast day. Most events last three to five days and include the *triduum*, the eve of the feast as well as the feast day itself. Marching bands, fireworks, and processions characterize the event.

August
throughout—Feast of the Assumption
This public holiday, commemorating the Virgin Mary's ascendance into heaven, is a national *festa* in this largely Catholic country. (August 15)

September
throughout—Our Lady of Victories
Every September 8th, Maltese traditionally celebrate the milestones in the island's history: the lifting of the four-month siege of 1565,

the ending of the French occupation in 1800, and the raising of the three-year siege of 1940-43. Though centuries separate these struggles, they were all bitterly fought and proved to be turning points in Malta's destiny. Additionally, the day commemorates the country's independence from Great Britain in 1964.

The five days of national celebrations are centered in Valletta and the Three Cities, considered the protagonists in Malta's history. On these days, Valletta is covered with red and white flags. Everyone participates in the festivities, which include speeches at the Great Siege Monument, church services, parades, a water carnival (on the 7th), and, of course, fireworks.

The towns along Marsamxett and Grand Harbour participate in a regatta, in typical Mediterranean rivalry. Most of the boats are new each year and are specially designed for races. The finish line of the 1,000-yard race course is Customs House Quay, where the coveted trophies are presented to the winners, who row home proudly carrying their prize. These traditional races commemorate the victory of the Maltese over the Turks in 1565, when hand-to-hand fighting in the shallow water around Senglea Point proved decisive. It's not known when the races were first held, but they were very popular by the turn of the 17th century.

This date also marks the feast day of Senglea (*Citta Invicta*—the Unconquered City—a name bestowed after the Great Siege of 1565), Naxxar, Mellieha, and Xaghra (in Gozo).

Off-Season
Pre-Lenten Carnival Days in Malta date to 1535 and feature grotesque masks, brass bands, and a folk dancing competition in Valletta's Freedom Square.

Holy Week and Easter are also celebrated with considerable ritual. Good Friday pageants, held in 14 towns, feature numerous life-size statues depicting scenes from the Passion and carried shoulder high along main streets. Men and women in the parade impersonate Biblical characters.

Maltese Holidays
New Year's Day, Feast of St. Paul's Shipwreck (Feb. 10), Feast of St. Joseph (Mar. 19), Freedom Day (Mar. 31), Good Friday, Workers Day (May 1), Sette Guigno (June 7), Feast of Sts. Peter and Paul (June 29), Assumption (Aug. 15), Feast of Our Lady of Victories (Sept. 8), Independence Day (Sept. 21), Immaculate Conception (Dec. 8), Republic Day (Dec. 13), Christmas.

For literature and further information, contact **Malta National Tourist Office**. In the U.S. the address is 249 East 35th St., New York, NY 10016 (212-725-2345).

8

Austria & Switzerland

"Festivals of Austria are not just summer finery, something to be taken out of the wardrobe at certain seasons of the year and cleaned and brushed for the occasion. They spring from the Austrian addiction to things artistic, from the possession of a precious heritage in which great works of art are preserved and venerated."
—Herbert Buzas, *Colorful Austria*

Still preserved, indeed revered, are the works of Austria's composers, to which other countries can only listen in awe: Mozart, Schubert, Beethoven, Haydn, Strauss, Mahler, Bruckner, Brahms. Operas, symphonies, waltzes, marches, operettas—Austria is where so much magnificent music was born that it is a place forever dedicated to preserving an incomparable heritage of sound.

Between music festivals there's another Austria, which pays homage to a less artistic life. In the "land of dancers, land of fiddlers," the return of the cattle from Alpine meadows is cause for celebration, as is the grape harvest, Corpus Christi Day, and Midsummer's Eve. Austria's neighbors—Switzerland, Italy, Yugoslavia, Hungary, Czechoslovakia, and Germany—have had considerable influence in Austrian life, even lending some of their own cultures to form Austria's traditions.

But at bottom, whether because of its high brow musical traditions, its rustic simplicity, its breathtaking landscapes, or its assimilation of bordering cultures, one word typifies Austria's attitude and lifestyle: *gemutlich*, a word that almost defies translation. A recent Austrian *Vacation Guide* says, "*Gemutlich* can be gregarious, relaxed, laid-back, cozy, easy-going, informal, open-minded, hospitable, unhurried, friendly, casual, welcoming, pleasant, comfortable. . . Moreover, the significance of the word often encompasses several of these meanings at the same time, in many dazzling variations."

But that's Austria for you, "the festive Europe."

Say this too loudly, though, and their peace-loving neighbors to

AUSTRIA & SWITZERLAND

the west might take issue with their claim to the festive life. After all, the Swiss, associated with cows, chalets, chocolate, cheese, and clocks, are a pretty lively bunch themselves who, despite remarkable diversity, are the most united and content of all Europeans. While they are fiercely loyal to Switzerland, there are no "typical Swiss"— though there may be typical Bernese, Genevese, or Ticenese.

Why? About 75% of Swiss speak German dialects, which can differ considerably in towns a few miles apart. About 20% speak French, although it's not like the French in France. The remaining population speaks Italian, except for a tiny group of Grisons who speak an ancient language called Romansch. To further confuse the situation, English is common throughout Switzerland.

A Swiss is first a citizen of his commune, then his Canton, then his country. This loyalty makes for a remarkable array of small-town festivals and observances of local and regional anniversaries. Perhaps the best example is the *Landsgemeinde*, the open-air assembly considered the oldest example of direct democracy in the world. The whole voting population meets in a meadow or marketplace on a spring Sunday to choose leaders and to speak up for the government.

A visitor may be surprised to learn how independent each Canton is, with its own government, laws, and taxes. But when a visitor is fortunate enough to be in Switzerland when the customs of the Cantons are being observed, then all else fades into the festive spirit that the Swiss—no matter how disparate they may be in language or loyalty—cultivate so ardently.

AUSTRIA

Austria

May

Vienna—Vienna International Festival

Founded in 1951, the Vienna Festival combines opera, symphony, choral concerts, chamber music, and sacred music. Held at various venues throughout the city—including the impressive State Opera, the Volksoper, Theater an der Wien, Konzerthaus, and the Church of the Augustinian Friars—the festival draws performers of the highest caliber. One year alone saw Mozart's *Abduction from the Seraglio*, a new production of Richard Strauss's *Elektra*, a new production of Johann Strauss's *Night in Venice*, the Vienna Symphony's performance of Mahler's Eighth Symphony, and appearances by the Cleveland Symphony, Chamber Orchestra of Europe, and countless recitals and solo performances. For more information, contact Bestellburo der Wiener Festwochen, Lehárgasse 11, A-1060 Wien (Vienna). (mid-May to mid-June)

St. Margarethen—Passio Domini

The Passion Play of St. Margarethen, performed every five years (next in 1996), takes place on an open-air stage at the picturesque quarry Romersteinbruch. Founded in 1926, the *Passio Domini* is based on the deep religious faith of the townspeople. When performed, it becomes almost a kind of worship.

Like the German passion play at Oberramergau, the St. Margarethen version uses almost 500 villagers to depict scenes from the New Testament. During the prologue, actors in modern dress, led by a cross, pass through the audience to the stage. After prayers at the crucifixion site, the procession vanishes behind the rocks, and a colorful tableau of life at the time of Christ unfolds, followed by a magnificent dramatic/religious pageant.

Proceeds from ticket sales are donated to projects in the Third World. For more information, contact Pfarrgemeinde St. Margarethen, Kirchengasse 20, A-7062, St. Margarethen. (weekends during the summer)

June

throughout—Samson Processions

Most everyone is familiar with the Old Testament story of Samson and Delilah. According to legend, Samson had enormous strength—as long as he never cut his hair. But his lover Delilah betrayed him, cut his hair, and sold him to the Philistines. When his hair grew back, he toppled the pillars of the Philistine palace, crushing himself and his captors.

In the Catholic countries of Europe, it has been the custom since the late Middle Ages to carry statues of Biblical heroes like Samson in church processions. But in the late 18th century, such show parades were forbidden, and in many areas of Austria, all the figures were confiscated. Fortunately, not Samson! On "Prang Day," Samson is raised and carried through the town with musical accompaniment. After taking a bow, he performs a little dance in front of every inn—no easy feat, since the Samson of St. Michael, for example, is 4.54 meters high and weighs 64 kg. The head of the carrier is attached to an iron rod to keep the figure balanced, and there's space in Samson's skirt for a small window through which the carrier gets refreshments like wine or brandy.

Samson Parades occur in seven Langau holiday towns, the most important being in early June in Mariapfarr, Mauterndorf, Muhr, St. Michael, and Tamsweg. These towns also host parades in July and August. For more information, contact Salzburger Land Tourismus Gesellschaft, Alpenstrasse 96, A-5033 Salzburg.

Salzburg—Whitsun Concerts

The weekend of Whitsun/Pentecost is dedicated to symphonic concerts at Grosses Festspielhaus. Local groups devoted to perpetuating the musical tradition of Austria perform the concerts. (See *Austria's Temples of Music* below.) For more information, contact Whitsun Concerts, Grosses Festspielhaus, Hofstallgasse, A-5010 Salzburg.

Neckenmarkt—Neckenmarkt Fahnenschwingen

This unique Austrian custom is the result of a historic event of 1620, when Burgenland (West Hungary) was attacked by soldiers from Siebenburgen. In the Battle of Lackenbach, Prince Esterhazy beat the Siebenburgen army with the help of the farmers of Neckenmarkt. As a special reward, the farmers received their own flag.

Today, the receiving of the flag is an annual event, when farmers in traditional costumes gather in the street and the main square and demonstrate with their flags. It's cause for a village celebration and for a great deal of Austrian merry-making. Neckenmarkt is famous for its red wine, so you can guess what beverage accompanies the feast! (first Sunday after Corpus Christi)

Bad Hall—Robert Stolz Festival
First begun in 1984, this festival is devoted to the operettas of Robert Stolz. These performances are held at Kurtheater, while waltz concerts are held at Gastezentrum. (mid-June to mid-July)

Hohenems—Shubertiade Hohenems
Traditionally the third week of June, the Shubert Festival is held in the town of Hohenems, on the Austrian side of the Rhine Valley about 10 miles from Bregenz. Initiated in 1976 by Hermann Prey, renowned German baritone and Schubert devotee, the festival is devoted to the symphonies, chamber music, and songs of the Austrian composer, with a sprinkling of Mozart, Mendelssohn, Handel, and Beethoven. Performances run in the Rittersaal (Knights Hall), in the courtyard of the Hohenems Palace, and in the Stadtsaal (Community Hall) in the nearby medieval town Feldkirch.

Considered a master of the Golden Age, Schubert was born in Vienna in 1797. At age 17, he wrote his first symphony, a mass, and several of his most famous songs. Though he spent most of his life in Beethoven's shadow, doubting his ability to produce anything worthy of that genius, Schubert not only created the genre of the German *Lied*, but also wrote more than 600 songs in 11 years. He wrote the *Unfinished Symphony* at age 25 and left a rich legacy of overtures, masses, string quartets, piano sonatas, chamber music, and dances. He died in 1828, within a year of gaining public acceptance.

For more information, contact Schubertiade Hohenems, Postfach 100, Schweitzer Strade 1, A-6845 Hohenems. (late June, for two weeks)

Baden—Sommerarena Baden
This operetta festival recently featured Fred Raymond's *Maske in Blau*, Franz Lehar's *Das Land des Lachelns*, and Fritz Kreisler's *Sissy*. For more information, contact Sommerarena Baden, Stadttheater, Theaterplatz 7, A-2500 Baden bei Wien. (late June to early Sept.)

Innsbruck—Tyrolean Summer
This event includes just about every kind of activity—musical or otherwise—that this beautiful Tyrolean city can muster. For musical offerings, there's brass band concerts, folk music, and sacred music. Venues include the Hofgarten, the Hofkirche (Court Church), Wilten Basilica, Igls Parish Church, the Spanish Hall at Ambras Castle, and the square at Golden Roof. (throughout the summer)

Vienna—Summer of Music
The Vienna Festival drifts quietly into Vienna's Musical Summer, providing performances through the months when opera and operetta theaters are closed. Concerts are offered in the courtyard of City Hall on Wednesday and Thursday, at the Musikverein, the Concert

Hall, Schönbrunn Palace, and in the homes of Haydn and Schubert. Organ concerts run Friday at the Augustinerkirche. For more information, contact Magistrat der Stadt Wien, Friedrich-Schmidt-Platz 5, A-1982, Wien. (June-Sept.)

Graz—Styriarte Graz

Each summer, this festival focuses on the work of one composer, and interpretations take on many proportions. For a recent festival featuring Beethoven, for example, his Symphonies 1-8, chamber music, and sonatas were performed by international ensembles and soloists. Graz is Austria's second largest city, located in wooded hills in the southeast of the country. For more information, contact Styriarte Graz Office, Palais Attems, 17 Sackstrasse, A-8010 Graz. (late June)

Ossiach and Villach—Carinthian Summer

Publicity from the Carinthian area exclaims ''Art knows no bounds!'' during festival time, and from the array on the festival schedule, they're not exaggerating. Operetta and comedy theater, competition between writers for the Ingeborg Bachmann Prize, symposia, and a kaleidoscope of theatrical productions make the Carinthian Summer an inviting event. Johannes Brahms described a holiday he spent in Carinthia in 1877: ''The first day was so lovely that I determined to tarry a second, but the second was so lovely that I have decided to stay here for the time being.'' You may be similarly delayed! The picturesque villages of Villach and Ossiach are located in the lake district of the Austrian Alps. (throughout the summer)

July

Bad Ischl—Operetta Festival

This summer-long event is devoted to the operetta, the musical genre that formed in the 1820's, when the middle class was growing. Hard to distinguish from the *opera comique* except by its longer spoken dialogue, the subjects and their treatment make an ''operetta.'' The stories are often pulp novel material, but once they've been set to great waltzes and polkas, and once the actors start singing those songs that make you hum, who cares about the content? The Bad Ischl event includes two of these charming pieces each season.

Known for its mineral springs, Bad Ischl became the summer residence of Emperor Francis Joseph I in the late 19th century. It's a delightful holiday destination, one hour east of Salzburg. For more information, contact Buro der Operettengemeinde Bad Ischl, Herrengasse 32, A-4820 Bad Ischl. (July through Sept.)

Salzburg—Summer Szene

Summer Szene, an international dance, theater, and music festival, is a pleasant complement to the famous Salzburg Festival in August.

The event began as an alternative to the classical (and expensive) Salzburg Festival. Theater and dance groups from around the world participate. For more information, contact Szene-Buro, Anton-Neumayr Platz 2, A-5010 Salzburg. (mid-July to mid-August)

Bregenz—Bregenz Festival

One of the highlights of this festival is the production on the floating stage in Lake Constance, where Wagner's *The Flying Dutchman* traditionally holds center stage. Another opera alternates with concerts in the new Festival Hall, with its modern stage, fine acoustics, and comfortable seating. In addition to the two operas, the Vienna Symphony offers concerts as well. Chamber music is performed at Hohenems Palace; *lieder* recitals at Festival Hall; and sacred music in various churches.

Bregenz is a picturesque community on the eastern shores of Lake Constance in western Austria. Its location on the Germany-Switzerland border makes it a convenient base for festival-going in other areas. For more information, contact Bregenz Festpiele, Postfach 311, A-6901, Bregenz. (mid-July to mid-August)

Mörbisch—Lake Festival

Like the Bregenz Festival, the event at Mörbisch also uses a floating stage on Lake Neusiedl. For over 30 years, it has presented operetta of the highest caliber. Performances run Saturday and Sunday, and during festival season Mörbisch has brass band concerts Sunday evening and folk events twice a week. Costumed villagers offer traditional music and dance, and food and wine exhibitions are everywhere. For more information, contact Seefestspiele Mörbisch, Schlob Esterhazy, A-7000, Eisenstadt. (mid-July to mid-August)

Wiesen—Jazz Festival Wiesen

The village of Wiesen, situated at the Region Rosalia, is well-known among lovers of both jazz and strawberries. Since 1976, it has hosted the biggest jazz event in Austria. Performers like Miles Davis, Herbie Hancock, and Dizzy Gillespie have performed here in the open-air, Woodstock-like atmosphere. Following the jazz event, there's *Weisen Sunsplash*, the only festival in Central Europe for African and Latin-American music and dance. Both festivals are held in an enormous tent, and many people camp in the meadows around the festival area. For more information, contact Jazz Pub Wiesen, Hauptstrade 140, A-7203 Wiesen. (mid-July)

Salzburg—Salzburg Festival

In 1313, the Archbishop of Salzburg created the town's first permanent musical ensemble, and during the 18th century, both father Leopold and son Wolfgang Amadeus Mozart were members. Drawn by the beauty of the city, its history, and its location, outstanding conductors and performers have made a pilgrimage here since the festival began in 1920 with a performance of Hofmannsthal's *Everyman*. The 70th anniversary festival included Beethoven's *Fidelio*, Mozart's *Don Giovanni*, and Strauss's *Capriccio*.

Symphonic concerts, instrumental and *lieder* recitals, ballet, and sacred music are all part of this prestigious festival. And the venues for festival events are unmatched: Kleines Festspielhaus, Felsenreitschule, Grosses Festspielhaus, and Mozerteum. With some tickets priced as high as $330, you can expect the performances to be superb! For more information, contact the Ticket Office of the Salzburg Festival, Postfach 140, A-510 Salzburg. (late July to late August)

Innsbruck—Festival of Early Music
During the 16th and 17th centuries, Innsbruck was the seat of the Tyrolean branch of the Hapsburg Dynasty, which made it the center of European music. The town's musical tradition was revived in 1963 with annual concerts of early music. In 1977, an entire festival was created exclusively for performances of music written before 1750. The festival offers Renaissance and Baroque works played on period instruments, with singers expert in the techniques of those periods. Since 1980, a highlight of the festival has been a production of a Baroque opera. (through early August)

August
A number of important festivals listed above continue throughout the month. August is also the month for many villages to hold community events, costumed parades, and Samson Processions.

September
Eisenstadt—Haydnfestspiele
Devotion to composer Joseph Haydn (1732-1809) highlights this week of concerts and performances. The composer's masses, string quartets, sonatas, and symphonies are featured each day, as well as a "musical roundtrip" with the Concilium Musicum, which visits places Haydn lived and worked. Paul Angerer and his ensemble perform on old instruments and give a chamber concert at Esterhazy Palace, where Haydn was Kapellmeister from 1761-90. The Concilium Musicum will also spend an entire day taking music lovers on a walk through Eisenstadt, home of the seven remaining organs on which Haydn performed. For more information, contact Buro der Burgenlandischen Haydnfestspiele, Schlob Esterhazy, A-7000 Eisenstadt. (early Sept., for 10 days)

Linz—Anton Bruckner Festival
"The Danube, Anton Bruckner, and the Linzertort are three Austrian treasures that color the soul of Linz"—something satisfying for

all tastes. Music lovers can hear the sounds of Bruckner throughout September in a festival devoted to this native son. In 1974, the city decided to honor him with a celebration of the 150th anniversary of his birth, and the festival was born. Bruckner's symphonies, masses, choral and orchestral works, and organ compositions are all played, along with works of other composers with Austrian ties—Beethoven, Brahms, Schubert, Mozart, and Mahler. Linz, the capital of Upper Austria, is 80 miles northeast of Salzburg. For more information, contact Bruckner Festival, Brucknerhaus, Untere Donaulande 7, A-4020 Linz. (mid-Sept., for 10 days)

October
Graz—Styrian Autumn Festival
For two months, the city of Graz, in the wine-growing half of Styria, celebrates the autumn harvest with an event that has become one of the foremost avant-garde festivals in the country, showcasing contemporary theater, music, and art, as well as mingling folklore and historic arts and crafts into the program. Graz, Austria's second-largest city, is a haven for writers and artists who treasure both its Alpine forests and its baroque/medieval atmosphere. For more information, contact Steirischer Herbst, Musikprotokoll, ORF, 20 Marburgerstrasse, A-8042 Graz, Austria. (Oct.-Nov.)

Austria's Temples of Music

Austria's music houses, where the setting is lovely counterpart to the performance, include a number of spectacular edifices in all the major cities.

In Vienna, the State Opera, with 1,642 seats, is located on Vienna's showcase boulevard, the Ring. First opened in 1869, most of the building was destroyed in World War II. One of the country's top post-war priorities, it re-opened in 1955 with Beethoven's *Fidelio*. Today, performances run daily from Jan. 1-June 30 and Sept. 1-Dec. 31 (except Good Friday and Christmas Eve, plus the day before and the day of the Opera Ball). The best seats for regular performances cost $125-$140; for premiere nights, special shows, etc., tickets cost up to $195. Lesser seats are available for about $50. (*Address:* Openring 2, A-1010 Wien.)

The Volksoper, considered Vienna's second opera house, generally stages operettas and light opera. Opened in 1898, the house seats 1,620. Performances are held Jan. 1-June 30 and Sept. 1-Dec. 31 (except Good Friday and Christmas Eve), and seats cost $16-$39. (*Address:* Wahringer Strasse 78, A-1090, Wien.)

For more information and tickets for the Vienna State Opera and the Vienna Volksopera, contact Bundestheaterverband, Hanuschgasse 3, A-1010 Wien.

The Theater an der Wien is now a haven for contemporary music in Austria (*Cats* and *A Chorus Line* recently had long runs), although it originally was the setting for performances like Beethoven's *Fidelio* and Strauss's *Die Fledermaus*. Beethoven actually lived in the building for a while. The house has a capacity of 1,170. (*Address:* Linke Wienzeile 6, A-1060, Wien.)

The Musikverein is the stage for the Vienna Philharmonic, and the Konzerthaus is geared to symphony, recital, and chamber performances. The Vienna Concert Season runs Jan. 1-June 30 and Oct. 1-Dec. 31, with concerts almost daily.

The Vienna Boys' Choir performs every Sunday and religious holiday from Jan. 1 to late June and from mid-Sept. to Dec. 31 at High Mass in the Chapel of Vienna's Imperial Palace (Die Burgkapelle). Tickets cost $4-$13 and can be reserved by writing to Verwaltung der Hofmusikkapelle, Hofburg-Schweizerhof, A-1010 Wien. The chapel is also the setting for masses composed by Haydn, Mozart, Beethoven, Schubert, and Bruckner.

Of course, Vienna is not the only Austrian city where music houses are nearly as important as the performances. Salzburg's Grosses Festspielhaus was built in the late 1950's. By carving into the face of a mountain and emphasizing width, it was possible to fit the festival hall behind the facades of the old stables (the West Gate is a Fischer von Erlach design from 1694) and to put a modern theater with state-of-the-art technology into the historic shell. With its superb acoustics and spacious stage, it has become the home of the big operas and large symphonies on the Salzburg Festival schedule.

Salzburg is home to two other magnificent venues, Kleines Festspielhaus (Old Festival House) and Felsenreitschule. The former, which dates to 1928, was created by adapting the former stables of the Prince Archbishops of Salzburg. The Felsenreitschule was created where material for the construction of the Cathedral had been cut in the early 17th century.

Finally, the Mozarteum, built and operated by the Mozart Foundation, hosts a major part of Salzburg's year-round musical life and the chamber concerts of the Festival (which are mostly dedicated to Salzburg's native son).

For more information on Salzburg music houses, contact Hofstallgasse, A-5010 and Schwarzstrasse 26-28, A-5010, Salzburg.

In Linz, the Brucknerhaus, named for the composer honored by a festival in September, opened in 1974 and has a seating capacity of 1,420. The program generally includes symphonic concerts, chamber music, and recitals. For more information, contact Untere Donaulande 7, A-4010, Linz.

The Festival Hall in Bregenz was added to the outdoor amphitheater complex on Lake Constance in 1982 and has helped elevate the standard of the Bregenz Festival to its present status. In the outdoor arena of the Festival complex, lavishly staged operas, operettas, musicals, and ballets constitute one of the mainstays of the annual celebration. For more information, contact Festspielhaus, Platz der Wiener Symphoniker, A-6901 Bregenz.

Austria Off-Season

Austrians really know how to celebrate through the winter—first with Advent activities in December, then with a round of balls between New Year and the start of Lent. Vienna alone offers over 300 spectacular balls, complete with evening dress, crystal chandeliers, debutantes, carnival masks, champagne, and of course, rooms full of charming couples dancing to the country's world-famous waltzes.

During Advent, there's an unequalled magic, a picture-book quality, to Austria's towns. Scenes from fairy tales grace village squares and store windows, outdoor markets offer native crafts, carillons peal Christmas music, and choir boys prepare special programs. And once the magic of Christmas is over, the Viennese take to ballroom floors in an elegant round of parties beginning on Dec. 31 with the Kaiser Ball at the Hofburg, followed by the Flower Ball at City Hall and the Vienna Philharmonic Orchestra Ball at the Musikverein (for which Richard Strauss composed the fanfare).

On the Saturday before Lent begins, the Masked Ball, set in the Hofburg's 18th-century halls, and the Opera Ball, set in the State Opera House, draw people from all over Austria. Other events, sponsored by trades and professions, draw hundreds of dancers. They include the Lawyer's Ball, the Pharmacist's Ball, the Engineer's Ball, the Physician's Ball, and even the Coffeehouse Owners' Ball.

These affairs are very formal, and balls prior to Carnival often require masks. Travelers who wish to experience the splendor of a bygone era at an Austrian ball can book tickets (alone or with "ball package tours") from several U.S. companies. Consult your travel agent, or contact Dailey-Thorp Travel, 315 West 57th St., New York, NY 10019 (212-307-1555).

Austrian Holidays

New Year's Day, Easter Monday, Labor Day (May 1), Ascension Day, Whitmonday, Corpus Christi Day, Assumption (Aug. 15), National Holiday (Oct. 26), All Saints Day (Nov. 1), Christmas, St. Stephen's Day (Dec. 26).

For further information, contact the **Austrian National Tourist Office**. In the U.S., addresses are 500 Fifth Ave., New York, NY 10110 (212-944-6880); 500 N. Michigan Ave., Suite 1950, Chicago, IL 60611 (312-644-8029); 1300 Post Oak Blvd., Suite 960, Houston, TX 77056 (713-850-9999); 11601 Wilshire Blvd., Suite 2480, Los Angeles, CA 90025 (213-477-3332).

SWITZERLAND

Switzerland

May

The Swiss greet the arrival of spring with a number of traditional events stressing renewal, the return of beauty, and the demise of winter. The end of the long, cold season is marked by maypoles, rites of spring, and fire called forth to "burn the winter."

Poschiavo—Gita a Selva

Basically a children's event of the Reformed School, this hike to the chapel on the Selva Alpine meadow revises a religious custom that dates to the 19th century, when the church was visited regularly every spring. After a speedy climb, the participants (accompanied by adults) gather for a church service and a meal of polenta and wine. The afternoon is time for drama presentations and sports competitions. (an early Sunday in May)

Begnins—May Day

May Day in this area of the VD Canton is also reserved for children who collect gifts on Saturday morning by going door-to-door singing songs. Later, they gather flowers to weave a crown for the May Queen and King, who are solemnly crowned on Sunday morning, then lead a procession through the village streets. Food and games, of course, are abundant. (second Sunday in May)

Beromuenster—Auffahrtsumritt

Unparalleled in Switzerland, the religious custom celebrated at Beromuenster in the LU Canton (also in Hitzkirch and Baselbiet) occurs on Ascension Day. The origin of the "Ascension Day ride on horseback" dates to the 1400's, but over the years, it has become more decorative and colorful than the original. A large group, mostly clergy and other clerics, leaves town for a ride around the fields. The priest, carrying the Most Holy Sacrament, is escorted by mounted soldiers, and the group is followed by large crowds on foot, a brass band, and a church choir. The procession takes several hours to complete as it follows the boundary of the village, and when the entourage returns to town, a benediction marks the end of the event. A village celebration follows. (Ascension Day is the 40th day after Easter.)

Baselbiet—Banntag

Like the Ascension Day ride in the LU Canton, this old custom in Baselbiet (BL Canton) is associated with the blessing of the fields and the checking of boundary markers. The religious character of the event has declined, however, and the celebration is now a community festival, where villagers walk the boundary lines accompanied by local officials, flag bearers, and musicians. A feast follows, along with a community meeting. Visitors are warmly welcomed! (Ascension Day)

Lausanne—International Festival

This festival invites artists and ensembles from five continents to the lovely area of French-speaking Switzerland on the northern shore of Lake Leman. The repertoire includes chamber concerts, ballet, opera, and jazz. Companies from as far as Tokyo and as close as Dresden participate. The 900-seat Théâter Municipale and 1,800-seat Theater of Beaulieu Lausanne are used for concerts. For more information, contact Festival International de Lausanne, c/o Théâter Municipale, Case Postale 3972, 1002 Lausanne. (through July)

June

Switzerland's summer calendar is greatly enriched by rural festivals, especially in its mountainous regions, where cows are led to Alpine pastures for summer grazing. Both the drive to the pasture in June and July and the return to the village in autumn spark much celebration. It's an ideal time for tourists to see traditional costumes, observe native customs, and sample local food.

Winterthur—Albanifest

The festival of St. Alban in Winterthur (ZH Canton) is somewhat exceptional since it's based on a historical event of the 13th century but was only re-instituted in 1971. On the last weekend of June, Winterthur is transformed into a Swiss fairground (a *Chilbi*), with rides, food stalls, music, and dancing. The festival dates to 1264, when the locale became a town by decree of Rudolf of Hapsburg. As it was St. Alban's Day, a day when political and military matters were discussed and settled, the festival was so named. Until the 18th century, the custom was regularly observed.

St. Gall—Kinderfest

Every three years (next in 1995), the city of St. Gall in eastern Switzerland celebrates its children's festival as a traditional event for both kids and adults. Dating from the 15th century, it originated in old school customs celebrated on St. Gregory's Day, in memory of Pope

Gregory I. Reorganized as a children's festival in 1824, today's festival has a colorful and relaxing atmosphere: bright costumes, flowers, a parade, and a fabulous culinary event featuring the St. Galler bratwurst—grilled sausage that's virtually a city symbol. Nearly 8,000 children participate in the fest, held traditionally on the days prior to summer vacation. (late June)

Zurich—Festival Weeks

This annual "toast to the arts," established in 1909, usually revolves around a particular theme. Recent festivals were "A Window on Europe—Traditions of Modernism in Russian and Soviet Culture" and "Zurich's Musical Life in the 19th Century." Visiting ensembles join Swiss performers at venues like the Tonhalle, the Zurich Opera House, and the Theater am Newmarkt, and performers have included renowned orchestras like the Leningrad Philharmonic, the Basel Sinfonietta, and the Bulgarian Male Choir. The Festival Weeks are well-known throughout Europe and are an enticement to travelers passing near or through Zurich in early summer. For more information, contact Prasidialabteilung der Stadt Zurich, 17 Stadthausquai, Postfach CH-8022, Zurich. (throughout June)

Thun (Bern)—Thun Castle Concerts

Held over a two-week period, the Castle of Thun concerts in the Rittersaal offer 12 classical concerts in several venues: the Castle, the Stadtkirche, and Bellevue Jugendstillsaal. (mid-June to early July)

Meiringen (Bern)—Music Weeks

This two-week festival presents concerts by a variety of artists. Groups and solo performers from throughout Europe flock to Meiringen, the principal town of the Hasle Valley. (late June to mid-July)

July

Montreux—International Jazz Festival

This famous resort city on the east end of Lake Geneva (the *Vaudois Riviera*) provides an extensive program of concerts, plays, and balls throughout the year, but no time is more exciting than July's two-week International Jazz Festival, when the jazz fan is guaranteed a wide-ranging program of musical entertainment, night after night. The Casino de Montreux, where the concerts are held, seats 4,000. Though billed as a jazz festival, other music is presented also; blues, rock, soul, fusion, African, and Brazilian sounds abound. A 12-hour overnight marathon concludes the festival, which has been going strong since 1966. The event traditionally begins on the first Monday of the month. For more information, contact Montreux Jazz Festival, Tourist Office, Case Postale Box 97, CH-1820 Montreux. (early July, for two and a half weeks)

Engandine—Engandine Concert Weeks

For 50 years, the Engandine Concert Weeks have been held in churches and concert halls throughout southeast Switzerland, radiating from St. Moritz. Swiss ensembles like the Camerata Zurich, Camerata Berne, and Festival Strings Lucerne are often joined by European groups from Amsterdam, Rome, and Milan. Soloists from throughout Europe also perform in recitals and concerts. (early July to mid-August)

Gstaad—Gstaad Menuhin Festival and Alpengala

In 1990, these two festivals were combined under one name. The 500-seat Saanen Church is the venue for chamber works, the Festival Tent in Wengen for symphonic concerts and operas in concert form. Yehudi Menuhin, who founded the event in 1956, often conducts or performs as a soloist, along with performers like Vladimir Ashkenazy and Anne-Sophie Mutter. Students from the Menuhin School in London and the International Menuhin Music Academy in Gstaad usually play at least one concert each season. For more information, contact Musiksommer Gstaad-Saanenland, Festival Office, c/o Tourist Office, CH-3780 Gstaad. (late July to mid-Sept.)

Wildkirchli—Schutzengelfest

Wildkirchli, a cave in the Alpstein range in Canton Appenzell Innerhoden, is renowned for its prehistoric finds. On the second Sunday in July, it hosts a modern treasure: the Festival of the Guardian Angel, which begins at 10:00am with a service led by a priest or Capuchin monk joined by the church choir and followed by a yodeler's chorus. The participants travel by foot to Ebenalp or Aescher, where they eat and dance for the rest of the day. This festival was the idea of a Capuchin monk who, in 1621, thought the cave ideal for a worship service. It has continued through the centuries and is a unique Swiss folk tradition that attracts a number of tourists.

August

throughout—Swiss National Day

Since the late 1800's, August 1 has been celebrated as National Day. The date refers to one of the first agreements made between the Cantons of Uri, Schwyz, and Unterwalden some five centuries ago: Canton leaders "at the beginning of the month of August" swore allegiance to one another, promising mutual help and assistance. From this, present-day Switzerland was built.

August 1 is celebrated exclusively in the communities, and the singing of the national anthem is especially moving. Fireworks, bonfires, decorated buildings, parades, and children's processions are all part of the festivities. Plus, the Rhine Falls at Neuhausen hosts a special celebration. The cascading water, rushing over the rocks before falling 75 feet to the Rhine, provides an impressive backdrop for the ceremonies. The waterfall is floodlit on this occasion as well, and a magnificent fireworks display attracts thousands.

Saignelegier—Horse Show

Founded at the end of the 19th century, the Saignelegier Horse Show promotes a native breed called Franches-Montagnes. Initially combined with a cattle market, the festivities have evolved largely into a horse show, as the animals are one of the principal attractions in this region dedicated to horsemanship. The show presents 400-500 horses before a jury on the afternoons of the second weekend in August, along with a colorful grand procession. Trotting events, straight racing, wagon races, and events featuring four-horse spans and bareback riding are all part of the program designed to provide a variety of top equestrian events. A Roman chariot race, which gives the proceedings a note of distinction, is a highlight.

Lucerne—Lucerne Festival

Lucerne's late summer festival, established in 1938 by Arturo Toscannini and Ernest Ansermet, draws conductors, soloists, and ensembles from around the world to Switzerland's most beautiful city. The Swiss Festival Orchestra, comprised of leading musicians from Swiss orchestras, is the centerpiece of the festival. Other prominent orchestras have been the Czech Philharmonic conducted by Vaclav Neumann, the San Francisco Symphony, and the Cleveland Orchestra. Festival-goers can also visit the Wagner Museum at Tribschen, where Richard Wagner lived from 1866-1872. Toscannini conducted the first Lucerne Festival concert in front of the museum as a special homage to Wagner. For more information, contact International Festival of Music, Postfach CH-6002, Lucerne. (mid-August to early Sept.)

Geneva—Summer Music, Geneva

Saluting a different country each summer, Geneva turns its attention to all cultural aspects of the featured nation during its summer festival. Guest composers, dance groups, and orchestras perform; native cuisine is served throughout the city; and, generally, the spirit of the guest country is alive throughout Geneva, distinguished as the European headquarters of the United Nations. For more information, contact Office of Tourism, Case Postale 440, 1211 Geneva. (throughout August)

Ascona—Music Weeks

The Moscow State Orchestra, Berlin Philharmonic, Czech Philharmonic, and Prague Symphony have all performed in this nearly two-month long festival of music. The resort town of Ascona, the setting for this prestigious event, began as a small fishing village, but the mild, sunny climate, coupled with an international music fest, have transformed Ascona into a prominent vacation spot. For more information, contact Ascona Tourist Office, 6612, Ascona. (late August to mid-Oct.)

Montreux-Vevey—Montreux-Vevey Festival

This shared-city festival began in 1944. As a center of artistic and intellectual life in this area of Switzerland, Montreux offers jazz in July, and later, with Vevey, classical music of international renown. The Festival Orchestra of Sofia, the Tokyo Philharmonic, and the National Choir of Bulgaria have been featured, along with a score of top soloists. Venues for performances include Montreux's Pavilion and Vevey's Theater and Salle del Castillo. Montreux and Vevey are situated on the shores of Lake Geneva. For information, contact Festival de Musique, Case Postale 162, CH-1820 Montreaux. (late August to early Oct.)

September

Autumn in Switzerland is a season of plenty; harvesting grain, gathering grapes, and going to market are typical fall activities. And how do the Swiss perform these tasks? By celebrating with a festival! Traditional celebrations are held in Neuchâtel, Lugano, Morges, and Spiez, and in the villages on the shores of the Lake of Bienne and in the Canton of Schaffhausen. Others of note are in Thal, La Neuveville, Lucarno, Murten, Mendrision, and Rorschach. Processions, visits to the wine cellars, and, of course, wine tasting, are all part of the joy of autumn.

Aarau—Bachfischet

Bachfischet means the catching of fish before the annual cleaning of the stream of mud and debris, usually on September 1. After the cleaning, performed by the entire community, a hearty meal was served as a reward. The annual cleaning still takes place, although much of it is now done by public workers. The tradition lives on, however, especially in Aarau, where children carry leafy branches and lanterns in a parade. Following the procession, there's a bonfire and the traditional shared meal. (second Friday in Sept.)

Zurich—Knabenschiessen

This traditional rifle match, or marksmanship contest, dates to the 17th century, when boys were required to practice their shooting during the summer holidays. Today, about 4,000 Zurich boys perpetuate the ritual, which culminates in the crowning of a King of the Marksmen and a large fair. (second weekend in Sept.)

Neuchâtel—Vintage Festival

Grapes have been cultivated on the hills of Neuchâtel since the 10th century, and residents honor their vineyards and wine with a colorful vintage festival, including a parade of floats covered with flowers and carts with traditional harvesting tools. For the entire weekend, the town is filled with wine and food associated with autumn, and many residents don regional costumes. (last weekend in Sept.)

October

Lugano—Vintage Festival

Introduced in 1932 in connection with the vintner's celebrations in French-speaking Switzerland, this festival, also known as *The Festa della Vendemmia,* is more of a reaction to an older flower festival in Locarno, since the two towns maintain a strong rivalry. As in Locarno, there's a parade of flower-covered floats carrying girls tossing blossoms to the crowd. The promenade along the bay is decorated with lights, and wagons pulled by oxen portray country scenes. A delightful feature are the numerous *grottino* (taverns) surrounded by grape arbors and a wagon serving polenta.

As the largest town in the Canton of Ticino, and thoroughly Italian in character, Lugano is a fascinating place to visit in Switzerland, especially during harvest time. (first weekend in Oct.)

Canton Unterwalde—Aelplerchilbi

To mark the end of the Alpine summer, many places in the Canton celebrate with a community festival. Dairymen and pasture owners join villagers in giving thanks to God for the bounty of the season. Dancing, a community meal, a church service, and a lot of old-fashioned fun complete the event. (last weekend in Oct.)

Folk Customs in Berner Mittelland

From Achetringele to Zibelmarit, the Bernese Mittelland boasts a wealth of folk customs and traditional festivals. Although they vary in age and origin, many dating back centuries, Bernese folk customs are as alive today as ever. And while the customs of the Bernese Mittelland are of a region, they are nonetheless unique.

A *Chilbi,* an Alpine festival, belongs to the Emmental area. Folk groups, yodelers, flag throwers, alphorn blowers, and traditional dancers add their special charm to these summer events. The *Luderenchilbi,* held every second Sunday in August, features hefty farm boys engaged in *Schwingen,* a contest similar to wrestling, held in a sawdust-covered ring. The winner takes home a flowed-decked heifer.

Like the *Alpchilbi,* a *Chasteilet* is held in Eriz and a *Schafscheid* (sheep separation) in Riffenmatt, on the first Thursday in September. On these occasions, the sheep, who spend the summer on the Alps, are sorted by their owners. Tradesmen, merchants, and carnival groups add color to the *Schafscheid.*

The *Zibelemarit* (onion market), dating to 1405, is the most popular market in the area. The privilege to sell their produce at the open-air market in Berne was granted growers of the Seeland in reward for their help during a big fire. On the fourth Monday of November, the center of Berne becomes a market and carnival grounds, and the scent of onions permeates the air, a reminder of other markets in other times.

For 250 years, *Solennitat* has been an important festival in Burgdorf. Always held the last Monday of July, it is a perpetually young festival of contests, games, songs, and a parade led by William Tell and his companions. Girls wearing large floral wreaths complete this rural Swiss event.

Wine festivals and grape-picking Sundays are organized during the harvest season in the towns on the north shore of Lake Biel. Plus, the city of Biel organizes a *Braderie* (summer festival) copied after an old medieval custom.

For more information on festivals in the region, contact Verkehrsverband Berner Mitteland, P.O.B., CH-3001 Bern.

Sechselauten: Zurich's Spring Festival

Possibly 650 years old, the historic rite of "chasing away Old Man Winter" is still celebrated in Zurich in a custom called *Sechselauten*. On the Sunday before the third Monday in April, there's a colorful children's procession through the streets, accompanied by the *Boogg*, an enormous snowman who is the symbolic figure of winter.

On Monday, Zurich's 25 guilds parade in their historic costumes with emblems, flags, lanterns, carriages, and bands. The city is completely decorated in blue and white. Following the procession, the members form into groups on the Sechselautenplatz by the lake, with the *Boogg* (full of fireworks) enthroned on a high pole. At the stroke of 6:00pm, a bonfire under the figure is lit, and all the city's church bells peal, officially announcing the end of winter, as riders from the mounted guilds circle around the blazing funeral pyre at a gallop. Once the flames reach the *Boogg*, he is blown apart by fireworks—a spectacular climax to the annual custom and a joyous welcome to spring. Dancing and celebrating continue throughout the city into the wee hours of Tuesday, and banquets are held at many guildhalls.

For more information, contact Tourist Office, Bahnhofplatz 15, P.O. Box CH-8923, Zurich.

Swiss Holidays

New Year's Day, Good Friday, Easter Monday, Ascension Day, Whitmonday, Christmas, and Dec. 26. Many Cantons also observe Labor Day (May 1) and Independence Day (Aug. 1).

For literature and further information, contact the **Swiss National Tourist Office**. In the U.S., the addresses are: 608 Fifth Ave., New York, NY 10020 (212-757-5944); 150 N. Michigan Ave., Suite 2930, Chicago, IL 60601 (312-630-5840); 260 Stockton St., San Francisco, CA 94108 (415-362-2260); and 222 N. Sepulveda Blvd., Suite 570, El Segundo, CA 90245 (213-335-5980).

9

Germany

"Germany spreads southward from the North Sea, the Danish Peninsula and the Baltic across the heart of north-central Europe. It reaches to the borders of Switzerland, Austria and Czechoslovakia. On the west it faces the Netherlands, Belgium, Luxembourg and France; on the east, Poland. . . One historian describes the shrinking and expanding of Germany this way: 'In a thousand years, geographic Germany has gone in and out like a concertina'."
—Wohlrabe and Krusch, *The Lands and People of Germany*

Though the geographic Germany seems in a continual state of flux, it has changed little in terms of tradition, and the legacy of German festivals (some of which date to pre-Christian times) remains constant, as do the legends and folk tales that cry "made in Germany!"

Germany has a "Fairy Tale Trail" (in the northern Hesse and Weser countryside), along which travelers are almost always greeted by "Once upon a time. . ." and where courageous princes, Puss-in-Boots, and Little Red Riding Hood once dwelled. Somewhere in the hills along the Weser, Snow White took refuge with the Seven Dwarfs. Sleeping Beauty lived in Sababurg Castle deep in the Reinhardswald. In 1248, the Pied Piper drove the rats (and later the children) from Hamelin, and the Brothers Grimm, responsible for collecting and preserving so many of these delightful German stories, are among Gottingen's most famous citizens.

Germany also has a "Romantic Road," a 180-mile stretch through Bavaria from Würzburg in the north to Fussen in the south. While dwarfs and golden geese may not reside there, legends are everywhere. Dinkelsbuhl has a fabulous children's festival commemorating the day the children saved the town from invading troops. And there are countless swans and enough castles to make a traveler feel royal—both were passions of King Ludwig II, who planned Scholss Neuschwanstein (the "new swan rock") and Linderhof.

Indeed, the marvels of German folklore are known everywhere, and many of the tales, so important to Germans, are equally important to travelers who seek genuine involvement with native traditions.

GERMANY

May

Harz Region—Walpurgisnacht

Actually celebrated April 30, Walpurgis Night is a popular tradition throughout Europe but especially in the Harz region of Germany. A night of revelry, believed in medieval days to be the occasion of a witches' Sabbath, it was immortalized by Goethe in *Faust* and is generally observed by nightmarish wildness.

Wiesbaden—International May Festival

One of the most famous and fashionable of the spa resorts, Wiesbaden lies in a sheltered valley between the Rhine and Taunus Mountains. Founded by the Romans, it offers thermal springs, a casino, and culture galore.

Throughout May, the festival (which traditionally begins May 1) presents eight or nine operas sung in their original language. Symphonies, ballets, dances, and dramas are all included in the festival schedule, the second oldest after Bayreuth.

Central to the festival is the Hessisches Staatstheater, where Verdi's *Don Carlos* and Monteverdi's *L'Inferno d'amore* were performed in 1990. Other renowned music, ballet, and opera compositions by international ensembles make the Wiesbaden event a delightful opening to the German musical calendar of events. For more information, contact International May Festival, c/o Hessisches Staatstheater, P.O. Box 3247, D-6200 Wiesbaden.

Constance & Friedrichshafen—Lake Constance Festival

Germany, Austria, and Switzerland share the shoreline of Lake Constance, and each country hosts some type of cultural offering each summer. Germany's contribution comes in late May (through late June), with a diverse five-week event that generally opens with a laser show and fireworks and continues with an incomparable offering of classical music and dance. Some of the highlights of past seasons have been performances by the National Ballet of Canada, Orchestre National de France, and the South-West German Radio Symphony conducted by Erich Leinsdorf.

Schwetzingen—Schwetzingen Festival

In the 18th century, the Palatine electors used Schwetzingen Castle (about 10 miles from Heidelberg) as their summer residence; later it became a hunting lodge. Today, this small village hosts a renowned music event with opera as well as contemporary music.

The first festival was held in 1952, but the tradition of music here was established in 1746, when a musical technique called the "Mannehein crescendo" was invented. Because of this, musicians from all over the world came here to study and practice.

The castle, which has spectacular gardens arrayed in the Versailles style, provides a charming setting for the festival, and there's a grand Rococo theater, which serves as the main venue.

An additional treat for visitors to Schwetzingen in early May is the Asparagus Festival, which draws gourmets along with music lovers. Schwetzingen's asparagus crop is celebrated throughout Germany, and people in the know (asparagus-wise) consider the festival a "must." For more information, contact Verkehrsverein Schwetzingen, P.B. Schlossplatz, D-6830 Schwetzingen. (May to early June)

Bonn—Bonn Summer

The birthplace of Beethoven, Bonn takes time from its hectic political schedule to host a five-month festival of music, theater, and cabaret. The whole city becomes an enormous festival venue, but the market square and the town hall are the main stages. Visitors who wish additional musical immersion might wish to visit Beethoven's house (now a museum) at Bongasse 20, where the composer was born in 1770 and where his musical works, portraits, and instruments (including his last piano) are displayed. (May to late September)

Würzburg—Wine Village

This former Roman outpost on the River Main is now a famous university city and headquarters of a number of wine producers. A lovely baroque city, Würzburg is considered the northern terminus of the Romantic Road, the 180-mile stretch through central Bavaria, ending in the foothills of the Bavarian Alps. Würzburg lies at the heart of Franken, one of the 11 specified wine-producing regions of Germany, and during the 10 days of the festival, over 100 Franconian wines and food specialties are served in 40 quaint cottages in the inner city. (late May to early June)

Cologne—Sommerköln

The fascinating city of Cologne (Köln), founded in 38 B.C. by the Romans, is located on a scenic section of the Rhine River. Its Dom (Cathedral), one of the largest Gothic structures in the world, serves as the geographic center of the Old Town. The city's "Romantic Summer" festival is a cornucopia of street theater, featuring dancing, music, and other forms of outdoor entertainment. Many events are held in Rheinpark, a large garden featuring sculpture and the famous Tanzbrunnen dancing fountain. (May-Sept.)

Hannover—Lichterfest

During the Festival of Music and Light, which takes place four times during the summer, the Great Garden in Herrenhausen is displayed at its best. From late afternoon through the evening, Europe's oldest baroque garden is the setting for dancing, singing, and music. The finale is the fireworks display set to Handel's *Music for the Royal Fireworks*. The Great Garden, with its fountains and cascades, is also illuminated throughout the summer. For more information, contact Tourist Office Hannover, Ernst-August Platz 8, D-3000 Hannover 1; or Hannover-Lower Saxony Tourist Office, 103 Carnegie Center, Princeton, NJ 08540. (early May, early June, mid-August, and mid-Sept.)

Hamelin—Pied Piper Pageant

Held every Sunday, the Pied Piper Pageant re-enacts the classic legend in which the Piper led the children away after not getting paid for ridding the town of rats. The story is presented in historical dress at midday on the Hochzeitshaus terrace. During the summer, the Pied Piper presentation is in the Bahnhof's restaurant daily at various times (see below). For more information, contact Tourist Office, Deister-allee, D-3250 Hamelin 1; or Hannover-Lower Saxony Tourist Office, 103 Carnegie Center, Princeton, NJ 08540.

June

Lüneburg—Lüneburg Bach Festival

The Hanseatic city of Lüneburg plays host to this event devoted exclusively to the works of Johann Sebastian Bach. Like other cities in the Lower Saxony region, Lüneburg has been an important town since the Middle Ages. For more information, contact Tourist Office, Rathaus, D-2120, Lüneburg; or Hannover-Lower Saxony Tourism Office, 103 Carnegie Center, Princeton, NJ 08540. (early June)

Göttingen—Göttingen Handel Festival

Not to be outdone in homage to German musical masters, Göttingen, like Lüneburg, honors Handel for a week in early June with a program devoted exclusively to his works. Music lovers will enjoy both the festival performances and the charming university city. For those who like additional folk participation, Göttingen is the city of charming little Ganseliessel, "the most-kissed girl in the whole world." According to tradition, every new doctoral student must kiss the cool, bronze beauty upon completion of the degree. (Ph.D.'s, of course, are not the only ones who succumb to the tradition.) For more information, contact Tourist Information Göttingen, Altes Rathaus, Markt 9, 3400 Göttingen; or Hannover-Lower Saxony Tourism Office, 103 Carnegie Center, Princeton, NJ 08540. (early June)

Würzburg—Würzburg Mozart Festival

Since 1922, renowned artists have come to Würzburg to commemorate Mozart in the festive surroundings of the Würzburg Residenz and Kaisersaal. Each festival season, Mozart lovers can hear his symphonies, concertos, sonatas, sacred vocal works, and one opera. Würzburg is a lovely place to enjoy his music in this three-week event. For more information, contact Mozart Festival Office, Haus zum Falken D-8700, Würzburg. (throughout June)

Schwäbisch Hall—Open-Air Theater
The medieval town of Schwäbisch Hall lies in the heart of the Swabian Alb, 40 miles east of Heilbronn. Its marketplace is one of Germany's most attractive, and on its northern side is St. Michael's Cathedral, the setting for plays performed through early August. The Cathedral is a 15th-century Gothic structure with 54 large, curved stone steps as its entrance. (late June to early August)

Bad Hersfeld—Bad Hersfeld Festival
Bad Hersfeld, northeast of Frankfurt near the border of what was East Germany, holds an annual drama festival in the ruins of its 1,000-year-old Abbey (Ruine der Abteikirch). Many of Germany's leading actors appear in the festival, which runs through early August.

Augsburg—Augsburg Mozart Festival
Mozart's father Leopold was born (in 1719) and bred in Augsburg, and family connections with the city remain strong. The eight-day festival upholds these ties with a "mostly Mozart" program and additions by some of his contemporaries. Concert venues include the Mozarthaus at 30 Frauentorstrasse, the 18th-century rococo festival hall of the Schaezler Palace, the Opera House, and the Kleiner Goldener Saal. Augsburg, the largest city on Germany's Romantic Road, also boasts Bertolt Brecht and Martin Luther as native sons. For more information, contact Deutschen Mozart-Gesellschaft, Karlstrasse 6, 8900 Augsburg. (early June)

Bogen—Procession with the Long Pole
This annual Whit Sunday pilgrimage dates back more than 500 years. The tradition, called Wallfahrt mit der langen Stang!, occurs every Whit Sunday, when a team of men, with the support of thousands of spectators, carries a 13-meter candle up the steep Bogenberg. This is a beautiful example of religious folklore. (Whit Sunday, also known as Pentecost, is the seventh Sunday after Easter.)

Kötzting—Kötzting Whitsun Ride
The color and splendor of the Kötzinger Pfingstritt is remarkable. This equestrian procession, really a pilgrimage by men on horseback as part of Whitsun festivities, dates from 1412 and attracts thousands of spectators annually to this Bavarian Forest area. (Whit Monday)

Aschau—Hohenaschau Palace Concerts
Matinee, evening, and courtyard concerts are held in the attractive surroundings of the 12th-century Hohenaschau Palace in Upper Bavaria. (June-August)

Rothenburg—Master Draught
This historic festival play, traditional procession, and military encampment are held annually at Whitsuntide. (See below.)

Heidelberg—Castle Illumination

Each year, the City of Heidelberg stages castle illuminations that have become world famous. Held three times during the summer (usually on Saturdays), they are accompanied by fireworks commemorating the terrible fire that consumed the Palace of the Electors during the War of Succession (1689-1693) and the lightning that struck the castle in 1764. In addition to the illuminations, open-air productions of *The Student Prince*, the popular operetta of life in this classic university town, are held in the castle courtyard during the Heidelberg Festival in late July and early August. For more information, contact Heidelberg Tourist Information, Am Hauptbahnhof, D-6900 Heidelberg. (early June, mid-July, and first weekend in August)

Hannover—Schützenfest

Historic Hannover, the city on the River Leine, has been making history for a millenia. The first settlement, which dates to 950, is now the core of Hannover's *Altstadt* (Old Town), which charms people of all ages. Hannover attracts over 200,000 spectators to its Schützenfest, the annual marksmen's pageant, carnival, and beer bash. The event, over 450 years old, features contests of marksmanship as well as Europe's longest procession, with participants in colorful garb from many countries, brass and pipe bands, decorated floats, and horse-drawn carriages. For more information, contact Tourist Office Hannover, Ernst-August Platz 8, D-3000 Hannover 1; or Hannover-Lower Saxony Tourist Office, 103 Carnegie Center, Princeton, NJ 08540. (late June to early July)

Bad Kissingen—Kissingen Sommer

This renowned spa town, considered the most attractive in the Franconian basin, also hosts an annual music event that includes classical orchestra and solo performances. The works of Mozart, Handel, Tchaikovsky, and Chopin are among those featured. In addition to the halls in Bad Kissingen, which date from the late 19th century, nearby castles, churches, and monasteries serve as festival venues. For more information, contact Kissingen Sommer, Box 2260, D-8730 Bad Kissingen. (late June to mid-July)

Schleswig-Holstein—Schleswig-Holstein Music Festival

The northernmost province of Germany, Schleswig-Holstein hosts this wide-ranging (geographically and culturally) musical event. Twenty-eight venues throughout the region, as well as in Denmark and areas of former East Germany, feature music everywhere. Events include orchestral and solo performances. For more information, contact Schleswig-Holstein Music Festival, Box 3830, 2300 Kiel 1. (late June to mid-August)

July

Munich—Munich Opera Festival

Munich, a city that loves festivals and celebrations, is at its musical finest in July, when it hosts this brilliant, first-class opera event. The festival presents six or seven operas—Strauss, Mozart, and Wagner are usually represented—in their original language, plus several ballets and a few recitals. The festival, first held in 1901, has seen some of the biggest stars in international music. Performances are staged in the National Theater, home of the Bavarian State Opera and the Cuvilliés Theater, Munich's 18th-century rococo hall, which offers an ideal setting for chamber music, recitals, and ballet. For more information, contact Münchner Opernfestpiele, Bayerische Staatsoper, Maximilianstrasse 11, 8000 München 22.

Bayreuth—Richard Wagner Festival

Germany's oldest music festival opened in 1876 with *Das Rheingold* in a festival house built by Wagner himself—the first composer to build a concert hall for his own works. Located in Upper Franconia, Bayreuth is a quiet town that becomes a magnet for Wagner fans for five weeks in the summer. His operas are performed in repertory with *The Ring* and have been conducted by impressive names like Horst Stein, Pierre Boulez, and James Levine. Along with the Salzburg Festival, tickets for this event are among the most difficult to obtain. Those interested should start at least a year in advance! For more information, contact Bayreuther Festspiele, Postfach 100262, D-8580 Bayreuth 1. (late July to late August)

Würzburg—St. Kilian Folk Festival

On the first Saturday in July, the biggest Volkfest in the area opens with a fabulous parade inaugurating the three-week funfair that includes a fairground, amusements, and the obligatory beer tent. Würzburg's Dom (Cathedral), dedicated to St. Kilian, an Irish missionary to Franconia in the 7th century, was begun in 1045. Destroyed by World War II bombs, it has been completely rebuilt. (throughout July)

Lindau—Children's Festival

This traditional children's event of the Allgäu/Bavaria-Swabia region dates to 1655. After a religious service, the children march in a colorful procession past the town hall, where the mayor makes a speech. Following the singing of *Lindau hoch*, there's food, drink, and a sports competition. (early Wednesday in July)

Neunburg vorm Wald—Vom Hussenkrieg

This spectacular open-air play commemorates the tragic fate of the border region of the Upper Palatinate Forest. The historical background is the assault of the Bohemian Hussites in the war from

1419-1434. The play is pure German history, but it's enlivened with costumes and spectacle. (July to late August)

Waldmünchen—Trenck der Pandur vor Waldmünchen

This historical open-air play is a reminder of the terrible times during the Austrian War of Succession (in the 18th century), when the soldiers of the notorious Col. Trench challenged the townspeople. It includes the war that raged from 1741-1748 and Prince Karl's condemnation to death. The play runs weekly from early July through mid-August.

Kaufbeuren/Allgäu—Tänzelfest

Bavaria's oldest children's festival features kids dressed in historical costume presenting the history of the town in a grand procession and production. The festival itself lasts 10 days, with the procession held on the weekend. (mid- to late July)

Memmingen—Wallenstein Summer

The Bavarian town of Memmingen comes alive at the end of July with several historical and traditional events. On a late July Thursday, a children's festival includes a parade and concert in the market square. A traditional *fischertag* is also held on a late Saturday, commemorating the time when the stream was cleared, allowing men to fish for trout. Today the honor belongs to men of the Fishing Club, and the guy who nets the largest trout is named "Fisher King." At 10:00am, the new king is crowned in a lively Bavarian tradition. Both events are annual.

"Wallenstein Summer," however, is held every four years, next in 1995. For one week, the whole town reverts to the year 1630, when Wallenstein, a great general of the Thirty Years War, reigned here for five months. Over 2,000 citizens act out the events of the era in authentic costumes and period entertainment. (late July)

Ulm—Folk Festival

The city of Ulm, lying at a point in the Danube where the stream becomes a navigable river, celebrates its fishing heritage with a *Fischertechen* (Fishermen's Jousting Match) and traditional procession on the river. Events are held for 10 days in late July, with the river procession on the two weekends that span the festival.

Hannover—Maschsee Lake Festival

The biggest artificial lake in Germany is Maschsee, a favorite recreation area for locals and visitors. In 1986, it was 50 years old—a good excuse to celebrate. They enjoyed the party so much that they now celebrate it annually, with countless activities on and above the lake. Windsurfers, yachtsmen, oarsmen, artists, clowns, jugglers, and theater groups offer entertainment throughout the three weeks. (late July to mid-August)

Schlob Kaltenberg—Kaltenberger Ritterturnier

Live through a day in the Middle Ages at the Kaltenberg Knights Tournament! The Black Knight, Robin Hood, D'Artagnan, and knights from all over Europe bring a taste of medieval life to modern Germany every weekend in July. Other events include folk dancing and displays of period entertainment. Schlob Kaltenberg is halfway between Augsburg and Landsberg, west of Munich. For more information, contact Fremdenverhehrsverband Ammersee-Lech, Von Kuhlmannstr. 15, 8910 Landsberg am Lech.

Hornberg—Das Hornbergger Schieben

Each year the people of Hornberg recreate the 1564 Hornberg Archery Tournament, just as their ancestors have done since the 16th century. A historical play is featured as part of this event, along with colorful costumes and entertainment befitting the period. Hornberg is between Freiburg and Rottweil. For more information, contact Walter Aberle, 1 Vorsitzender, 7746 Hornberg. (July-August)

August

Heidelberg—Heidelberg Festival

With its beautiful Renaissance castle and university both cherished by the people of Heidelberg, it's no wonder the two are combined in a festival. Romberg's operetta *The Student Prince*, based on life at the university (the oldest in Germany, founded in 1386), is produced annually on the castle grounds. It alternates with musical productions both classical and contemporary. For more information, contact Tourist Information, Postfach 105860, D-6900 Heidelberg. (through August)

Volkach—Franconian Wine Festival

At the Franconian Wine Festival, growers show their finest wines, particularly highlighting the year's young wines. Like most wine events, conspicuous consumption is very much in order. (early August)

During August, wine festivals and markets run throughout Germany in the 11 specified growing regions. The better-known fests are at Wiesbaden, Rudesheim, Stuttgart, Winningen, Mainz, and Bernkastel-Kues.

Fürth im Wald—Der Drachenstich

East Bavaria's *Fürther Drachenstich*, over 500 years old, is Germany's oldest popular play. Over 1,000 costumed participants, 200 horses, and a number of music groups take part in the procession and play, which portrays the eternal struggle against evil—represented by an enormous dragon that winds through the streets of town while being battled by costumed horsemen. (second or third Sunday in August)

Staubing—Gäubodenfest

Another popular festival in Bavaria, the Gäubodenfest is an enormous funfair that attracts nearly a million visitors, most of whom manage at least one or two stops at the ubiquitous beer tents. (11 days in mid-August)

Hannover—Old Town Festival

During the last weekend of August, the historic Old Town section of Hannover becomes an enormous stage for rock and jazz musicians, circus artists, and street performers. An estimated 300,000 people visit the area for this exciting event.

Worms—Backfischfest

This old Rhine town is important in religious history as the place where the Imperial Diet of Worms issued its edict against Martin Luther in 1521. It is also important in secular history as the site of the Backfischfest, one of the Rhineland's liveliest wine festivals—a showcase for area wines and an excuse for capping off the summer with entertainment, eating, and drinking. (late August to early Sept.)

September

Berlin—Berlin's Festival Weeks

This event, founded in 1951, kept culture alive when Berlin was a divided city. Originally, the five- to six-week-long event offered opera, symphonic, chamber, and choral concerts, plus film and art exhibitions, in West Berlin, while East Berlin hosted theater, music, and ballet. Since reunification, the festival format has changed, but it remains an important cultural event. For more information, contact Berliner Festspiele, Budapester Strasse 50, 1000 Berlin 30. (early Sept. to mid-Oct.)

Seesen—Schuttenfest

Like so many other areas of Germany that celebrate historical events, Seesen, in the Harz region, recalls the days of the Renaissance with dramatic pageants, historical markets, jousting, and period music. The Schuttenfest of 1428 is remembered by the entire village and is a splendid display of native folklore and tradition. For more information, contact Seeses Tourist Information, Markstrade 1, D-3370 Seeses/Harz. (first weekend in Sept.)

Heilbronn—Wine Village

Another round of wine festivals begins in September in the wine-growing regions. In addition to the annual event at Heilbronn (for one week in mid-month), other fests occur at Trier, Offenburg, Würzburg, Lake Constance, and Boppard on weekends throughout Sept.

Nürnberg—Altstadtfest

The "Old Town" festival of Nürnberg is one of the biggest music and folk festivals in Germany. Once considered the ideal medieval city because of its architectural splendor (much of it ruined, unfortunately, by World War II bombings), the city has undergone restoration, and its Old Town is still a beautiful venue for this early autumn event, which includes Dixieland, jazz, rock, and pop music for 10 days. (mid-Sept.)

Bad Dürkheim—Dürkheim Sausage Fair

The Dürkheim *Würstmarkt*, among the best-known of the public festivals in Germany, has been called "the greatest wine festival in the world." The giant feast actually has religious origins: over 560 years ago, local vintners served pilgrims wine, sausage, and bread as they made their trek on St. Michael's Day. Eventually, the pilgrimage evolved into a wine drinkers' tour.

The fest still uses the symbol of the wheelbarrow (used to transport the wine casks), a pan to heat the sausages, and a basket with homemade bread. Today, 36 booths maintain the tradition. These small wine taverns are covered but open on the sides and fitted with narrow tables and benches. In addition, large pavilions become dance halls, where German bands play traditional music. The wine (traditionally from the previous year) is served in glasses (*Schoppen*) that hold half a litre (about a pint), and chicken and sausages are abundant. No one goes hungry at the *Würstmarkt*.

The event runs Friday-Tuesday on the second weekend, and Friday-Monday on the third weekend of Sept. As well as food and drink, there's an amusement park, a procession with decorated floats and vineyard proprietors, and a ceremonial tapping of the first cask by the mayor of Bad Dürkheim and the German Wine Queen.

Munich—Oktoberfest

No offense to Bad Dürkheim, but Munich's *Oktoberfest* makes the *Würstmarkt* look like a Cub Scouts' meeting. This epic bash is discussed in detail below. (runs 16 days from mid-Sept. to early October)

October

Fürth—St. Michael's Fair

The high point of all the Fürth festivals and an 800-year-old tradition, this Franconian harvest celebration features a procession with over 3,000 participants. The entire event lasts about two weeks and draws nearly 100,000 visitors. (mid-Oct.)

Schwangau—Colmansfest

On the Sunday before October 13, the Schwangau horse owners ride in traditional costume to St. Colman's Church. Ministers, servers, and honored guests sit in decorated coaches before the open-air Mass. The horses are blessed and then led three times around the church.

Neustadt—Wine Harvest Festival

Here's another opportunity to sample the fine wines of the Rhein-pfalz region. (mid-Oct.)

For additional information on the 11 specified wine-growing regions of Germany (Ahr, Baden, Franken, Hess, Bergstrasse, Mittelrhein, Mosel-Saar-Ruwer, Nahe, Rheingau, Rheinhessen, Rheinpfalz, and Wurttemberg), contact Deutscher Weinfonds— Pressestelle, Postfach 1707, Gutenbergplatz 3-5, 6500 Mainz 1.

Darmstadt—Frankenstein Festival

This annual festival takes place at Castle Frankenstein, the inspiration for Mary Shelley's novel. The event, organized by two American soldiers who were stationed in Germany, takes place on three weekends around Halloween and celebrates the famous monster who lived in this part of Germany, south of Frankfurt. For more information, contact Darmstadt Tourist Office, Luisenplatz 5, 6100 Darmstadt. (late Oct. to early Nov.)

A Year-Round Array of Folk Festivals

The many folk festivals held throughout the year are more than just celebrations. Several of the major fests—such as the Oktoberfest, the Christmas Markets, and the summer and fall wine festivals—are major tourist attractions, and visitors are welcome to participate. In addition to native crafts and foods, Germany's festivals display the country's riches in music, dancing, and seasonal celebrations.

Germany greets the spring with a variety of colorful festivals, including the historic *Master Draught* and *Shepherds' Dance* in Rothenburg. The festival dates to the 17th century:

Master Draught and Shepherds' Dance

The great historical plays, the Master Draught (*Der Meistertrunk*) and the Shepherds' Dance were originally performed in Rothenburg-on-Tauber every Whitsuntide. Special trains bring spectators to this memorable presentation, in which citizens become actors and the most famous of all medieval towns, Rothenburg, becomes a stage.

The **Master Draught** commemorates the historic feat of 1631, when Burgermeister Nusch prevented General Tilly from giving the town to the invading soldiers for pillage and burning. Accepting the challenge of the General, Nusch emptied a beaker that held four quarts of wine—in one long gulp. *Der Meistertrunk* is re-enacted in the large assembly room of the city hall where it actually happened.

In the afternoon, the **Shepherds' Dance** takes place in the ancient market square. This custom can be traced to 1516, when the Town Council granted shepherds, freemen, and servants of the

Shepherd's Guild the right to replace the Little House of Prayer outside the *Klingentor* (city gate). This house of worship, also known as the Shepherd's Church, was ordained in 1483 in honor of St. Wolfgang, patron of shepherds.

Colorful costumes and a convincing performance of both the Master Draught and the Shepherds' Dance make a profound impression, especially with their mass scenes depicting the entry of the imperial troops into the town and their encampment outside the city wall. Although *Der Meistertrunk* recalls the grave danger the town faced during the Middle Ages, it is spiked with wit and humor. (Whitsunday, also known as Pentecost Sunday, occurs on the seventh Sunday after Easter.)

The Pied Piper of Hamelin

The quaint town of Hamelin, on the banks of the Weser River, retains the look of bygone days in its carefully preserved Old Town. Half-timbered houses and exuberant architecture present an outdoor stage for a lively pageant performed from May to September to honor Hamelin's most famous visitor—the Pied Piper.

According to legend, in 1248 the people of Hamelin hired the Pied Piper (so named because of his multi-colored, or pied, garments) to rid them of rats. He did so by playing a tune that enchanted the vermin, who followed him to the river and drowned. But the town refused to pay the Piper. In revenge, he played another tune the next Sunday, one that lured all the children out of town and deep into a hill where they disappeared, never to be seen again.

Though Hamelin is now the economic and cultural center of the area, it continues to honor its legend with an outdoor pageant, featuring children in period costumes, statues, exhibitions, and a local drink known as Rat Tail Flambe, or "Rat Poison," which only the most adventurous dare consume! The event runs on Sundays from May-Sept.

Many summer celebrations in Germany pay homage to the art and history of marksmanship with special festivals staged in Lower Saxony, Bavaria, and North Rhine-Westphalia. The largest, the Marksmen's Fair, takes place in Hannover at the beginning of July, with 10 days of merrymaking. Tents, rides, sausage grills, and all the elements of funfairs are featured.

The arrival of autumn heralds a round of wine festivals and the ultimate beer bash, Oktoberfest, which is in a class by itself (see below). At the end of August, the Moselle Wine Festival, Germany's oldest, takes place in Winnigen and features rows of wine and food stands with the best of the region's harvest. For two weekends in September, the town of Bad Dürkheim, on the German Wine Road south of Frankfurt, holds its Sausage Market, Germany's biggest wine festival. Dating back to medieval times, the *Würstmarkt* serves over

50,000 gallons of wine and tons of traditional snacks, including sausage, chicken, and pork, to half a million people each year.

Some of the most elaborate and culturally significant celebrations in Germany happen around Christmas. At year-end, all of Germany becomes a winter wonderland with *Christkindlsmarkts*—processions, musical programs, and displays of seasonal crafts. The traditional Yuletide fairs begin in late November and reach their peak on Christmas Eve. In Hamburg, an important folk tradition at this time is the Hamburg Dom:

Hamburg Dom—The Folk Festival of the North

With a bang that reverberates through the Rhineland and Hesse, the Netherlands and Westphalia, the Jutland peninsula and the Danish Islands, Copenhagen, Stockholm, and Oslo, the Christmas Dom of Hamburg opens on November 5th to become the grand folk festival of the North. The festival continues at a breathtaking pace until December 4th.

The festival began shortly after the consecration of the Mariendom (St. Mary's Cathedral) in 1339. As was customary in the Middle Ages, the Dom was an enclave in the city-republic of Hamburg, with special privileges and its own market jurisdiction beyond the reach of Hamburg law. In its outer halls, a market ran continually, and no one thought it was wrong that selling and buying extended into the church proper at Yuletide. Hence, the name *Weihnachts* (Christmas) *Dom* was coined. Only when the goings-on became too boisterous, and traders sold smuggled and stolen goods, did the city put its foot down.

The Dom Chapter, unwilling to lose the revenue from the brisk business, hatched a compromise: traders were permitted in the church only in very bad weather so their goods wouldn't spoil. This compromise, by the way, is the oldest record of the Christmas Dom still preserved in the Hamburg archives.

Trouble with the traders remained, however. Youngsters of the guilds and ruffians often fought in the dusk of the church interior. Churchgoers who got in their way did not always fare well. No wonder, then, that some traders moved their activities to the broad Jungfernstieg (Maiden Lane, now one of the city's finest boulevards). In 1804, secularization brought the Mariendom into the possession of the city, which had the church torn down but preserved the Weihnachtsdom. When there was no longer sufficient room in the inner city, the Hamburg Dom was transferred to the Holy Ghost Meadow. On this large field, one of the world's most interesting festivals developed, with all the paraphernalia of a great amusement park.

Karneval

Every year, Germany shakes off the winter doldrums with *Karneval*, the colorful pre-Lenten party festival and parade that rivals Rio's Carnival and New Orleans' Mardi Gras. *Karneval* is a national extravaganza in hundreds of locations, especially in the Rhineland, Bavaria, and Hesse. Although most festivities begin in November, they reach their peak in post-New Year's fancy-dress balls and other celebrations and ceremonies.

Different regions in Germany celebrate the season with their own customs. Munich's *Fasching* allows the city to display its creativity and artistic flair. *Karneval* in the Black Forest, called *Fasnet*, dates to the Middle Ages and was developed by the craftsmen's guilds. Throughout the ages, *Karneval* Associations in the Black Forest have used the same wooden masks and traditional costumes in their parades.

Periodic Festivals

In addition to annual festivals and celebrations, Germany observes special events periodically, the most famous of which is the **Oberammergau Passion Play**, last performed in 1990 and not scheduled again for another 10 years.

Performed against the spectacular backdrop of the Bavarian Alps, the *Passion Play* is a centuries-old tradition that began as a plea for God's help during the Black Plague in the 17th century. Villagers pledged that if Oberammergau were spared, they would show their appreciation to God by re-enacting the Passion of Christ every decade. According to legend, no plague deaths occurred after the pledge was made. To this day, Oberammergau has kept its promise.

By tradition, only village residents can perform the Passion Play. The cast of approximately 1,600 invests two years of preparation in the production, which is performed four times a week from mid-May through late September.

The production was originally staged in a meadow. In the early 20th century, the 5,000-seat Passion Playhouse was built. Although the stage is in the open, the seats are covered. While other areas of Europe perform Passion Plays (see Austria and Norway), few can compare in scope and grandeur to the Oberammergau event.

Another event performed only periodically is the **Landshut Wedding 1475** in Landshut (East Bavaria), staged every four years (next in June/July, 1993). With almost 2,000 participants in medieval costume, it's the biggest historical festival in Germany and relives the splendor of the late Middle Ages when Prince George and Princess Hedwig were wed. When last enacted, feasters consumed 333 oxen, 275 hogs, 40 calves, 12,000 geese, and hundreds of gallons of beer and wine!

The **Agnes Bernauer Festival** in Straubing (East Bavaria) is held only at four-year intervals also. This event commemorates the tragic fate of Agnes of Augsburg, a commoner who married Duke Albrecht of Straubing. She was accused of witchcraft and sentenced to death by drowning in the Danube. The historical implications of the wedding are more the occasion for the festival, however, and like countless other German folk events, it offers a brilliant display of costumes and regional traditions. (July, next in 1993)

Munich's Oktoberfest

"Ozapft is!" (*"It's tapped!"*) exclaims the Lord Mayor of Munich after broaching the first barrel of brew. And with that, the world's biggest beer bash begins!

The figures are staggering: six million liters of beer (the equivalent of three million six-packs); 500,000 broiled chickens and at least as many pork sausages; 60 oxen roasted on a giant rotating spit; tons of fish, *würsts*, and ham hocks; 11 huge beer tents, each holding up to 6,000 people; 40 smaller beer, wine, and coffee houses; 200 carnival attractions and 55 rides; 7,000 participants in the Costume and Marksmen Parade on the first Oktoberfest Sunday; countless brass bands; and five million party-goers—all crammed into the most famous and fun-filled 16 days on earth, *Oktoberfest*.

It began in 1810 with a horse race to honor the wedding of Crown Prince Ludwig to Princess Therese von Sachsen-Hildburghausen. The site was an open field at the gates of the city christened the *Theresienwiese* (Therese's Meadow) in honor of the bride. Even today, citizens of Munich don't go "to the Oktoberfest" but *"Auf die Wies'n"* ("to the meadow"). In 1811, an Agricultural Fair joined the race, and though the race disappeared in 1938, the Agricultural Fair still runs every three years.

During the first decade, the amusements were slim. In 1818, the first merry-go-round and a set of swings were set up. Small booths began to supply beer, and in 1896, the first great beer tents, run by entrepreneurs in collaboration with the breweries, appeared. To this day, Munich breweries supply the staple of the event, German beer—often brewing special "Oktoberfest beer" just for the fair.

Festivities begin at 11:00am (usually on a Saturday in mid-Sept.) with the entry of the Oktoberfest Landlords and Brewers in decorated carriages, ornate wagons of the Munich breweries, waitresses on floats, and all of the beer tent bands. The parade, which begins at Schwanthalerstrasse and winds to the fairgrounds, involves over 1,000 participants. At 8:00pm on Saturday, the Folklore International takes place in Circus Krone (Marsstrasse 43) and includes German and international groups who perform in original costumes.

The Costume and Marksmen's Parade, held on Sunday at 11:00am, features folk costume groups, historical uniforms, marching bands, oxen, and floats representing various parts of Bavaria. The four-mile parade route runs from the Max II Monument through the city center to the Oktoberfest grounds.

The Oktoberfest really is terrific fun. The carnival rides are great: the Ferris Wheel in particular gives a wonderful view of the madness below, and don't miss the peculiar form of Bavarian sadism called "The Devil's Wheel" (don't be shy—jump on!). Inside the beer tents, oom-pah bands play German favorites, busty waitresses carry armloads of foamy steins, and everyone makes lots of new friends. The beer tents don't serve food, so buy a roasted chicken from a vendor outside and take it into the tent with you. Grab a seat wherever you can, shout for a beer, and pretty soon you'll be singing along and doing the "chicken dance" with the rest of the happy crowd. One hint: Get the carnival rides out of your system *before* you hit the beer tents, or that won't be all you'll get out of your system!

Most beer tents start to close around 11:00pm, and the fairgrounds are cleared by midnight. A few tents may stay open until 2:00am, and there are some beer halls near the fairgrounds that serve the late-night crowd until 4:00am. If you get too drunk to make it home, the police maintain a shed on the fairgrounds with cots.

For more information, contact City of Munich, Postfach, 80000 Munich 1.

The Rhine: Germany's Great Entertainer

Of course, hearts of romantics beat a little faster on the Rhine, but even the unromantic find it worthwhile. Connoisseurs, casual tourists, history buffs, friends of good drink—all love the atmosphere of Germany's Rhine River, sometimes called "flowing history."

Fed by Alpine springs as the Hinter Rhine and Vorder Rhine, the river travels 1,011 kilometers before reaching its Dutch delta. Lined by German countryside for 850 km, it leaves Lake Constance at Stein am Thein as the High Rhine. As the Upper Rhine, it flows north between the Black Forest and the Vosges. Blocked by the Taunus, it then turns west through the wine-growing region of the Rhinegau. It cannot, however, resist the pull of the North Sea, and after the Rhinegau, the river stays on a northerly course until the estuary.

The 126 km stretch of the Middle Rhine to Bonn is a water gap in the slate hills of the Rhineland, reaching a depth of 300 meters. Here's where the Rhine belongs to the romantics—a region celebrated in song and poetry by German, English, and French writers. From Cologne to the start of the delta behind the German-Dutch border, it flows through lush lowlands, though still in close contact with the industrial region on the Ruhr. At Wesel, it's almost a kilometer wide.

Though its wine and song have made it famous throughout the world, it has more to offer than *joie de vivre* from grape juice, more than renown from Romanticism. The Rhine was and is the great entertainer of all European rivers, and never is the river more entertaining than in summer, when she erupts into flames for an unparalleled spectacle of illumination, fireworks, and ships.

Rhein in Flammen

Along one of the most beautiful stretches of the romantic Rhine—between the colorful town of Linz and Bonn—the traditional Rhine embankment illuminations known as "The Rhine in Flames at the Seven Mountains" are staged every year on the first Saturday in May, with the grand closing fireworks along the banks at Bonn. As part of the larger program of entertainment, the towns along the Rhine offer music, dancing, and a cheerfulness typical of the region. Opening fireworks in Linz are at 9:30pm; closing fireworks at Bonn start about 11:00pm.

"The Rhine in Magical Fire," the second summer illuminations around the Bingen Loch on the first Saturday of July, is arranged by the towns of Bingen, Rudesheim, Assmannshausen, and Trechtingshausen. Starting at 8:30pm, about 50 ships from the lighted fleet sail to a point near Trechtingshausen. At 10:00pm, the first fireworks from the Castle Reichenstein explode, followed by six more fireworks shows from the Castle Rheinstein, Assmannshausen, the ruins of the Ehrenfels Castle, the Castle Klopp in Bingen, and the old quarter of Rudesheim. The closing fireworks erupt from the middle of the Rhine between Bingen and Rudesheim. Lights illuminate all the churches, castles, and monuments on both sides of the 12 km stretch of the river. The program ends about midnight.

On the second Saturday of August, the third *Rhein in Flammen* takes place, when 70 decorated passenger ships glide down the Rhine in an incomparable spectacle. You can watch from the banks or the hillside on either side of the 17 km route. While the brightly lit fleet floats downstream, the historic buildings of the adjacent towns are illuminated by Bengal lights. Eight displays of fireworks along the way light up the evening sky—from Spay to Braubach (Marksbsurg Castle), Brey, Rhens, Lahnstein, Koblenz (Stolzenfels Castle and Konigsbacher Brewery), with the closing fireworks at the fortress Ehrenbreitstein at the mouth of the Moselle River. The opening fireworks in Spay begin at 9:30pm; closing fireworks at Koblenz at 11:00pm.

The fourth Rhine illumination occurs on the third Saturday in September. The sister towns Katz and Rheinfels, with their castles St. Goarshausen and St. Goar, face each other across the Rhine and serve as a lovely setting for a magical evening of fireworks. The illuminations begin at 8:30pm, with the house facades, castles, towns, and hillsides all bathed in lights. The hilltop fireworks begin at 8:45pm from the Castles Katz and Rheinfels; the final grand display erupts from the middle of the Rhine.

For more information, contact Verkehrsamt, Rheinstrasse 16, 6220 Rudesheim.

German Holidays

New Year's Day, Epiphany (Jan. 6), Good Friday, Easter Monday, Labor Day (May 1), Ascension Day, Whitmonday, Corpus Christi, Unity Day (June 17), All Saints Day (Nov. 1), Repentance Day (Nov. 20), Christmas, and Dec. 26.

For literature and further information, contact the **German International Tourist Office**. In the U.S., address are 747 Third Ave., New York, NY 10017 (212-308-3300); and 444 S. Flower St., Suite 2230, Los Angeles, CA 90071 (213-688-7332).

10

The Iberian Peninsula: Spain & Portugal

"Life in Spain gives off a note which, like Spanish guitar music, is both sweet and melancholy. . . The Spanish take joy in the bloody spectacle of the bullring, but they are gentle and kindly to foreign visitors. Absorbed in the mysteries of their religion, they have always the consciousness of death—and respond by being sharply, explosively alive!"
—John Davis Lodge

Napoleon once said "Europe ends at the Pyrenees," and in many ways, for many years, the Iberian Peninsula (four-fifths Spain, one-fifth Portugal) was removed both geographically and historically from Europe. For several hundred years, Spain associated far more with North Africans than Europeans—in fact, Spain was occupied for eight centuries by the Moors—and this too contributed to the country's separateness and diversity.

Spain is profoundly Catholic, and religious *romerias* (pilgrimages) play an important role in the life of the Iberian Peninsula. Spain is quite Moslem as well, and countless *fiestas* (festivals) and *ferias* (fairs) evoke the centuries-long Moorish rule.

Spanish festivals are almost always a colorful mix of the pious and profane, with more than 150 celebrations occurring from January 5 (the Feast of the Holy Child) to December 28 (the Festival of the 'Moorish King'). One especially interesting fest—the Moors and Christians Pageant in Alcoy on April 23—includes parades, "battles," historical presentations, and, as always, spectacular costumes.

Another unique cultural mixture is observed on Book Day/Lovers Day (also April 23), when both St. George and Cervantes are honored. Since 1714, the people of Barcelona have visited St. George's Chapel in the Palau de la Generalitat to pray before his statue. Since the same day marks the anniversary of the death of Spanish author Miguel de Cervantes, the custom of giving a book and a rose to a

175

THE IBERIAN PENINSULA

loved one has developed into a long-standing—and delightful!—tradition.

Portugal, Spain's neighbor, is also filled with a great tradition of celebration. Tourist material claims, "when people come to Portugal they find Europe as they expect it to be—old world culture, old world tradition, old world charm"—and nowhere are these qualities more obvious than in a Portuguese festival. Like Spain, many events have a religious nature, but in Portugal an equal number honor the land, sea, and people who till the soil and fish its waters.

For example, the Red Waistcoat Festival in Vila Franca de Xira honors the cowboys who handle the bulls of the Ribatejo, and in Nazaré, fishermen take the spotlight in Our Lady of Nazaré Festivities. Harvest and flower festivals also offer the regions of Portugal a chance to bask in their traditional folklore and culture. Spectators can thrill to the spectacular warrior dances of the *Pauliteiros* of Miranda and the *Viras* and *Malhoès* of Minho. They can wonder at the intricate rhythms of the dances of Povóa and Nazaré, smile at the gaiety of the *Corrindinho* of the Algarve, and reflect with the somber strains of the Alentejo choirs or the *Fado* of Lisbon. But everywhere in Portugal, when festival time comes, the sardines are grilled, the bulls run through the streets, and the wine flows.

SPAIN

Spain

March
Valencia—Fallas de San Jose
The Festival of Fire of St. Joseph, patron saint of carpenters, is celebrated in Valencia March 12-19 (the 19th being the feast of St. Joseph). The festival begins at sunrise, with the city awakened by thousands of firecrackers, and ends a week later at midnight, with hundreds of floats set ablaze. The floats, beautiful examples of Spanish craftsmanship, are constructed throughout the year by local carpenters and artists. The *falla* monuments and their *ninot* figures are usually satirical portrayals of the human condition, while the floats tease local citizens, international figures, and famous events. The celebration ends with the *Nit del For*, when all the floats are set on fire while Valencians toss firecrackers into the blaze.

In addition to the parade of floats and the daily round of festivities and bullfights (*Las Fallas* marks the beginning of the bullfight season in Valencia), one of the most delightful events is the *crida*, a public announcement made from the Torres de Serrano by the Queen of the Fallas and the Mayor of the City.

Although the event has its origins in the Middle Ages, when carpenters honored the saint by saving small pieces of wood and setting them on fire at midnight on St. Joseph's Day, it is thoroughly modern in its excitement and revelry.

April
Seville—April Fair
Another of Spain's major spring festivals is Seville's "April Fair," in which a tent city (the pavilions are called *casetas*) is constructed in the Los Remedios district. Many locals camp there throughout the fair, eating and drinking the whole time! The entire event is a showcase of Spanish folklore and customs, from bullfighting to flamenco.

Over the past century, the Fair has developed into one of the most fascinating spectacles Spain has to offer. Originally a 19th-century livestock show, the five-day event is now an extravaganza, with daily parades renowned for impressive horsemanship, followed by all-day dancing, music, and feasting. After a siesta, matadors perform in the Plaza de Toros, and the merry-making continues. Throughout, the fair blazes with multi-colored tents, wreaths, and paper lanterns.

Seville is a charming, romantic city, made famous by *Don Giovanni*, *Carmen*, and *The Barber of Seville*. If you wish to be among the millions under its spell, the last week of April is the best time.

May

Jerez de la Frontera—The Horse Fair

Over the centuries, this festival has evolved from a livestock fair into a dynamic event that includes bullfights, singing and dancing in the Gonzalez Hontoria Park, and the Horse Fair itself, with riding demonstrations and competitions. A market runs in conjunction with the fair.

A visit to Jerez de la Frontera, about 60 miles south of Seville, should also include a stop at one of the *bodegas* to sample the excellent golden sherry produced nearby. (early May for one week)

Madrid—San Isidro Festival

As is the general custom in Latin countries, every city and town has a patron saint. While some choose bishops and martyrs, Madrid has chosen to live under the guardianship of a peasant, San Isidro (St. Isadore), patron saint of farmers, born in Madrid in the 11th century and canonized on May 15, 1630 in Madrid's Plaza Mayor.

The festival usually begins on the Friday before May 15, at 10:30pm in the Plaza. After a speech by the mayor, a rocket blast sets off ten days of cultural events, singing, dancing, drinking, and eating. The Plaza, the focal point of events, hosts an outdoor concert every evening. Throughout the night, people gather to socialize and enjoy flamenco and *zarzuelas*, a unique Spanish form of operetta. Families use this event as an excuse to don the traditional Castilian costumes of their ancestors as well. Women and young girls parade in polka-dot dresses, fringed shawls, and carnations in their hair, while men and boys wear black trousers with black-and-white caps and vests.

Other venues for concerts and activities are Las Vistillas park and the Casa de Campo, Madrid's largest park. Evening picnics are also featured throughout the festival, along with cultural programs at Madrid's theaters.

Of course, no Spanish festival would be complete without a bull-fight, and the San Isidro event marks the beginning of Madrid's month-long season. Over 20 bullfights are held each year at Plaza de Toros las Ventas, with Spain's finest matadors performing daily at 5:00pm. The festivities end with fireworks in Retiro Park. (mid-May)

Madrid—Opera Festival

The Madrid Opera season, running through mid-July, features a number of special performances during its festival time in May and June. Recent fests have offered a rich and varied selection, including Wagner's *Walkure*, de Falla's *Atlantida*, and Bellini's *Puritani*. For more information, contact Teatro Lirico Nacional la Zaruela, del Banco Popular Espanol, Oficina Principal, Calle Alcala, 26 Madrid.

Barcelona—Barcelona Opera Festival

The Barcelona Opera season starts in November and runs through the end of June. Featured performances have included Strauss's *Ariadne auf Naxos* at the Gran Teatre del Liceu and the recent recording of Janacek's *Jenufa*, conducted by Vaclav Neumann. Verdi's *Simon Boccanegro* and Offenbach's *Tales of Hoffman* have also enlivened the program.

Running concurrently with Barcelona's opera festival is a portion of the *Barcelona Mozartiana*, which begins in January and concludes in early June. Three separate programs are devoted to the famed Austrian composer.

For more information, contact Gran Teatre del Liceu, Department d'Abonaments i Localaitats, Carrer Sant Pau, 1 baixos 08001 Barcelona.

June

Almonte—The Rocio Pilgrimage

The Rocio Pilgrimage, an ancient Corpus Christi celebration, brings participants from Huelva, Cádiz, and Seville. Hundreds of riders on horseback and girls in typical Andalusian dress cross the countryside to the sound of flutes and tambourines on their way to the Sanctuary of *Nuestra Senora del Rocio*. Carts drawn by oxen and decorated with flowers and wax figures accompany the pilgrims. Once at the sanctuary, the religious ceremonies begin, the most impressive being the evening rosary processions (featuring pilgrims crossing the marshes with lighted candles) and the procession of the Virgin. Participants continually dance and sing the Rocio *seguidillas* and *sevillanas*. (early June)

throughout—Feast of San Antonio de Padua

Many Spanish villages pay homage to St. Anthony, a native of Lisbon who lived in Padua for years. He died on June 13, 1231, and is revered by the country. (June 13)

Toledo—Corpus Christi

The feast of Corpus Christi brings special events to most of Spain. Since 1317, this feast has been celebrated everywhere with processions and mystery plays. In Toledo, Spain's best-preserved and most mysterious medieval city, a solemn procession bearing the Arfe monstrance (reportedly made with silver from the New World) passes among the faithful. The Illescas nobles in their red habits, the Mozarbic Knights in their blue habits, the Knights of the Holy Sepulchre dressed in white, and the Knights of the Corpus Christi dressed in green evoke memories of medieval times. (June 14)

La Laguna, Tenerife—Corpus Christi
In the Canary Islands, where the Corpus Christi feast has been celebrated since 1496, festivities are linked closely to the old custom of covering the procession route with aromatic herbs and flowers called *alfombras de flores* (flower carpets), which are themselves great works of art and beauty. (June 14)

Granada—Corpus Christi
The celebration of Corpus Christi in Granada is especially famous for the splendor of its processions, festivities, and bullfights. The celebrations, which last for 10 days, begin with a true spectacle in which the gigantic *Tarasca*, a papier-mâché female figure dressed in the latest fashion, is surrounded by other large *cabezudos* figures, carriages, and colorful banners. (June 14)

throughout Spain—Feast of San Juan
For this feast day, many towns decorate their streets with branches and leaves, hold *romerías* (pilgrimages) and bonfires, and celebrate age-old rituals like bull-running and street-dancing. In Alicante, the "St. John Bonfires" feature colorful figures satirizing human vices, which are usually burned on the night of June 24 (the *crema*). Other important events include fireworks, competitions, bullfights, and various religious celebrations, especially the outstanding floral offering to the Virgin del Remedio, patron of the city.

San Pedro Manrique (Soria) holds the Passage of the Fire and the *mondidas* festival. On the evening of June 23, the men of the town each hoist someone on their shoulders and walk across a pile of coals—barefoot! The *mondidas*—women dressed in white costumes called *cestanos* and *arbujuelos*—parade to the main church, where the *mondidas* leader offers the first *arbujuelo* to the priest. (June 24)

throughout—Feast of San Pedro
The patron saint of fishermen is usually taken on a procession at sea in a number of coastal areas. He's also the subject of other celebrations, such as the unique *Kaxarranca* dance in Haro (Rioja) or the "Dance of the Fan and Branch" in Barcelona. (June 29)

Granada—Granada Music and Dance Festival
One of the most important music festivals in Europe, this event features an array of international orchestras and performers in settings of incomparable grandeur—the Alhambra, the Palace of Charles V,

the theater of the Gereralife Gardens—as well as modern facilities like Manuel de Falla Auditorium. Offerings at a recent festival included a concert by José Carreras followed by a performance of the Chamber Orchestra of Israel and Strauss's *Salomé*. For more information, contact International Music and Dance Festival, Apartado de Correos, No. 64, 18080 Grenada. (mid- to late June)

July

Pamplona—San Fermín Festival

Considered one of the three most important Spanish festivals (along with *Las Fallas* and "The April Fair"), the running of the bulls in Pamplona also ranks among the world's great parties (along with Munich's *Oktoberfest* and Rio's *Carnival*). For more information, see below. (July 6-14)

San Sebastian—International Jazz Festival

Like so many jazz events around Europe, this one in San Sebastian offers high-quality performances by renowned jazz artists. The festival has been a tradition since 1965. (last two weeks of July)

Hita (Guadalajara)—Medieval Theater Festival

This delightful festival begins early in July, with jesters and dancers of Somosierra, who perform accompanied by bagpipers and other musicians. There are medieval feasts and dinners in the Cerro, as well as contests and bull-lancing exhibitions in the Palenque. In the evening, actors perform scenes from medieval dramas. (throughout July)

Santander—International Festival of Santander

From late July to late August, Santander is an exceptionally exciting place, thanks to the sparkling Music and Dance Festival, one of the most important artistic events in Spain. At times, the festival coincides with religious fests honoring Santiago, the patron saint of Spain, making it even more exciting. Some opening night performances have included arias by the American bass Samuel Ramey and overtures by the Metropolitan Opera Orchestra. Concert pianists and soloists from an international cadre of performers are regularly on the Santander menu to add luster to the program.

Santiago de Compostela—Feast of St. James

Under a special privilege granted by Pope Calixtus II, every year that the feast of St. James (July 25) falls on a Sunday is a Holy Year (next in 1993). As such, it is marked by special celebrations, beginning with the opening of the Puerta Santa on the preceding New Year's Eve. The *Fiestas de Santiago Apostol* is also celebrated each July with a great procession and the swinging of the huge censer known as Botafumeiro.

Villajoyosa (Alicante)—Festival of Christians & Moors

This festival in honor of Santa Marta begins at dawn, when the entire town rushes to the beach to see the Christian and Moorish ships "battle." The Moors win, the battle moves to the beach, and the Saracens take the town. At the end of the day, the Christians have recovered and drive the invading forces back to the sea, whereupon the participants triumphantly parade the statue of Santa Marta through the streets. Similar celebrations run throughout the summer in villages of Alicante and Valencia provinces. (July 25-28)

Throughout the year, almost 150 celebrations of Moors and Christians take place. Starting January 5-9 with the feasts of the Holy Child in Valverde de Jucar (Cuenca) and ending with the festival of the Moorish King (Rey Moro) in Agost (Alicante) on December 28, Spaniards celebrate their dual heritage. Most events occur in Alicante, with processions, speeches, plays, ancient dances, and mock battles.

August

Mérida (Badajoz)—Classical Drama Festival

Once ranked as the ninth town in importance in the Roman Empire, Mérida is sometimes called "Rome in miniature." This western town contains some of the finest Roman ruins on the Iberian Peninsula, including the Roman Amphitheater where the drama festival is held. One of the town's greatest treasures (along with its Roman bridge, Circus Maximus, and Trajan's Arch), the theater was built in 18 B.C. by Agrippa to seat 5,000. (throughout August)

Elche (Alicante)—Mystery Play

While most Spanish towns have patron saint festivals in the summer, the Feast of the Assumption (August 15) is celebrated nearly everywhere and exceeds all others in solemnity and fervor. Perhaps the most beautiful celebration is the mystery play called Mary's *dormicion*, performed in the Cathedral of Santa Maria de Elche on the 14th and continuing through the feast day.

September

Almagro (Ciudad Real)—Festival of Drama & Comedy

Almagro hosts an annual "Festival of Classical Drama & Comedy" the first two weeks in Sept. Like other towns with ancient Roman heritage in the Salamanca area, the setting for classical music and drama is perfect. For more information, contact Instituto Nacional de las Artes Escenicas y de la Musica, Jose Antonio 11, Almagro (Ciudad Real).

Villena (Alicante)—Festival of Christians & Moors

Held in honor of Our Lady of Virtue, this festival begins with a grand entrance: 2,000 participants welcome the statue of the Patroness outside the city as she returns from her pilgrimage. The "battles" last two days and end on the feast day, with the "victory" of the Christians and a solemn procession. (usually Sept. 4-9)

Jerez de la Frontera (Cádiz)—Grape Harvest Festival
This typical Spanish wine festival includes the blessing of the grapes and the first wine before the statue of San Gines de la Jara, patron saint of wine growers in the region. In addition, a cavalcade, flamenco festival, and, of course, bullfights are featured. (mid-Sept.)

Barcelona—Feast of Virgin de la Merced
Although religion is the primary reason behind most Spanish festivals, each has a unique regional flavor and additions. In Barcelona, the city celebrates its patroness with a parade of "giants" from Catalonia. (Sept. 24)

October
Barcelona—International Music Festival
Orchestral and chamber concerts, recitals, contemporary and Catalan music—all are part of this celebrated event, first held in 1962. The Palau de la Musica hosts all performances. (throughout Oct.)

Consuegra (Toledo)—Saffron Rose Festival
Held in the shadow of Consuegra's conspicuous castle, the Saffron Rose Festival celebrates the harvest of the rare flower with exhibitions of the region's folklore. Saffron, the world's most expensive spice (about $2,000 a pound), is made from the two-tine stamens of the crocus. A key ingredient in Spain's best dishes, saffron is cheaper in Spain than anywhere else in the world. (late Oct. weekend)

From Carnival to Christmas

The people of Spain take their celebrating very seriously, especially their religious observances. They regard the feast days as both obligation and justification for reviving an ancient form of worship or regional practice. To call these observances "colorful" or "traditional" seems almost trite, since they are grand historic, religious, and dramatic spectacles. From Carnival (Shrovetide in Spain) to Christmas, religious holidays are celebrated passionately.

Shrovetide festivities are held everywhere, with some places beginning preparations as soon as Christmas is over! They are usually characterized by subversion of the *status quo*, with masks and disguises and permissiveness. In general, Carnival celebrations are no-holds-barred events that welcome visitors and provide an ideal pre-Lenten splurge before the 40 days of fasting.

Cádiz, Santa Cruz de Tenerife, and Villanueva de la Vera hold especially brilliant Carnivals. Cádiz is famous for its fancy-dress balls, pranks, disguises, and float parades. Santa Cruz de Tenerife hosts perhaps the ultimate Carnival, with a notorious "Brazilian-style" procession, fancy-dress parades, and street musicians. The events climax in the Arena on Shrove Tuesday. Villanueva de la Vera's Pero Palo Festival has origins in an ancient tradition of parading a dummy representing the devil (*Pero Palo*) around town. He is carried on the shoulders of young men, who beat him and dance to drums until they knock him down. Once down, he is carted away in a wheelbarrow to his grave, and the village has a community feast.

The greatest outbursts of religious fervor take place during Semana Santa (Holy Week), the last week of Lent. Religious splendor aside, Holy Week offers a grand show, beginning on Palm Sunday. In Elche, the Palms procession has special significance with palm fronds handwoven into intricate designs. The Palms Fair in Palma de Majorca is also worth seeing. In Castille, the festivals of Valladolid, Zamora, and Cuenca are notable for their display of the masterworks of Castilian imagery shown in the solemn *pasos*, platforms bearing sculptured scenes from the Passion. In Murcia and Cartagena, Holy Week activities are the setting for the splendid Salzillo sculptures.

But without a doubt, the Holy Week events in Andalusia, the best known outside of Spain, typify this type of religious activity. Seville and Malaga rival one another in the splendor of their processions and pageantry. In fact, every city in Andalusia outdoes itself to express devotion to the ceremonies marking the death of Jesus. Holy Thursday and Good Friday, especially, offer the most intriguing spectacles. In Tobarro (Albacete), the *tamborrada* employs over 5,000 drums, and in Ulldecona (Tarragona), the Passion Play has been performed in exactly the same manner since 1595.

Easter processions and rituals are also unique in Spain, where Easter is the zenith of the liturgical calendar. Emotional "reunion" ceremonies between the resurrected Christ and his mother usually occur during processions in Coria del Rio (Seville), Pilas (Seville), Elche (Alicante), and Villanueva de la Serena (Badajoz). Other communities burn an effigy of Judas, stage plays depicting the resurrection, or hold painted egg and cake festivals. Some places celebrate Easter Monday and Tuesday as well, with outdoor festivals and chocolate cakes in abundance.

Fifty days later, on Whitsunday (also called Pentecost), pilgrimages and other celebrations are held. In El Rocío in the Huelva region, thousands trek across the field of Andalusia on foot or horse, carrying the Virgin del Rocío in solemn procession, and then celebrate in the town. In Atienza (Guadalajara) and Sant Feliu de Pallerols, some pilgrims carry huge, heavy crosses while running 10-15 kilometers. The people of Peñas de San Pedro perpetuate this *Cristo del Sahuco* pilgrimage on Whitsunday and again on August 28.

Trinity Sunday follows Pentecost and is observed in some areas with processions devoted to the Christian Trinity. On the next Thursday, special events observe Corpus Christi (Corpus Domini in some places).

In 1317, Pope John XXII declared that the body of Christ should be part of a solemn, public procession, and ever since, the day has received great attention in Spain. In the procession, the main feature is the Host, which takes precedence over everything else and is usually held in a richly decorated container. Mystery plays are performed in some regions; in Valencia, they are staged on wooden floats called *roques* dating from the 15th century. Seville, Berga, and Redondela are also known for Corpus Christi performances.

Flower carpets, which cover procession routes with aromatic herbs or flower petals, are also a Corpus Christi tradition. The artists take great pride in their carpets, even though they'll be trampled in the solemn processions. The flower carpet tradition is especially popular in Catalonia, Galicia, and the Canary Islands. On the Island of Lanzarote, the carpets are made of salt; in Elche de la Sierra (Albacete), artists use sawdust and wood shavings.

For Christmas, celebrations take many forms, and most involve some type of music—handbell-ringing, caroling, even *divinos*, individuals who go caroling with mandolins, tambourines, and guitars. Nativity Plays run in many cities, with live animals for authenticity.

While all these observances have solemn religious foundations, they are also vehicles for recreating age-old traditions that make Spain such an exciting country to visit.

Fiesta San Fermín

"The fiesta was really started. It kept up day and night for seven days. The dancing kept up, the drinking kept up, the noise went on. The things that happened could only have happened during a fiesta. Everything became quite unreal finally and it seemed as though nothing could have any consequences."

—Ernest Hemingway, *The Sun Also Rises*

Fiesta San Fermin is a religious festival honoring the patron saint of Pamplona, but like most Spanish celebrations, it's also an annual excuse to revive native traditions and indulge in good food and wine. In 1926, when Hemingway and his pals went to Pamplona, the running of the bulls had only regional renown. But since the publication of *The Sun Also Rises*, the festival has attracted an international crowd, some of whom journey to Pamplona every year.

At exactly noon on July 6, the mayor announces, *"Senores y senoras, viva San Fermin!"* He might as well simply say, "Let the party begin!" because at 12:01pm, rockets explode, champagne corks fly, bands begin playing, and dancing in the streets becomes *de rigueur*. It doesn't stop until midnight on the 14th.

In between, excitement is everywhere. At exactly 8:00am each day, the real highlight of the fest—and the part that most people associate with Pamplona—occurs. The *encierro*, or running of the bulls, is the old-fashioned method of getting six 1,200-pound fighting bulls from a corral at one end of town to a holding pen behind the bull-fight plaza for the afternoon *corrida*.

From the *encierro* (which means "enclosure"), the bulls, led by six steer, run the half-mile through the narrow, barricaded streets of the city to the bullfight plaza. The unique aspect of the running, however, and what makes Pamplona such a spirited and reckless place, is that young men (and some women) use it as a test of manhood by running with the bulls—or trying to. Runners are allowed to carry only rolled-up newspaper for protection.

Theoretically, bulls run in herds and follow a direct path behind the steers and behind the runners. It's when one is separated from the herd that the danger—the risk of being gored or trampled—occurs. Most runners do not attempt the entire course; in fact, the experienced run for a few seconds then jump atop a barricade while the herd passes. Most hope to run again the following day. Some don't want to try their luck again, and some can't.

After the *encierro*, which lasts only two or three minutes, people begin the daily round of parties. *Aficionados*, most clad in the traditional white pants and shirt with red waist sash, will be drinking at the Cafe Txoco or the Iruna Cafe, which, according to Hemingway, "did not make this same noise at any other time, no matter how crowded it was." Everything is different during San Fermín!

The official program of the fiesta lists countless daily events between the *premier encierro* at 8:00am on July 7 and the *acto final de las fiestas* at midnight of the 14th, which is a candlelit parade and singing of *Pobre de Mi y Traca* (*Poor Me*), a lament that the festival is over for another year. Highlights include the official procession of the statue of San Fermín on the 7th, the folklore parade *Salida de la Comparsa de Gigantes y Cabezudos* (devoted to a different "giant" each day), the daily presentation of the matadors and *caballeros*, and the *corrida de toros* (bullfight) at 6:30pm each evening. There are also musical events all day and dancing until 3:00am.

Spanish Holidays

New Year's Day, Epiphany (Jan. 6), St. Joseph's Day (March 19), Maundy Thursday, Good Friday, Easter Monday, May Day, Corpus Christi (June 14), Feast of Santiago (July 25), Assumption (Aug. 15), National Day (Oct. 12), All Saints Day (Nov. 1), Constitution Day (Dec. 6), Immaculate Conception (Dec. 8), Christmas.

For literature and further information, contact the **Tourist Office of Spain**. In the U.S., addresses are 665 Fifth Ave., New York, NY 10022 (212-759-8822); 845 N. Michigan Ave., Chicago, IL 60611 (312-643-1992); San Vicente Plaza Bldg., 8383 Wilshire Blvd., Suite 960, Beverly Hills, CA 90211 (213-658-7188); and 1221 Brickell Ave., Suite 1850, Miami, FL 33131 (305-358-1992).

Portugal

May

Barcelos—Festas das Cruzes

These festivities are among the most exciting in northern Portugal. The outstanding event of the weekend-long fest is the Procession of the Holy Cross on the final day. The program includes a great fair with an impressive exhibition of handicrafts, concerts, and a fireworks display on the Cavado River. The well-known good luck symbol of Portugal, the Barcelos rooster, originated in this Minho district town, 50 km. from Porto. (first week in May)

Fatima—Annual Pilgrimage

Fatima, where the Virgin Mary is said to have appeared to Francisco, Jacinta, and Lucia, calling for world peace, is considered one of the most important Catholic shrines in the world. Hundreds of thousands of pilgrims travel here to commemorate the first apparition of the Virgin on May 13, 1917. Beginning May 12, believers arrive on every conceivable means of transportation—from tour buses to donkey carts—to await the passing of the statue of the Madonna through the central square (larger than St. Peter's in Rome!). As many people as possible then visit the Chapel of the Apparitions, where the alleged appearance took place. The faithful also hold all-night vigils by candlelight, and many walk on their knees to the shrine—quite a poignant sight.

Although many European festivals are religious in origin, few are so devout. Most of the participants are devoted Catholics in town for one purpose only. There are no costumed folk dancers, no acrobats, no musicians. It's strictly religious—but quite spectacular in the sheer numbers it attracts.

Fatima is 36 miles east of Nazare and 88 miles north of Lisbon.

Viana do Castelo—Festival of Our Lady of Roses

The towns around Viana do Castelo are known for their lavish spring

PORTUGAL

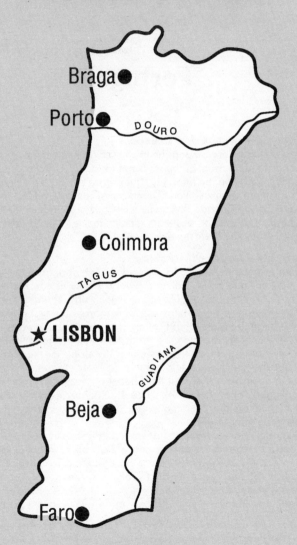

flower pageants. This *Festas da Senhora do Rosas* is a flower parade in which the village women walk through the town displaying intricate rose tapestries carried above their heads. (early May)

Alvares—Festasdos Andores Floridos
Like the flower pageant in Viana do Castelo, this event includes floats covered entirely with roses. Participants draw the floats over streets laden with rose designs (similar to the Corpus Christi processions held throughout southern European countries). (late May)

Algarve—Algarve Music Festival
Leading Portuguese and foreign musicians are featured in over 40 concerts held throughout the lovely seaside resorts of the Algarve. (May-June)

June
Santarem—National Agricultural Fair
This great fair—no, not just an agriculture fair—is the most important of its type in Portugal and a good place to understand how important the land is to the Ribatejo, an area devoted to cattle, vineyards, olive groves, and corn. In addition to the exhibitions of Portugal's farming and livestock activities, the fair also includes a colorful program of bullfights, folk songs, dances, and a large amusement fair. (early June, for 10 days)

Lisbon—Festas dos Santos Populares
Every June 12, the Alfama area of Lisbon adopts a carnival atmosphere that lasts until June 29. The reason, supposedly, is to honor the saints Anthony (June 13th), Peter (20th), and John (24th) on their feast days. But what's a Portuguese feast day without singers, dancers, and sardines roasting on open fires in the streets?

Lisbon honors its favorite saint, Anthony, born in the Alfama in 1195, with an impressive show of *marchas* (walking groups of singers and musicians), who parade in costume down the Avenida da Liberdade from the Praça Marquês de Pombal to the Praça dos Restaurados. They then move to the Alfama to dance, drink, and enjoy *fado* music until daybreak. The festivities continue nightly until St. John's feast.

With or without a saint to honor, the Alfama is a fascinating area of Lisbon, with a history dating to the time when it was the Saracen sector of the city.

Sintra—Summer Music Festival
Byron's "glorious Eden" is even more lovely in June and July, when the annual summer music festival highlights the splendid national palaces in Sintra, Quelez, and Pena. Piano is the dominant musical genre, with performers like Maria João Pires, Ian Fountain, Catherine Collard, and Peter Donohoe featured recently. Just 18 miles from

Lisbon, Sintra is one of the country's most romantic spots and one of the oldest towns in Portugal. Home to a number of spectacular palaces and castles, it's an ideal setting for a summer music event. (June to mid-July)

Sintra—Great Fair of St. Peter
In Sintra as in Lisbon, St. Peter is honored in a variety of unique ways on his feast day, June 29. A popular fair features regional products and handicrafts, especially the famous Sintra cheesecakes.

Porto—Festas de São João
Although great festivals in honor of St. John are held elsewhere, Porto offers the most colorful. On every corner of the city there are *cascatas* (arrangements of religious motifs), bonfires, and groups of merrymakers singing and dancing all night. Most events are held at the great amusement fair of Fontainhas. Considered Portugal's second city, Porto is the home of port wine, and like the sherry lodges of Spain's Jerez de la Frontera, the port lodges here shouldn't be missed. (June 23-24)

Vila do Conde—Festas de São João
Bonfires throughout town, thousands of lights, and fireworks erupting anywhere and everywhere pay homage to St. John the Baptist on June 23 and 24. The two days of parties end with a candlelight procession to the beach, led by lacemakers and women dressed in traditional costumes of the Minho area.

Braga—Festas de São João
Festas of Christian saints are celebrated ostensibly under the banner of the Church. However, some non-Christians prefer to mark the occasion as an observance of the summer solstice. Whatever your persuasion, all-night parties, raging bonfires, flowing wine, and roasting sardines are all part of the celebration of St. John's feast day in Braga. (June 23-25)

Ponte de Lima—Festas dos São João
This small Minho district town on the banks of the Lima celebrates the feast of St. John with similar revelry as Braga.

July
Vila Franca de Xira—Colete Encarnado
This "Festival of the Red Waistcoat," Portugal's answer to Pamplona, honors the *campinos*, the Portuguese cowboys who tend the bulls in the pasture lands of the Ribatejo. The three-day event includes a colorful parade of cowboys in traditional stocking caps and red vests, bullfights, folk dances, a fair, and lots of sardine-eating and wine-drinking on the "Nights of the Grilled Sardine." The resemblance

to Pamplona is only slight, for the nightly *esperas de toiros* (running of the bulls) is tame compared to the Spanish event, with fewer people involved and a shorter course. The streets are heavily barricaded, though, and the bulls sometimes make it exciting when they decide to shift direction! Vila Franca de Xira is about 20 miles north of Lisbon. (first week in July)

Estoril—Estoril Music Festival

Leading Portuguese and foreign musicians brighten this annual music festival in the seaside towns of Estoril and Cascais. Celebrated since 1974, the festival offers daily concerts (except Sunday) at palaces and manor houses. Performers have included the Chamber Orchestra of Moscow, the Gulbenkian Orchestra, and the Ballet Victor Ullate of Spain. (July through early August)

August

Guimarães—Gualterianas Festivities

Centuries old, this traditional festival in honor of St. Walter coincides with the Free Fair of St. Walter, which dates to 1452, and includes a spectacular procession called ''The Procession of St. Walter'' on the first Sunday of August. On Monday, another procession, the *Marcha Gualteriana*, is based on traditions of medieval folk criticism. Music and folk dance groups participate, as well as residents who perform medieval plays. Guimarães, the country's first capital, is in the northwest corner of Portugal, 25 miles north of Porto.

Fundao—Folklorico de Silvares

An annual folklore event is held in Fundao in the Sêrra Da Estrêla region, famous for its folklore and skiing. The event welcomes international performers and crowds. (early weekend in August)

Alcochete—Feast of Green Caps and Salt Pans

This folklore festival is actually a funfair, but it includes the release of bulls through the streets in typical Portuguese fashion. Alcochete is located on the estuary of the Tagus, where salt pans have been exploited since Roman times. (mid-August weekend)

Viano Do Castelo—Our Lady of Agony Festivities

Portugal's ''city of folklore'' is the venue for one of the country's most colorful festivals. The event includes a sumptuous procession where Our Lady is carried over carpets of flowers, a fair, dancing and singing all night, and an allegoric procession enlivened by the rich display of farm women in native costumes of orange, scarlet, and Prussian blue. Layers of golden necklaces with heart- and cross-shaped pendants complement their traditional clothing. Brilliant fireworks over the Lima River close the event, held on the weekend nearest August 20.

Viseu—St. Matthew's Fair

One of the most important agricultural and livestock fairs held in Portugal each year since the Middle Ages, the St. Matthew's Fair is today an International Fair and Exhibition. Folk dancing and singing, popular amusements, and other traditional events are also part of the program. Viseu, the capital of the Beira Alta province, is where Dão wines are made. (late August to late Sept.)

Miranda do Douro—Festas da Santa Barbara

During this festival, held annually on the third Sunday in August, visitors can observe some of the most exciting examples of Portuguese folk dancing: the *pingacho* (rough ballet), the *Geribalda* (a round dance), and the *Mira-me Miguel* (a square dance). Even more exciting is the *pauliteiro* troop—men dressed in white flannel shirts, aprons, and flower-covered hats who perform ritualized sword fights to bagpipes, cymbals, and drums. The dance, similar to the pyrrhic dance of the ancient Greeks, is appropriate to the culture and folklore of this Trás-Os-Montes region, where the people speak their own dialect, *mirandes*, a form of Low Latin.

September

Palmela—Wine Harvest Festival

Palmela, one of Portugal's leading wine-producing regions, celebrates its harvest every year with colorful events that include a parade of harvesters, folk songs and dances, an amusement fair, and lots of wine-tasting. A huge fireworks display called the "Burning of the Castle" is held near Palmela Castle, the place from which Alfonso Henriques, the first king of Portugal, drove out the Moors. (early Sept. weekend)

Lamego—Our Lady of Remedies Festivities

An important religious occasion in the far northeastern region of Portugal, this festival's most impressive feature is the Triumphal Procession on the last day. There's also a torchlight procession, a "battle of flowers," a folklore festival, a funfair, fireworks, and sporting events. (early Sept. weekend)

Algarve—Folk Music and Dance Festival

This weekend event, held in all the larger towns of the Algarve (Faro, Lagos, Albufeira, Silves), ends Sunday evening at Praia da Rocha with marvelous performances by groups from all over Portugal. (early Sept. weekend)

Moita—Our Lady of Good Voyage Festivities

An outstanding festival occurs in the old town of Moita do Ribatejo on the banks of the Tagus. The highlight of the five-day event is the blessing of the fishing boats in a unique procession. No Portuguese festival, religious or not, would be complete without bull-running, bull-fighting, folk-dancing and -singing, sardine-roasting, and, of course, wine-drinking! This one is no exception. (second weekend in Sept.)

Nazaré—Our Lady of Nazaré Festivities
This quaint fishing village, a booming tourist area in summer, becomes relatively quiet again in September for this important local event. The Nazaré fishermen, being the greatest devotees of Our Lady, carry her image on their shoulders in three festive processions held throughout the week-long celebration. Bullfights, concerts, folk dances, and singing are included. (early to mid-Sept.)

Vila Franca de Xira—October Fair
Like "The Festival of the Red Waistcoat" held here in July, the October Fair is centuries old. Since the area's main attractions are farming activities, it's essentially an agricultural fair. Of course, all the obligatory festive trappings are included: the traditional release of bulls in the streets, would-be bullfighters trying their hands at capework, exhibitions, singing, dancing, eating, and drinking. (late Sept. to early Oct.)

Braga—Vinho Verde Fair
This week-long event, held in the Palaçio Municipal de Esposicaos (industrial fair ground), features the region's wine producers and smaller estate bottlers and their products. Lots of tasting! (late Sept.)

October
Fatima—Pilgrimage to Shrine of Our Lady
Crowds of pilgrims again converge on Fatima to celebrate the last apparition of the Virgin to the little shepherds on October 12th.

Portugal's Atlantic Gems

The Azores
- *São Miguel*—the transparent waters of lagoons with legends of kings and lost cities;
- *Santa Maria*—green fields, yellow crops, white-washed houses with lace-like chimneys;
- *Terceira*—the constant presence of ancient history, the gentle undulation of a green countryside;
- *Pico*—the black of basalt, the deeds of whalers, a mountain that suddenly rises on the sea's horizon;
- *Faial*—a town mirrored on the sea, ocher walls of a fortress, hydrangeas framing houses and roads;

- *São Jorge*—broad green pastures sprinkled with wildflowers, yellow circles of cheese, fertile *fajas* of vineyards and orchards;
- *Graciosa*—undulating wheat fields, windmills, the nectar of wines;
- *Corvo*—a green drop in the expanse of turquoise ocean;
- *Flores*—basalt petrified in eternal threads, picturesque customs, the harmony of life floating on the foam of the sea.

These are the Azores, believed to be the remains of the lost continent of Atlantis. This archipelago in the Atlantic spans 500 miles across nine separate islands, with its main island of São Miguel over 750 miles west of Portugal (and 2,110 miles east of New York). They are the most isolated islands in the entire Atlantic.

Uninhabited when discovered in the early 15th century, the Azores grew mainly as a Portuguese settlement. As such, religious celebrations have always played an important part in the lives of residents, and many pilgrimages and processions occur throughout the year.

The Festivals of the Holy Ghost, among the most traditional on the archipelago, run April to June. Said to have medieval origins, the festivals are common to all the islands, though they have slight local adaptations. The celebrations at the village of Rabo de Peixe on the north coast are considered the most colorful, with decorated carts and oxen.

On the first Sunday after Easter, the *Senhor dos Enfermos* (Our Lord of the Sick) procession takes place on São Miguel and other islands, with the most impressive parade at Furnas.

On the fifth Sunday after Easter, the annual festival honoring the image of *Senhor Santo Cristo* proceeds through the streets of Ponta Delgada, the capital of São Miguel, also called *Ilha Verde* (Green Island) because of its lush vegetation—hydrangeas, azaleas, and cannas grow profusely. The procession passes through the decorated town on streets carpeted with flowers. A small 16th-century image of Christ of the Miracles, accompanied by its fabulous treasure, is the central focus of the procession. All the buildings and trees along the route are decorated with small lights, and a fair, fireworks, and a weekend of merry-making are part of the festival.

From mid- to late June, Saints Peter, John, and Michael are all honored with festivals in their names. As *Cavalhados de São Pedro* is a colorful folk event and pilgrimage honoring St. Peter, the patron saint of Ribeira Seca (Riabeira Grande) in the northern portion of São Miguel. A parade of masked riders—the King and his knights and lancers—takes to the streets in an event dating to the 15th century. It's generally held on the 29th and is a municipal holiday.

The *Festas Sanjoãninas* (St. John's Festivals) at Angra do Heroismo or Praia de Vitoria (Terceira) are animated with folk dancing and a peculiar form of bullfighting called *tourada a corda* in which the beast is led around by ropes. The fest lasts for ten days, usually concluding on the feast day, the 24th.

The Procession of St. Michael at Vila Franca do Campo on the south coast of São Miguel is also a curious event, with origins in medieval times. Representations of the various classes of workers are displayed around their patron saints.

These early summer events are among the more important fests on the islands. However, most summer Sundays offer a *romaria*, a pilgrimage to a chapel in the hills or through the streets of a city, and these are equally beloved by residents. *Romaria* are followed by an *arrial* (a funfair with singing, dancing, and fireworks), and throughout the summer, an encounter with one of these Azorean festivals is probable.

Madeira

Madeira, the main island of the small archipelago of the same name, is Portugal's second Atlantic gem, lying a bit closer to the mainland, 530 miles to the southwest, off the coast of Morocco. Only 35 miles long and 13 miles across at its widest point, it is a mountain peak of a volcanic mass. Like the Azores, the island was discovered by Portuguese sailors and claimed for their country. It was named Madeira, meaning ''wood,'' because of its dense forests.

Madeira's capital, Funchal, is the center of the island's wine industry and host to many interesting folk events, the most important on the Feast of the Assumption, August 15. Festivities in honor of Our Lady of the Monte run throughout the many hilltowns of Madeira, but the Monte closest to Funchal is the site of the best-known. In addition to an imposing procession in honor of Our Lady, there's a traditional fair with burning charcoal fires preparing the typical *espetadas* (meat on spits) in the open. Music and dancing fill the streets throughout the busy capital city.

All the other major places on the small island hold *romarias* and *arrials* on other religious feast days, especially in late June in honor of St. Peter. The people of Ribeira Brava celebrate Peter with a solemn procession followed by sword-dancing, an age-old tradition.

Two secular festivals are noteworthy as well. In May, the Flower Festival is a magnificent exhibition of the exotic flowers grown on Madeira, and in mid-June, the Madeira Bach Festival, founded in 1979, delights the composer's devotees. Each season one of Bach's major choral works is presented, along with concertos, cantatas, suites, and organ and harpsichord works. The 15th-century Sé (Cathedral) and the Municipal Theater host the concerts.

For New Year's, the End of the Year Festival, also called St. Sylvester's Festival, is one of the most exciting events on the island, with a fireworks show over the lovely bay at Funchal. Many cruise ships dock here for the celebrations.

Portuguese Holidays

New Year's Day, Good Friday, Liberty Day (April 25), Labor Day (May 1), Portugal and Camoes Day (June 10), St. Anthony's Day (June 13), Corpus Christi (May 30), Assumption (Aug. 15), Day of the Republic (Oct. 5), All Saints Day (Nov. 1), Independence Day (Dec. 1), Immaculate Conception (Dec. 8), Christmas.

For literature and further information, contact the **Portuguese National Tourist Office**. In the U.S., the address is 590 Fifth Ave., New York, NY 10036 (212-354-4403).

11

Scandinavia: Denmark, Finland, Sweden, & Norway

"What is Scandinavia? There are a number of definitions. Geographically, it is simply the great mountainous peninsula which droops for 1,200 miles like a curved nose from the northernmost reaches of Europe, and which includes only Norway and Sweden. In common usage, Scandinavia encompasses three kingdoms—Denmark, Norway, and Sweden. It is also said to include Finland and Iceland."
—Hammond Innes

In a more poetic mood, Innes also called Scandinavia, "a land of fjords and the midnight sun. . . The fjords of the Norwegian coast are one of the scenic wonders of the world, great glacier-scored gashes up which the largest liners sail; it is a world where the sun does not set and people sleep with their blinds drawn against the unending summer day; it is a fairy-tale world composed of sea and rock and forest, where the mountains are capped by eternal snows and great glaciers push their icy snouts to the edge of sheer precipices." This, too, is Scandinavia.

And: There are the sand dunes and treacherous tides of the west-facing coast of Jutland in Denmark. There's the most sophisticated of all the capitals, Copenhagen. There are Stone and Bronze Age monuments and Viking artifacts in Sweden. This, too, is Scandinavia.

Innes, however, has not been the only one to ask this question. Even tourist office material has an inquiring start: "So what exactly is Scandinavia? It is the Top of Europe geographically and the Continent's last undiscovered tourist destination. Sophisticated travelers are discovering Nordic charm, clean living, great cuisine, and good value ... and best of all, Scandinavians are happy about sharing this bounty with international visitors.

"Scandinavia is Denmark, where the people in Hans Christian Andersen's hometown of Odense recount his fairy tales in a setting little changed over the years. Where Hamlet's castle at Elsinore still radiates the beauty and mystery Shakespeare intended. And where

wonderful, wonderful Copenhagen's ballet, opera, concerts, and festivals can never quite outshine the twinkling lights and simple pleasures of an amusement park called Tivoli, where everyone is a kid again.

"Scandinavia is Finland, an unspoiled paradise of dense forests, 188,000 islands where breathing the cleanest air on earth is an exhilarating experience. Where people can visit one of the most exotic places on earth, a peaceful kingdom called Lapland. Where even the nation's capital, Helsinki, 'Daughter of the Baltic' has the special feeling of a seaside town punctuated with parks and open spaces.

"Scandinavia is Norway, an inspirational land whose coastline stretches more than a thousand miles from sunny beaches in the south to the Arctic Sea in the north, and whose majestic fjords have inspired geniuses from Grieg to Ibsen. This is a land of 12th-century stave churches and Viking lore.

"Scandinavia is Sweden, a spacious land with great varieties of landscape—mountains and fells, lakes and forests, islands and archipelagos, idyllic small towns, and one of Europe's premier capitals, stimulating Stockholm."

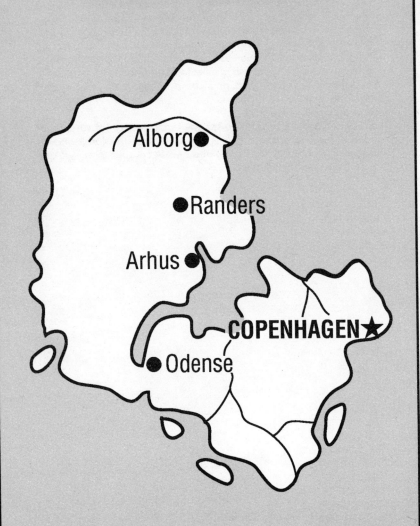

Denmark

It is impossible to begin Denmark's calendar in May, because several important fests occur earlier and are, in the true spirit of Hans Christian Anderson, real "events" to the Danes: the opening of three of the most famous amusement parks this side of Disney World—Tivoli Gardens, Bakken Park, and Legoland!

Copenhagen—Tivoli Gardens Opening

Tivoli Gardens, probably the world's most famous amusement park, has hosted over 250 million people since 1843. Set on 20 acres of garden in the center of Copenhagen, Tivoli is a flower-filled world with all the excitement, beauty, and adventure anyone could desire.

There are 25 amusements and a children's theater *Valmunen*—unlike any other in the world. The Chinese-style Pantomime Theater, the oldest building in Tivoli, features the world's only original Commedia dell'Arte performance with Pjerrot, Harlequin, and Columbine. And there's a 1,930-seat Concert Hall, where world-famous artists meet Tivoli's Symphony Orchestra in concerts, guest ballet performances, and festive music. The famous Tivoli Concerts start in early May. An Open-Air Stage, where performers can entertain 50,000, is also part of the complex.

The famous Tivoli Guard—110 boys in the uniform of the Danish Queen's Royal Life Guard—parade on weekend evenings at 6:30pm and 8:30pm, complete with their band, color guard, royal coach, and naval detachment. The band gives concerts at 3:30pm on Saturday afternoons.

In the evening, 110,000 lamps are lit over the stunning flower arrangements, enchanting fountains, and time-honored, stately buildings. An enormous fireworks display appears four times weekly, and 29 restaurants and a beer garden will keep you happy between rides, concerts, and parades. Tivoli is open daily 10:00am-midnight. For more information, contact Tivoli Gardens, Vesterbrogade 3, DK-1620, Copenhagen. (late April to mid-Sept.)

Copenhagen—Bakken Park Opening

Founded on the site of a sacred well, Bakken Park, seven miles north of the city, is probably the oldest amusement park in the world. Its first season was in 1583!

Just a gentle walk through beautiful Deer Park, once an 18th-century hunting lodge, is reason enough to visit Bakken, "a much more Danish and older institution than sophisticated Tivoli," according to its publicist. Bakken is a good, old-fashioned fairground, with merry-go-rounds, big dippers, candy stalls, hot dog stands, beer halls, bumper cars, restaurants, variety shows, and *palais de danse.* Said to be a place for "real Copenhageners," but no one will mind an outsider or two. The best thing about Bakken? There's no admission fee! Open daily noon-midnight from late March to late August.

May

Billund—Legoland Opening

You'll have to venture out of Copenhagen for a visit to Legoland, billed as "an amusement park for the whole family." Its main attraction, Miniland, is made of 33 million Lego "bricks," those multi-colored, multi-shaped plastic connectors that parents find all over the house a week after Christmas. Imagine 33 million of them all in one place! Ingeniously, they re-construct famous buildings and landscapes from all over the world.

Legoland, open May 1 to mid-Sept., is near the factory where the bricks are made and Arhus, Jutland's capital. Arhus is the country's second-largest city and the site of another version of Tivoli Gardens: Tivoli-Friheden offers amusements, an open-air theater, art shows, concerts, and an interesting forest setting.

For more information, write Legoland, DK-7190, Billund. The address of Tivoli-Friheden is Marselisborg Skov, DK-8000, Arhus.

Randers—Castle Concerts

The Randers Orchestra gives six concerts of chamber music at Clausholm, Tjele, Ulstrup, Gammel Estrup Castles, and Overgaard Estate. Top performers from around Denmark perform. (early May to early Sept.)

Ribe—Watchman's Round of Ribe

Denmark's oldest town, full of red-roofed, half-timbered medieval houses, narrow lanes, and cobblestone streets, is the perfect setting for the nightly reenactment of the watchman's rounds, making sure "all's well" for the night. This ancient custom, revived in 1936, is a charming example of Jutland folklore. Mainly a tourist attraction now, the ritual is performed May 1 to Sept. 15.

Copenhagen—Danish Ballet and Opera Festival

During the last two weeks of May, the Old Stage of the Royal Theater in Copenhagen hosts both classical and modern dance and two operas. The festival features the world-famous Royal Danish Opera and Ballet companies, as well as visiting artists. Recent offerings have included *The Taming of the Shrew* danced by the Stuttgart Ballet, Verdi's *Otello*, and Offenbach's *Tales of Hoffman*. For more information, contact Royal Theater, P.O. Box 2185, DK-1017, Copenhagen.

Aalborg—Aalborg Festival

Founded over 1,000 years ago by Vikings, Aalborg has retained much of its ancient feel, despite the fact that it is the largest city in North Jutland. Its annual festival combines both old and new, with a wide range of activities and entertainment for a week in late May.

June

Hjallerup—Hjallerup Fair

Hosting over 200,000 visitors in four days, the Hjallerup Fair is considered the largest festival in Northern Europe. It includes a horse fair, stalls, a funfair, and traditional Danish entertainment like "tilting at the ring." (first weekend in June)

Salten—Salten Fair

The Salten Fair, which dates to 1850, began as a horse fair, but today it includes 300 different stalls, a funfair, and traditional entertainment. The Fair is a great chance to see authentic Danish crafts and exhibits. (mid-June)

Aalborg—Aalborg Jazz Festival

Shortly after its town festival closes, jazz takes over in a weekend festival throughout the city. Jazz musicians perform in every conceivable indoor and outdoor location. (mid-June)

Ebletoft—Watchman's Rounds

Like Ribe, Ebletoft is a well-preserved town of half-timbered houses and cobblestone streets, and it, too, has made the ancient tradition of the watchman's nightly rounds into a production during the summer. After each striking of the hour, the watchman and his staff sing their songs outside the Old Town Hall, then go on their evening rounds. The tiny Town Hall, built in 1576 and rebuilt in 1789, is now a museum with a collection of archaeological and cultural items. The nightly rounds, along with the opening of a pedestrian street in the Old Town, runs late June to late August.

throughout—Midsummer Night

June 23 and 24 are the year's most fun-filled days in Scandinavia, as everyone celebrates the summer solstice with bonfires, torchlight parades, and midsummer songs and dancing. In Copenhagen, *Sante Hans*, meaning "burn the witch," dates to the brutal time when "witches" really were burned. Today, only witch dolls are thrown into the bonfires, and the atmosphere is joyous, as are all the midsummer festivities throughout Copenhagen.

Frederikssund—Viking Festival
The town of Frederikssund is noted for its annual 16-day Viking Festival, when over 200 townspeople produce Viking plays and historical reenactments. Nordic legends about heroes like Erik the Red and Leif Ericsson are performed in an exciting pageant, followed by a Viking banquet. Frederikssund is 30 km. northwest of Copenhagen. For more information, contact Tourist Information Office, 22 H.C. Andersens Boulevard, DK-Copenhagen V. (late June to early July)

Skagen—Skagen Festival
This major folk event in the seaside resort of Skagen offers Scandinavian and British rock, folk, and jazz in various venues. The entire Jutland peninsula, from Arhus and Aalborg in the north to Ribe in the south, is full of spectacular scenery and lovely beaches, and Skagen's musical event is a real vacation bonus. (late weekend in June)

Roskilde—Roskilde Festival
The biggest rock festival in northern Europe draws over 50,000 fans to this suburb 20 miles west of Copenhagen. Supposedly one of the oldest such events in Europe, the fest also offers folk music, theater, film, and video. Besides luring thousands of rock 'n roll fans, Roskilde is also the country's major religious pilgrimage site, as its 12th-century cathedral is the final resting place for 38 Danish kings and queens. (late June to early July)

July

Copenhagen—Copenhagen Summer Festival
This festival features concerts of classical, chamber, and church music in the Great Hall at Charlottenborg (throughout July), at the Kastel Church (Sundays in July and August), and at the Church of the Holy Ghost (July-August).

Aalborg—Fourth of July Celebrations
Ribald National Park, 18 miles south of Aalborg, is the site of one of Scandinavia's largest Independence Day celebrations. On July 2, there's a lavish garden party, and on July 3, a gala concert. Fireworks, of course, mark the evening of the 4th, when Americans, Danes, and Danish-Americans celebrate U.S. independence. Ribald Park, part of Denmark's largest forest, contains the Lincoln Memorial Log Cabin and Immigrant Museum, with mementos of Danish immigration to the United States.

Copenhagen—Copenhagen Jazz Festival

Every summer, an international cast of jazz musicians visit the major cities of Europe to perform in indoor and outdoor venues. Copenhagen hosts them for ten days in mid-July, with more than 130 concerts scheduled. For more information, contact Copenhagen Jazz Festival, City Center, Norregade 7A, 2, DK-1165.

Hasle—Herring Festival

Sweden celebrates its crayfish, Holland its mussels, and Ireland its oysters. Denmark's fish of honor is the herring, and a parade and funfair occur in Hasle annually to celebrate the catch. Even a "Miss Herring" (lucky girl!) is selected to adorn the weekend activities of dancing, music, and lots of eating and drinking. (mid-July)

Kramnitze—Garfish Festival

Kramnitze's reply to the Hasle festival above is a popular local event. The specialty is hot smoked garfish, and appropriate entertainment accompanies the feasting. (mid-July)

Arhus—Viking Meet

This traditional market is for the locals who greet the Viking ships on their return from summer expeditions. The exchange of home-made goods for items from foreign countries makes for an interesting and unique Danish event. (late July weekend)

August

throughout—Harbor Festivals

Throughout the month, usually on weekends, a number of towns hold Harbor Festivals with entertainment, drinking and eating, and aquatic events. Some are genuinely local affairs (though tourists are welcomed warmly) with mostly native entertainment and participation, while others, especially in the larger cities, are somewhat more sophisticated. Whichever, they are always a good party and a great chance to encounter Danes in a relaxed atmosphere.

Faborg, Assens, and Kerteminde hold the most traditional harbor events. Svendborg, an old port and boating center on the island of Funen, features a lively fest with an old-style Market Day, traditionally held on the first Thursday of August. Every Saturday morning, there's a fish and flower market as well.

Copenhagen—Copenhagen Water Music

The city's impressive harbor is the venue for this mini-music festival sponsored by the Copenhagen Harbor Authority and Carlsberg Breweries. It includes family entertainment, jazz concerts, a film screening, and classical music. (late August weekend)

Logumkloster—Kloster Maerken

This country fair, one of the biggest in Denmark, boasts a meeting of the knights of the road from the whole county, a horse fair, funfair, and flea market. The three-day event ends with a giant fireworks display. (mid-August)

Bandholm—Herring Festival

Yet another fish fair! This time, the island of Lolland, where most people make ferry connections from northern Europe to Copenhagen, hosts a traditional event, which features salted and grilled herring with bread and butter. Non-herring-lovers can try other local foods, but herring is really queen for this day in late August. There's music and dancing, too.

September

Arhus—Arhus Festival

Denmark's most comprehensive program of cultural and traditional events—concerts, theater, opera, ballet, cabaret, sports, and exhibitions—comprises this fabulous week-long event. A Medieval Fair, held concurrently at the fairgrounds of Moesgaard Prehistoric Museum, lets children and adults watch a medieval jousting tournament and crossbow competitions, buy medieval goods, food, and drink (prepared using original recipes), and be entertained by jesters and period music. The entire town becomes a living arena of performances and exhibitions. The event, held since 1965, grows in popularity and scope each year. For more information, contact Arhus Tourist Office, DK-8000, Arhus. (early to mid-Sept.)

A Danish Sampler: Hamlet & Hans

Two favorite sons of Danish history are the real Hans Christian Andersen and the fictional Hamlet. Places associated with them are famous sites in Denmark and capitalize on their literary associations.

Hans Christian Andersen

Odense, the provincial capital of Funen Island, is the childhood home of Andersen, who was born there in 1805. His old home (39 Hans Jensensstraede) is now a museum featuring fairy tale memorabilia, documents, manuscripts, and reprints of his books. Andersen struggled as a writer, but his effort was rewarded, as his timeless tales are now available in 80 languages.

The towns and villages of his native island and its archipelago bear a striking resemblance to England, with their magnificent manor houses, beautiful parkland, and half-timbered homes. By the acre, Funen is the most castle-rich province in Europe and includes the romantic Egeskov Castle at Kvaerndrup and Nyborg Castle at Slotspadsen. No wonder Andersen was so inspired by history! On the outskirts of Odense, Funen Village features heritage homesteads, venerable chestnut trees, and the Hans Christian Andersen Festival, in which his fairytales are performed on an open-air stage from mid-July to mid-August.

For more information: Tourist Association, Radhuset, Odense.

Hamlet

For England's William Shakespeare, all the world was a stage, including Denmark's Kronberg Castle in Elsinore, immortalized as the setting for *Hamlet*. The 400-year-old fortress, at one time the key to the Baltic, is full of lacy spires, imposing towers, and secret passageways. There's considerable doubt that a Danish prince named Hamlet ever existed, or that Shakespeare ever saw the castle. Regardless, Elsinore, 25 miles north of Copenhagen, has become a popular tourist spot by touting its medieval lanes, half-timbered houses, and ''Hamlet's Castle'' (history be damned!). English productions of *Hamlet* are staged frequently at the castle during the summer.

For more information, contact Tourist Office, Havnepladsen, Elsinore.

Danish Holidays

New Year's Day, Maundy Thursday, Good Friday, Easter Sunday, Easter Monday, Prayers Day (April 26), Ascension Day (May 9), Whitsunday and Whitmonday, Christmas, Boxing Day (Dec. 26).

For literature and further information, contact the **Danish Tourist Board**. In the U.S., the address is 655 Third Ave., New York, NY 10017 (212-949-2333).

FINLAND

Rovaniemi

Kuopio

Savonlinna

Tampere

Pori

Lahti

Turku

★ HELSINKI

Finland

May

Kajaani—Kainuu Jazz Spring

Kainuu Jazz Spring, a four-day jazz event in Kajaani the last weekend of May, offers several concerts in Kaukametsa Hall, plus late-night jams. Blues is featured for three days at the Blues Marathon, and Cafe Jazz is everywhere in downtown Kajaani. Since 1983, the event has brought a cosmopolitan feeling to the northern countryside emerging from the long winter.

June

Riihimake—Riihimake Summer Concerts

According to its organizers, the goal of the Riihimake concert series is to "approach the riches of music without presumption, enabling the music of (Finland) to be heard alongside the works of old masters." It's a multicultural event, where the listener encounters both fine music and precious works of sculpted glass in the Tapio Wirkkala Finnish Museum of Glass, the main concert venue. (early June)

Mantsala—Sepan Soitto

This traditional folk music festival in the idyllic grounds of a handicraft museum brings together nearly 1,000 musicians and dancers. The program also includes performing groups from abroad and the Finnish Championships for traditional folk groups. The fest is a prime opportunity to see Finnish folk culture at its best. (early June weekend)

Tampere—Pispalan Sottisi

Pispalan Sottisi is Finland's largest international folk dance festival. Nearly 2,000 dancers from Finland and abroad perform at the celebration, which has a different theme each time and includes a central production with all the groups, a folk dance contest, concerts, and informal gatherings. The festival runs in even-numbered years in early June.

Seinajoki—Province Rock
A rock festival and world music festival all in one, this event is a cross-section of popular music, presented in a "global village" constructed on the festival site. Dozens of musicians from throughout the world perform during this weekend jam. (early June)

Kuopio—Kuopio Dance and Music Festival
Each year, this week-long festival focuses on a different theme, ranging from Mediterranean and African dance to Scandinavian music. Groups from the featured countries perform native dance, opera, and ballet and present exhibitions of their culture. Finnish dance companies also create compositions in the spirit of the honored country. Jazz and light music is offered daily in the marquee at the steamship harbor on Lake Kalavesi. For more information, contact Kuopia Dance and Music Festival, Tullinportinkatu 27, SF-70100, Kuopio. (early June)

Ilmajoki—Ilmajoki Music Festival
This week-long event presents two operas each season—a Scandinavian opera usually runs with a popular work like *Madame Butterfly*—and 20 concerts in four different locations. A high-tech sound system, seating for 3,000, and a large marquee create a splendid backdrop for the top-notch productions. The towns of Ilmajoki, Seinäjoki, Nurmo, and Kurikka also serve as venues for evenings of classical and popular music. For more information, contact Ilmajoki Music Festival, Kahmankuja 6, SF-60800, Ilmajoki. (early June)

Ikaalinen—Sata-Häme Accordion Festival
The accordion, Finland's national instrument, is the centerpiece of this unique festival celebrated ten days in June in the idyllic town of Ikaalinen. Apart from delightful Finnish accordion music, top international performers of light music are showcased. As in other Finnish festivals, a different theme is featured each year. For more information, contact Sata-Häme Accordion Festival, Hanuritalo, P.O. Box 37, SF-39501, Ikaalinen. (mid-June)

Helsinki—Helsinki Seajazz
This international jazz festival offers a high quality and varied program during the three days before Midsummer. Concert venues include Koff Park, the best open-air theater in the city, and the old Katajannokka engine factory, which becomes a jazz club for the event. (mid-June weekend)

throughout June—Midsummer
Like the other Scandinavian nations that joyously celebrate the summer solstice, Finland revels in Midsummer with bonfires throughout the country, dancing in the streets, and dozens of local festivities featuring good, old-fashioned revelry. (June 22-23)

Naantali—Naantali Music Festival

Organizers of this two-week concert series in the monumental 15th-century Naantali Abbey claim the setting "will attune the visitor's mind to listen to the message of the great composers mediated through the performance of virtuoso chamber musicians." Whether this is true or not, the high quality music, performed by orchestras like the Academy of St. Martin-in-the-Fields, the Ensemble Vienna-Berlin, and the New Helsinki Quartet, makes the Naantali festival a delightful event. For more information, contact Naantali Music Festival, P.O. Box 46, SF-21101, Naantali. (mid- to late June)

Jyväskylä—Jyväskylä Arts Festival

This arts event at Jyväskylä, in the lakeland area of central Finland, is the oldest multi-arts discussion forum in the country. Each year it takes a different theme and examines aspects of art related to it. While the seminars attract intellectuals throughout Scandinavia, the tourist may find the films, theater, dance, and music more alluring. The festival runs for ten days in mid-June. For more information, contact Jyväskylä Arts Festival, Kramsunkatu 1, SF-40600, Jyväskylä.

Joensuu—Joensuu Song Festival

While music is always central to this song festival, it aims to be a "cultural carnival" of art. A variety of concerts provide the fest's framework, with a major classical event on the Laulurinne stage. There are also chamber music concerts and recitals, rock and jazz concerts, club events, and circus plays. The festival culminates on Midsummer Eve (June 22) with a concert held on the Russian side of the border in Sortavala. Joensuu, the district capital of northern Karelia, is only a few miles from the border. For more information, contact Joensuu Song Festival, Koskikatu 1, SF-80100, Joensuu. (mid-June)

Tornio & Haaparanta—Midnight Sun Jazz Fun & Accordion Festival

Tornio, on the northern tip of the Gulf of Bothnia in Lapland, is the site of two successive music festivals on either side of the 12-mile border there between Finland and Russia. While both events feature performers chiefly from Scandinavia, musicians from around Europe also participate. (late June to early July)

Porvoo—Summer Sounds

The second-oldest town in Finland, Porvoo hosts a Summer Sounds program that stretches from the baroque to the most contemporary of musical styles. Porvoo is 30 miles northeast of Helsinki. (late June weekend or early July)

Imatra—Big Band Festival

An internationally renowned fest of big band music—and a unique meeting of East and West—the Imatra program features big bands from Russia, Europe, and the U.S. Concerts are held all over the city, and the festival includes a competition of orchestras from around Scandinavia. Imatra is in the lake region of eastern Finland. (late June weekend or early July)

Taipalsaari—Kalenat
This South Karelian provincial festival is based on local folk traditions, although folk song and dance groups from Scandinavia and Europe are often invited to add an international flavor. (late June weekend or early July)

July

Savonlinna—Savonlinna Opera Festival
About 225 miles from Helsinki, Savonlinna grew around the three-towered medieval castle Olavinlinna, founded in 1475. Built on islands, Savonlinna is the oldest town in eastern Finland and one of the country's most popular tourist areas, thanks to the castle and the beautiful Saimaa lake district.

The castle is the venue for one of Europe's most important and best-known music festivals, the Savonlinna Opera Festival. Started in 1912 as an "opera week" and disbanded in 1930, the event was revived in 1967. The great courtyard within the castle is an ideal setting for the operas, which have included Verdi's *Aïda*, Wagner's *Flying Dutchman*, and Prokofiev's ballet *Romeo and Juliet*. Performances by visiting international troupes and Finnish companies are always first-class. Further, Suruton Villa on nearby Kasinonsaari Island offers an exhibition on the history of the opera festival. For more information, contact Savonlinna Opera Festival, Olavinkatu 35, SF-57130, Savonlinna. (throughout July)

Ruovesi—Ruovesi Witch Trial
The first witch trials in Ruovesi were held in 1643, and today the trials are reenacted in a four-day festival in early July, bringing considerable excitement to Ruovesi. The program includes drama, music, and events associated with local folk traditions. For more information, contact Matkailutoimisto, SF-34600, Ruovesi.

Harma—Harma Mischief
Probably the Finnish festival with the most exotic-sounding name, *Harmalaaset Hajyyly* is a local cultural festival that depicts the past and present of Alaharma in music, song, and drama. Like most heritage festivals, it promotes and preserves local folk customs and involves hundreds of participants. (early July weekend)

Turku—Ruisrock
The oldest city in Finland hosts the country's newest music at Ruis-

rock, the world's oldest regularly scheduled rock concert. The venue for this unique, raucous event is the public park on the island of Ruissalo, near the center of Turku. The concert attracts thousands of young people annually. For more information, contact Turku Music Festival Foundation, SF-20500, Turku. (early July weekend)

Lapua—Etelapohjalaiset Spelit
While the name may be unpronounceable, the event is quite simple: a gathering of folk musicians, choirs, bands, and dancers who make their way to Lapua, a South Ostrobothnian town, each year for a weekend of music and dance. (mid-July)

Pori—Pori Jazz
The idea for a jazz festival in Pori, 150 miles northwest of Helsinki, was first hatched in the mid-1960's. Though the location is magnificent, an American reporter asked, "Who'll ever find it?" At first, only 1,500 people attended. Today, over 60,000 come annually to hear music day and night on Jazz Street in Pori, on the island of Kirjurinluoto, in the Cotton Club, and in many Pori restaurants. The music ranges from traditional to contemporary jazz, Dixieland, blues, and swing, with performers like Chuck Mangione, B.B. King, and the Woody Herman Orchestra. With 19 hours of summer sunshine and 24 hours of music, Pori is truly a magnificent place for a week-long jazz fest. For more information, contact Pori Jazz 66 ry, Eteläranta 6, SF-28100, Pori. (mid-July)

Kaustinen—Kaustinen Folk Music Festival
During Scandinavia's largest folk music festival, Kaustinen rings with the sound of music from around the world for eight days and nights. The venues range from intimate farmhouses to smoky clubs to full-scale concert arenas. Over 2,000 Finns play, sing, and dance to both traditional and contemporary music. Plus, groups from six continents join the Finns for one of the largest reviews in the area. One year, the audience exceeded 90,000! First held in 1968, the festival today is the most significant event for Finnish folk musicians. For more information, contact Kaustinen Folk Music, P.O. Box 24, SF-69601, Kaustinen. (mid-July)

Kuhmo—Kuhmo Chamber Music Festival
Kuhmo, 420 miles from Helsinki in the northeast corner of Finland, probably hosts the most remote chamber music festival in the world. The town is surrounded by the stark wilderness of the Kainuu forest near the Russian border. But the location belies the quality and quantity of the festival, which presents over 65 concerts in two weeks, with a selection more eclectic than one might imagine: One year, the dual themes were "Hungarian Music Today and Yesterday" and "The Complete Chamber Works of Johannes Brahms." Other years have

celebrated Felix Mendelssohn-Bartholdy and vocal music from Europe, Africa, and Georgia. For more information, contact Kuhmo Chamber Music Festival, Kontiokatu 2 A 6, SF-88900, Kuhmo; and Lutherinkatu 12 A 2, SF-00100, Helsinki. (mid-to late July)

Viitasaari—Time of Music

In late July, the town of Viitasaari presents eight days of modern music in Finland's only summer festival devoted to the contemporary. The festival invites both Finnish artists and others from around Europe. For more information, contact Time of Music, SF-44500, Viitasaari. (late July)

Lahti—Lahti Organ Festival

This prestigious event is a renowned venue for organists and all fans of organ music. The program also includes other kinds of music, from orchestral concerts to solo performances. Ristikirkko Church and the Lahti City Theater, as well as churches in surrounding towns, host the concerts. Lahti is 64 miles north of Helsinki. For more information, contact Lahti Organ Festival, Kirkkokatu 5, SF-15110, Lahti. (late July to early August)

Lieksa—Lieksa Brass Week

The annual Brass Week festival, held the last week of July, has become a prime site for brass music and musicians from around the world. As you might guess, it's the biggest thing to hit Lieksa all year. For more information, contact Lieksa Brass Week, Koski-Jaakonkatu 4, SF-81700, Lieksa.

August

Turku—Turku Music Festival

Sometimes called "the cradle of Finnish culture," Turku, on the southwest coast about 100 miles from Helsinki, is Finland's oldest city. Its 30-year-old festival—a key event on the country's culture calendar—offers music ranging from the medieval era to first-time performances. Festival organizers hope that "within a medley of styles and periods, listeners will identify features that make a work of art interesting, communicative, even a work of genius." Performances are held in such evocative locales as the courtyard of Turku Castle (built in the late 13th century), the 13th-century Cathedral, and the Sibelius Museum. For more information, contact Turku Music Festival Foundation, SF-20500, Turku. (early to mid-August)

Savonlinna—Olujaiset Beer Festival

After its opera festival in July, the beautiful Olavinlinna Castle courtyard hosts a great beer bash in mid-August! Arranged "to foster the drinking and brewing traditions of Olavinlinna Castle," the fest includes musical performances and competitions, and lots of beer-drinking. For more information, contact Savonlinna Tourist Office, Puistokatu 1, SF-57100, Savonlinna.

Mariehamn—Aland Culture Festival

This wide-ranging cultural event is held each year in the Aland Islands, between Sweden and Finland. Though they belong to Finland, the islands are more Swedish at heart and operate autonomously, with their own flag and stamps. The festival combines a bit of both cultures, along with international artists performing jazz, classical pieces, and drama. For more information, contact Trobergsgrand 1, SF-22100, Mariehamn. (late August to mid-Sept.)

Helsinki—Helsinki Festival

The largest cultural event in the Nordic countries, the Helsinki Festival is an outgrowth of the Sibelius Festival started in 1951. Then, its primary focus was the works of Jean Sibelius, the Finnish composer. The Sibelius Weeks ended in 1965, and in 1967 the Helsinki Festival Foundation created a more broadly-based program, keeping classical music as its cornerstone. Today, the festival includes music commissioned from several Finnish composers, as well as plays, jazz, rock, and visual arts.

The theme of a recent Helsinki Festival was "St. Petersburg—Leningrad," hosting artists and composers from that city. Many events are free and in public places throughout the city. Since Finland has 20 hours of daylight in late August, the outdoor performances are unforgettable! Indoor venues include the Sibelius Academy, the Finnish National Theater and Opera, the House of Culture, the House of Nobility, and the lovely Finlandia Hall. The summer concert season in Helsinki officially begins in mid-July as a "warm-up" to this spectacular event. For more information, contact Helsinki Festival, Unioninkatu 28, SF-00100, Helsinki. (late August to early Sept.)

Finnish Holidays

New Years Day, Epiphany (Jan. 6), Good Friday, Easter Monday, May Day, Ascension Day (May 4), Midsummer Eve (June 21), All Saints Day (Nov. 2), Independence Day (Dec. 6), Christmas, Boxing Day (Dec. 26).

For further information, contact the **Finnish Tourist Board**. In the U.S., the address is 655 Third Ave., New York, NY 10017 (212-949-2333).

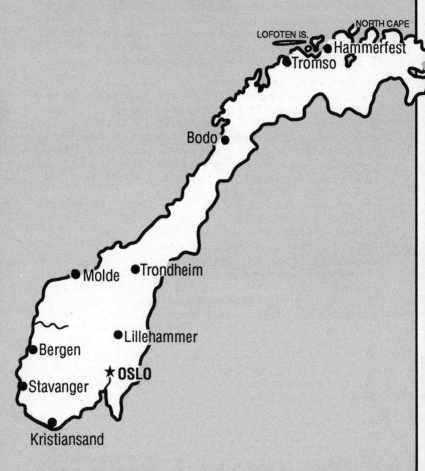

Norway

May

Kristiansand—International Church Music Festival

Choirs, orchestras, and ensembles from churches and religious institutions from many countries venture to Kristiansand Cathedral to perform all types of liturgical music at this week-long event. Almost completely destroyed during World War II, Kristiansand is today a modern city with numerous cultural events throughout the year. Located in the great stretch of coast toward the North Cape between Molde and Trondheim, the town is full of music lovers. Indeed, many consider it the center of opera in Norway, since it features Opera Week in February. (early May)

throughout—Constitution Day

On May 17, Norway's national holiday, citizens don their Sunday best—often national or regional costumes—throughout the country. In Olso, everyone heads for the park just below the Royal Palace. King Olav V and his family appear on the balcony to hear the King's Anthem, a moving tribute to monarchy, followed by the national anthem and a parade of children up the grand avenue Karl Johansgate to the Palace Gardens. Everyone then enjoys a fine Norwegian lunch, and dinner parties are de rigueur in the evening.

Bergen—Bergen Night Jazz

You can hear jazz concerts throughout Bergen the last week of May. A city surrounded by seven mountains, Bergen was the first capital of Norway during the 13th century and the seat of the medieval kingdom. It's thoroughly modern now, and jazz is king during this festival, which attracts artists from around the world. The concerts begin at 11:00pm and last until morning.

Bergen Night Jazz runs concurrently to the prestigious Bergen International Festival below:

Bergen—Bergen International Festival

This world-class music event features a stellar range of artists. The largest annual musical event in Scandinavia, it coincides with both Bergen Night Jazz and the Fjord Blossom Time, when Norway's fjord country is bursting with spring hues.

Classical and modern dance, two operatic masterpieces, drama, film, recitals, and major symphony concerts are all included in Norway's finest cultural showcase. While the festival seeks to offer international cultural events to Norwegians, it's also a vehicle for presenting Norwegian culture to an international audience. One of the programs that accomplishes this is the Fana Folklore Concert, held in 800-year-old Fana Church outside Bergen. There, participants hear folk music played on an ancient organ, eat Norwegian national dishes, and dance to traditional folk instruments. From jazz to traditional music, the Bergen Festival has it all! For more information, contact Bergen International Festival, P.O. Box 183, N-5001, Bergen. (last week of May to early June)

Rosendal—Rosendal Music Festival

Brass band concerts, national and international artists, open-air concerts, and all-night jazz sessions characterize this multi-faceted concert in Rosendal by the Hardangerfjord. As tulips are to Holland, the fjords are to Norway, and none is more beautiful than the Hardangerfjord near Bergen. For more information, contact Kvinnherad Tourist Office, N-5020, Rosendal. (late May weekend)

June

Nesbyen—Folk Music Festival

No visit to a Scandinavian country is complete without attending at least one folk dance or music event. At the Nesbyen festival, you can enjoy traditional Norwegian folk music all over town in mid-June.

Stavanger—Emigration Festival

This festival celebrates Norwegian emigration to North America with concerts, theater, folklore, and exhibitions. A Norwegian Emigration Center (Bergjelandsgt. 30, N-4012, Stavanger) can help you trace your roots if you are of Norwegian descent, and it provides information on Norwegian families who relocated to America. (mid-June)

Harstad—North Norway Festival

Performers from all over Norway come to Harstad, in the middle of the island of Hinnoya, to perform in concert, dance, and theater pieces. Art exhibitions are also featured at this week-long event. (late June)

throughout Norway—Midsummer Night

Midsummer is an important holiday throughout Scandinavia, and Norway celebrates it joyously. Bonfires are an especially festive aspect of the events. (June 22-23)

Kongsberg—Kongsberg Jazz Festival

This five-day international event is considered one of Scandinavia's most important jazz festivals. Several concerts are held outdoors in lovely settings. (early June)

Molde—Molde Jazz Festival

Molde, the picturesque town on the shores of the Romsdalfjord, 500 miles from Oslo, hosts Norway's oldest jazz event. Located in the shadow of the Romsdal Alps, Molde is also called "the city of roses" because of its attractive parks and gardens.

The week-long jazz fest, founded in 1961 as a three-day jam for amateur Norwegian musicians, now attracts international stars and thousands of fans each year. During the festival, two concerts a day are held in the 587-seat town cinema, and more intimate sessions continue throughout the night at various hotels and pubs. For more information, contact Molde Jazz Festival, P.O. Box 261, N-6401, Molde. (mid-June)

Trondheim—St. Olav Festival

Known as Norway's "Royal Town" because the nation's kings are crowned in its Nidaros Cathedral, Trondheim is the principal city in the north-central region of the country, 425 miles north of Bergen. Founded by the Viking king Olav Tryggvason in the 10th century, Trondheim's cathedral has been the major ecclesiastical building in Scandinavia since the 11th century. It's Scandinavia's equivalent of England's Canterbury, as medieval believers made frequent pilgrimages there.

Indeed, the centerpiece of the St. Olav Festival is the *Nidaros Play*, a nine-act drama about a blind peasant who journeys to St. Olav's shrine to be healed. The play incorporates numerous actors, as well as the audience and the St. Olav Choir. Another interesting aspect of this historical drama is that St. Birgitta, the founder of the monastery at Vadstena, Sweden, is a character in the play.

In addition to the drama, presented five times during the ten-day event, over 60 concerts, lectures, organ recitals—even an opera—are offered. Plus, on June 29, St. Olav's Day, there's a service commemorating the day Olav Haraldsson died on the battlefield in 1030. For more information, contact Festivalkontoret, Kongasgardsgt. 2, N-7013, Trondheim. (late June to early August)

August

Vinstra—Peer Gynt Festival

In 1867, playwright Henrik Ibsen published *Peer Gynt*, a drama based partly on the exploits of a Norwegian folk hero noted for such daring deeds as riding reindeer bareback. Later, Norwegian composer Edward Grieg set the play to music. Vinstra's ten-day festival honoring Ibsen's masterpiece offers music, parades in national costumes, and other events celebrating the character Gynt. For more information, contact Peer Gynt Festival, Vinstra Turistkontor, N-2640, Vinstra. (early August)

Bo—Telemark Festival

This international festival, a meeting place for Norwegian and international folk musicians and dance groups, is held in Bo. The Telemark region, where folk arts have long traditions, is the home of many famous fiddlers, dancers, and singers. (mid-August)

Oslo—Jazz Festival

This annual event features jazz from around the world and an international cast of performers. It overlaps Oslo's Chamber Music Festival, which also lures a notable roster of musicians to perform in the 14th-century Akerhus Castle and Fortress, located on a cliff over the Oslo fjord. Both events attract people from throughout Scandinavia. All visitors, of course, are welcome! (mid-August)

Lillehammer:
Site of 1994 Winter Olympics

Just 112 miles from Oslo, Lillehammer, at the northern edge of Lake Mjosa, has long been a popular winter playground for Norwegians. In 1994, the world will discover Lillehammer too, as the XVII Winter Olympic Games bring athletes from around the globe—the first time since 1952 Norway has hosted the Games.

In Lillehammer, many Olympic venues will be within walking distance of the city center. The Lillehammer Stadium, the main arena, will host the ice hockey and figure skating events in four ice halls (the main hall seats 10,000). Speed skating events will run in an outdoor stadium at the main arena. All alpine events except the men's downhill will be held in Hafjell, nine miles from Lillehammer. Other sites are Hamar (58 km. south) and Kvitfjell (50 km. north).

Norwegian Holidays

New Years Day, Maundy Thursday, Good Friday, Easter Monday, May Day, Constitution Day (May 9), Whitmonday (May 20), Christmas, Boxing Day (Dec. 26).

For literature and further information, contact the **Norwegian Tourist Board**. In the U.S., the address is 655 Third Ave., New York, NY 10017 (212-949-2333).

Sweden

May
Uppsala—Walpurgis Night
Actually celebrated on the eve of May 1, Walpurgis Night is believed to be the traditional medieval occasion of a witches' sabbath and is, therefore, a night of wildness and revelry, somewhat like Halloween in the U.S. At the university town of Uppsala, 42 miles northwest of Stockholm, students and alumni don white caps and celebrate the rebirth of spring and the death of winter with a torchlight parade and a night of revelry and singing. A lively songfest is held on the grounds of the castle at Uppsala, founded by Gustavus Vasa in 1540. Although basically a student celebration, everyone is invited. Other celebrations of Walpurgis Eve are held in Lund, Stockholm, Göteborg, and Umea.

Stockholm—Drottningholm Court Theater
Located on an island in Lake Malaren, seven miles from Stockholm, Drottningholm (Queen's Island) Palace is the home of the Swedish royal family. Nearby is the Drottningholm Court Theater, an 18th-century theater that has retained its original settings and machinery. Europe's oldest rococo theater, it presents 28 opera and ballet performances from late May to early Sept. A recent season included the Royal Opera's production of Vogler's *Gustav Adolf och Ebba Brahe*, first produced in Stockholm in 1788. Other productions have included two Mozart operas and Gluck's *Iphigenie en Tauride*. Visitors interested in the history of the stage can also visit the interesting museum there. For more information, contact Drottningholm Court Theater, Box 27050, S-10251, Stockholm.

June
Göteborg—Happy Göteborg Festival
Mostly a local musical event organized by civic groups, this early June event is a "warm-up" to the larger international fest with over 4,000

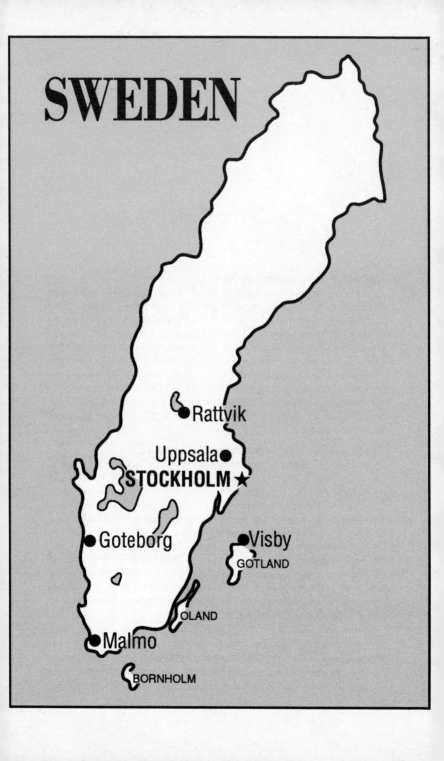

musicians from 12 nations in late June. As Sweden's second largest city, Göteborg easily—and hospitably—hosts both events.

Vadstena—St. Bridget of Sweden

This chronicle play in three acts depicts the life of St. Birgitta, a popular Swedish saint who founded the Abbey Church here between the mid-14th and 15th centuries. The abbey housed the nuns of St. Birgitta's order until their expulsion in 1595. (Nuns from the order returned here in 1963.) As in the *Oberammergau* tradition in Germany, over 150 residents of Vadstena act in the play with orations, song, music, and dancing. (mid-June weekend)

Kalmar—Sweden-America Day

The first Swedish immigration to the United States, over 300 years ago, began in Kalmar and ended in Wilmington, Delaware. To commemorate this event, Kalmar hosts a day-long celebration on June 17, beginning with a service in English in the chapel of Kalmar Castle in Smaland.

throughout—Midsummer Eve

Wherever you go on Midsummer Eve, Swedes are celebrating. The summer solstice is the true climax of the Swedish year, and maypoles are raised in city parks, village greens, and private gardens. The name "maypole" comes from an old Swedish word *maja*, which means "to make green." Leafy birch branches and rings of flowers hang from the pole, and the entertainment includes games and dancing to fiddles and accordions.

Traditional celebrations run throughout Sweden on the closest Saturday to June 21 or 22—the actual date of the solstice. The event, a public holiday, is especially festive in the province of Dalarna, at Naas Manor House; at Gammelgarden, Bengtsfors (Dalsland), where there is also a traditional Midsummer wedding; at Hogbobruk, Sandviken; and at Fatmomakke (Lapland).

Arjeplog—Lapland Festival of Music

In addition to the spectacle of six summer weeks when the sun never sets in Lapland (it just dips close to the horizon), there's a great chamber music festival with world-famous conductors, orchestras, and soloists. Arjeplog was colonized in the 16th century, when silver mining started on the Norwegian border. Its music festival is a unique addition to the incredible landscape. (late June to early July)

July

Halmstad—Sweden America Day

Like Kalmar, Halmstad pays homage to Swedish-American ties with a 4th of July celebration of fireworks and festivities.

Hova—Medieval Festival and Tournament

A number of areas in Sweden are home to splendid medieval and Renaissance castles and fortified cities. In Hova (Vastergotland), the only jousting competition in the Nordic countries occurs at its festival and tournament during the second week of July.

Rattvik—Music on Lake Siljan

Music fans head for Lake Siljan during the first week of July to attend Sweden's largest music festival. Hundreds of musicians performing jazz, folk, classical, and pop are available throughout the week in churches, schools, old barns, and sports arenas in the area.

Visby—Visby Festival

The mystic pageant opera *Petrus de Dacia* by Friedrich Mehler is staged in the impressive ruins of St. Nicholaus Church, the 13th-century Dominican monastery where Petrus de Dacia served as prior in the Middle Ages. Since 1929, this annual festival has staged a mystical opera in a setting that makes the Middle Ages come alive in the moonlight-filled evening performances. In addition to its thrice-weekly opera productions, the walled city of Visby is the most popular place in Scandinavia to sample medieval life. It's a lovely town for a walking tour. For more information, contact Visby Festival, 47 Tranhusgatan, S-621 55, Visby. (early July to early August)

Karlshamm—Baltic Sea Festival

All of Karlshamm joins this festival of music, yacht races, bistros, and dancing in the harbor quarters. A market fair and carnival add to the weekend activities. (mid-July)

Ekanas—Renaissance Festival

Ekanas Castle, one of Sweden's best-preserved Renaissance buildings, is the marvelous setting for a festival of Renaissance music. Additional activities of the period, both at Ekanas Castle and the nearby towns of Linkoping, Norrkoping, and Soderkoping, make a visit here delightful in late July/early August.

August

throughout—Kraftskiva

The Swedish crayfishing season officially opens at midnight on the second Wednesday of August. Sound boring? Hardly! Crayfish season means party time, as the entire Swedish population gets involved in the catching, preparation, and devouring of over three million tons of crayfish during the brief season. Most Swedes, in fact, attend at least one *kraftskiva* (crayfish table) each season to renew an ancient Swedish tradition.

The crayfish, which resemble tiny American lobsters, are boiled, then served cold in the dill, vinegar, and salt in which they are cooked.

This juice enhances their flavor and is often considered the tastiest part of the meal. In the finest Swedish tradition, each crayfish is consumed with a *nubbe*—a shot of aquavit after each claw is eaten. An additional Swedish accompaniment is toast and *knackebrod* with butter and cheese. Delicious!

Visby—Medieval Week

If you enjoy cheering armored knights in tournaments, attending medieval plays, and participating in activities from a time long passed, head to Visby, the capital of Gotland, in August. Hundreds of islanders in costumes create in this week-long event, which include both music and period festivities. Visby, which dates from 2000 B.C., is a medieval city surrounded on three sides by a 13th-century stone wall. You can get there by ferry from Stockholm. (early August)

Stockholm—Stockholm Festival

Operas, concerts, ballet, drama, exhibitions, and other cultural events flood the streets, concert halls, and theaters of Sweden's capital for this three-week event. (mid-August to early Sept.)

Folk Culture in Sweden

In Sweden, as in most European countries, folk culture has probably been best-preserved in music and dance. Folk musicians gather throughout the summer in *spelmansstamma* to encourage the preservation of folk culture and to prove the old traditions aren't dead. Likewise, dance festivals are held from early spring to late autumn and include both Scandinavian groups and dancers from around the world.

Popular folk music gatherings are held in June at Malmköping, Bingsjö, and Gammelstrang; in July at Delsbo, Film, Bingsjö, Gavle, Bjuraker, and Lerum (near Nass Castle). At Bingsjö, Sweden's largest *spelmansstamma* hosts 40,000 musicians and visitors annually for a nine-day music festival called *Musik vid Siljan* (early July). Väsby is the site of a gathering in early August.

Well-known dance festivals are held in Hallefors (a weekend in mid-June), where 1,000 participants from the Nordic countries perform; at Rättvik (late June), with participants from many European countries; at four different locations in Halsingland, as part of the Halsinge-Hambo Festival (early July); and at Falun (weekend in mid-July).

Another unique form of folklore preservation in Sweden is the homestead museum. As the name implies, country homesteads and farms have become museum-quality places where native songs, dance, crafts, and traditions are maintained. The also host special theme days called *hembygdsdagar*:

Rättviksveckan is a mid-June week of various activities tied to the community's old traditions. Days at hill farms, handicraft days, church-boat rowing, the Rättvik wedding, folk music, and dance are included. (In Rättvik, Boda Kyrkby, and Furudal in Dalarna.)

"Church-Boat Rowing" in local costume takes place every Sunday at 10:00am from late June to mid-August in Enabron, Rättvik (Dalarna). Sunday Boats, originally designed to transport 20 people to church, are vehicles unique to Sweden.

"Life on a Hill Farm at Stampen" provides a look into a self-sustaining household from the 19th century. There's a working press for homespun cloth, a water mill, and an alpine meadow with livestock. Entertainment is offered some evenings. (In Hamara, Vadmalsstamp, and Eksharad in Varmland, through July.)

Klarhalja recreates life in the Klaralven Valley as it was 100 years ago. Charcoal-making, timber floats, and handicrafts, as well as activities in the surrounding hill meadows, are offered at Karnasens Hembygdsgard, Norra Rade (Varmland) in the second week of July.

"Festival Week at Dal" (late July) offers folk entertainment of various types, including demonstrations of traditional skills like blacksmithing. (In Baldersnas, Herrgard, and Bengtsfors in Dalsland.)

"*Gammelvala*—The Old World" includes demonstrations of 40 traditional trades and skills in authentic surroundings, plus musical plays, during the last week of July. (In Hembygdsgarden, Skutboudden, and Brunskog in Varmland.)

"Culture Days" at Vastanfors, Fagersta (Vastmanland) are hosted by residents in turn-of-the-century dress who provide market stalls, metalworks demonstrations, a mini-circus, and trips by steamboat and carriage in the last weekend in July.

Finally, the Whitefish Festival at Kukkolaforsen pays homage to a favorite Swedish delicacy. The festivities begin with netting whitefish in the waterfalls, followed by smoking and grilling the fish, boat rides through the falls, and traditional entertainment. (last weekend in July)

Swedish Holidays
New Years Day, Epiphany (Jan. 6), Good Friday, Easter Monday, Labor Day (May 1), Ascension Day, Whitsunday and Whitmonday, All Saints Day (Nov. 2), Christmas, Boxing Day (Dec. 26).

For literature and further information contact the **Swedish Tourist Board**. In the U.S., the address is 655 Third Ave., New York, NY 10017 (212-949-2333).

12 ▌Greece

> "Merely the mention of such key words as mythology, philosophy, democracy, points immediately to their Greek source. So also do the familiar forms of architecture, sculpture, painting, poetry, drama, and music have their taproots in the . . . land where the Hellenic style was nurtured and brought to fruition."
>
> —William Fleming, *Art, Music and Ideas*

As the Greek National Tourist Organization (GNTO) says, in Greece one can "travel through antiquity with uninterrupted ease." It's a country whose beginnings can be traced to 3000 B.C., when the Minoans developed a language and buildings. In 1500 B.C., the Mycenaean civilization gave the world heroes like Achilles and Helen of Troy. Democracy can be traced to about 700 B.C., and names like Sophocles, Aristophanes, Plato, Aristotle, and Socrates emerge about 400 B.C. In Greece, antiquity is taken for granted.

The GNTO also notes the vast range of Greek culture: "The Greeks established contact at a very early stage with the people of Asia, Africa, and Europe. They learned, taught, gave, and received from those they met, and attempted distant journeys not merely to trade but also to explore and learn. In short, they were the first tourists."

Few societies have provided such a heritage to the western world—a heritage pervasive wherever modern tourists travel in Greece. On the mainland—Attica, Peloponnese, Central Greece, Thessaly, Epirus, Macedonia, Thrace—and in the 1,400 islands, there is a profound sense of history, and Greek festivities are usually outstanding examples of this cultural tradition. From the renowned theater festivals at Athens, Epidaurus, and Epirus, to the spectacular "Sound and Light Shows" that focus on Greek architecture and history, travelers are continually reminded of the debt they owe to Greece's past.

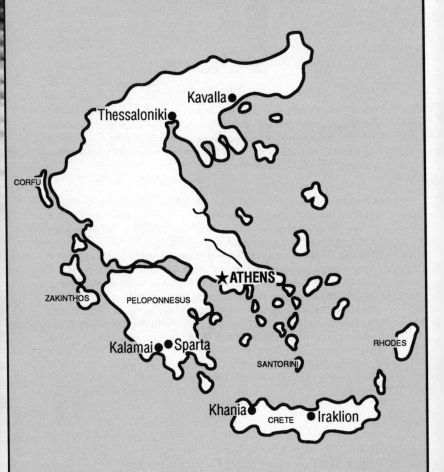

May

Athens—Sound and Light Show

The Acropolis, which some consider the most splendid group of antique buildings in the world, is the scene of sound and light shows
from April to October. Like the French *son et lumière*, the Greek shows
feature illuminated monuments as a text is read with musical accompaniment. The Acropolis (the word literally means "an easily defen-
sible upper city") rises 200 feet above the surrounding plain and
originally served as a fortress and sacred sanctuary of Athena. The
Parthenon (built as a temple to Athena), the Sanctuary of Zeus, and
the Erechtheum (the sanctuary of Athena, Poseidon, and Erechtheus)
are some of the backgrounds for the show. Audiences view the show
from the Pnyx, the semi-circular terrace on the northwest hill of
Philopappos, on the periphery of the Acropolis. An English performance runs at 9:00pm nightly.

Also, traditional Greek dances are held at Dora Stratou (Philopap-
pou Hill) nightly at 10:15pm. The combination of sound/light/dance
is a wonderful introduction to Greek culture and folklore.

Corfu—Sound and Light Show

Corfu, one of the northern Greek islands near Albania, offers many
unexpected British elements, vestiges of the days when it was under
English rule. One of the most impressive reminders is the large central square, the Esplanade. Bordered by the Palace of St. Michael
and St. George on the north and the Old Fortress on the east, the
Esplanade is a splendid setting for sound and light shows and traditional dancing. Programs in English run at 9:30pm from May 15-Sept.
30. Dance programs are nighty at 9:00pm at the Old Fortress.

Rhodes—Sound and Light Show

Rhodes is considered Greece's most cosmopolitan resort. One of its
most spectacular architectural treasures is the Grand Master's Palace,
a copy of the Pope's Palace at Avignon. Though criticized as osten-
tatious, the Palace is a magnificent setting for the sound and light
shows held there from April 1-Oct. 31. The English program alternates with Greek, French, German, and Swedish at 9:15pm, 10:15pm,
and 11:15pm. Also, traditional Greek dancers perform daily (except
Saturday) in Rhodes at the Old City Theater at 9:15pm.

Limnos, Arahova, Assi Gonia, Kos—Feast of St. George

To honor St. George on May 1, the village of Kalliopi on the island
of Limnos celebrates with grand horse races. Arahova features a
three-day, non-stop feast, and Assi Gonia, near Hania on the island
of Crete, the feast is followed by a sheep-shearing contest and the
enactment of old customs by local shepherds. On the island of Kos
at the village of Pili, traditional music and dancing follow a spirited
horse race.

Langadas, Agia Eleni—Feasts of Constantine & Helen

Located 13 miles northeast of Thessaloniki, Langadas is the scene of a unique pagan tradition called *anastenarides* (fire-walking), held May 21-23, the feast of St. Constantine and his British-born mother, St. Helen. The celebration features a group of barefoot dancers who perform on hot embers while holding icons of the saints above their heads. Apparently, they don't get burned.

In Agia Eleni near Serres, similar ceremonies honor the saints, but in addition to the firewalking, the residents sacrifice a calf and burn candles in its ears. Visitors who wish to experience Greek mythology firsthand and witness ancient sacrificial rites shouldn't miss this unusual observance.

June

Athens—Athens Festival

The Athens Festival of Music and Drama is a recreation of the Dionysia, a succession of tragedies about an ancient Greek family. Originally, the plays of Aeschylus, Sophocles, and Euripides were performed in the Theater of Dionysus on the southern slope of the Acropolis and would last from early morning to nightfall. Thousands of Athenians attended the Dionysia in early summer to watch the tragedies unfold and be amused by the comedies of Aristophanes as well. Naturally, all the trappings of a true bacchanalia came with the drama.

Founded in 1955, the Athens Festival has allowed thousands of Greeks and visitors to enjoy the performances at the Odeon, erected in 161 A.D. Originally covered with a cedar roof, the Odeon is now open-air, with seating for 5,000. It's an incomparable setting for the festival.

Programs include orchestral and chamber music, classical and popular theater, grand opera, and both modern and classical ballet. In recent years, the festival has seen Wagner's *Ring* danced by the Bejart Ballet and Martha Graham's Company in *Phaedra*, *The Rites of Spring*, and *Errand into the Maze*. The Greek National Opera performed Verdi's *Nabucco*, and the Opera of Hungary staged Puccini's *Madame Butterfly*. Of course, ancient Greek drama is also a highlight. For more information, contact Athens Festival, Box Office, 4 Stadiou Street, Athens. (early May to late Sept.)

Athens—Lycabettus Theater

Supplementing the Athens Festival, various artists perform in the summer in the open-air theater on Lycabettus Hill. There's usually traditional Greek music and songs; a concert by blues legend B. B. King; Irish folk music; and many popular stars. The theater seats 4,000. Performances usually begin at 9:00pm. For more information, contact Athens Festival Box Office (address above).

Epidaurus—Epidaurus Festival

The great event of the Peloponnese region is the festival of Greek drama at Epidaurus, held on weekends in July and August. Inaugurated in 1954, the festival gained world renown for its performances of ancient Greek drama. The theater at Epidaurus, the best-preserved of all Greek theaters, was built in the third century B.C. and seated 14,000. This superb creation, attributed to Polycleitos the Younger, is famous for its acoustics, making it magnificent for ancient drama.

Recent offerings included Euripides' *Phoenician Women*, *Medea*, *Iphigenia at Aulis*, and *Iphigenia in Tauris*, Sophocles' *Antigone*, Aeschylus' *The Persians* and *Oresteia*, and Aristophanes' *Frogs*. The National Theater of Greece and the Northern Greece State and Art Theater produce the plays, held Fridays and Saturdays at 8:00pm.

Epidaurus, 20 miles from Nafplion on the Saronic Gulf, can be reached easily from Athens. For more information, contact Athens Festival Box Office (address above). (late June to late August)

Patras—Patras International Festival

The Patras Festival offers jazz, chamber ensembles, percussion octets, string quartets, piano and guitar recitals, and electronic music. Theater presentations, actors' workshops, poetry readings, and art exhibitions create a "fringe" atmosphere. (mid-June to late August)

throughout Greece—Navy Week

Closely linked with the sea throughout its history, Greece celebrates Navy Week with special displays and entertainment at many coastal towns. Navy Week also serves as the occasion for fishermen to stage festivals around the country. At Volos, on the last day, sailors re-enact the launching of the Argonauts' Expedition. (last week of June)

July

Kavala—Philippi and Thassos Festival

As you might expect of a country so closely linked with drama, wherever there's an antique theater, a theater festival follows. The northern Greek theaters at Philippi near Kavala and on the island of Thassos are both venues for ancient drama throughout the summer. The festival has been an annual event since 1957. (July-Sept.)

Dodona—Epirus Festival

The town of Dodona in northwest Greece is also the site of an ancient drama event. Its theater, recently discovered and restored, was buried for centuries, as were temples and priests' houses. In 1876, the site was unearthed, and the theater is now alive again with high-quality Greek drama. (early July to early Sept.)

Daphni, Rethymon, Patras—Wine Festivals

As the home of Dionysus, God of Wine, Greece hosts numerous wine festivals noted for revelry, dancing, and singing. All visitors are encouraged to sample regional foods and beverages. The event at Daphni (near Athens) takes place at the Byzantine Monastery from late July to early Sept. The Rethymon festival (Crete) is held at the Municipal Garden in the last week of July, and Patras (Peloponnese) holds its event throughout the city and on its festival grounds in late August/early Sept.

August

Katerini—Olympus Festival
Held at the nearby village of Lithoro, the Olympus Festival includes various artistic events on the grounds of Platamona Castle. (mid-August)

Kos—Hippokrateia
The island of Kos celebrates the Hippokrateia Festival with performances of ancient drama, musical evenings, a flower show, a display of popular art, and a special re-enactment of the Hippocratic Oath, still adhered to by physicians. (mid-August)

Corfu—Feast of the Savior
At the annual pilgrimage to Pontikonissi on August 6 (the Feast of the Savior), hundreds of pilgrims venture by boat to honor Christ and enjoy a traditional fair on the isle.

Corfu—Feast of St. Spyridon
On August 11, Pontikonissi is again the scene of a religious festival, this time in honor of St. Spyridon. A colorful procession and traditional fair highlight the observance.

throughout Greece—Dormition of the Virgin Mary
Greeks celebrate the major religious holiday of the Virgin Mary with processions, pilgrimages, and church services on August 15. The island of Tinos, especially, is known for festivals with great ceremony and colorful traditions.

Lefkas—Festival of Art and Literature
Music and theater, folk singing and dancing, and native food and wine are all part of this popular event in the capital of Lefkada. The Homeric associations of the Ionian Islands, of which Lefkada is a part, make them an interesting venue for a festival of this type. (mid-August)

September

Thessaloniki—Greek Song and Film Festival
This festival takes place in the Palais des Sports as part of the International Trade Fair, the largest of the annual trade fairs in Greece. The Fair, held the second week of Sept., is the beginning of a series

of cultural events in the capital of northern Greece and includes Greek and foreign films, as well as Greek folk musicians. The events continue through October in conjunction with the Demetria Festival.

Athens/Sparta—Spartathlon

This international marathon covers 250 kms., from the Panathenian Stadium in Athens to Sparta. It commemorates the athleticism of young men from the two rival cities of ancient Greece. For more information, contact Spartathlon Association, Box 3851, 10210 Athens.

October

Marathon/Athens—International Open Marathon

This 42-kilometer marathon attracts athletes of all ages who wish to retrace the ancient route from Marathon (northeast of Athens) to the capital. It commemorates the young warrior Pheidippidis' run to announce the Athenian victory over the Persians in 490 B.C. The finish line is Panathenian Stadium. For more information, contact SEGAS, 137 Sygrou Avenue, 17121 Athens. (mid-Oct.)

Thessaloniki—Demetria Festival

The Demetria Festival, a revival of the tradition of Byzantine festivities in the capital of Macedonia, is now part of the broader program following the International Trade Fair. The event is a series of theatrical, musical, and operatic performances given by Greek and foreign companies. Additionally, the Greek Song and Film Festival, with top Greek and foreign films, is held with the Demetria Festival. (throughout Oct.)

Olympia & the Olympic Games

The coast of the western Peloponnese and the area from Patras to Olympia are among the world's most scenic spots. The entire area is strewn with the ruins of ancient sites, including Olympia, one of the most important sanctuaries of antiquity, where human strength was worshipped and beautiful myths and legends were born. Olympia was dedicated to Zeus, and the famous games (and many feasts) were held in his honor.

The first Olympian Games were held in 776 B.C. (Pindar associates their origin with the burial rites performed on the grave of Pelops, who had won a chariot race and the right to marry the king's daughter.) Two centuries later, the Games had considerable prestige. Prior to the week of contests, special messengers would cover the country to announce the suspension of all disputes and warfare among the Greek city-states. The event, held in July or August every fourth year, lasted five days and included foot races, wrestling, chariot and horse racing, and the pentathlon. For a millennium, the Games occurred every four years.

The advent of Christianity inspired radical social and religious reforms, and soon the pagan monuments at Olympia were dismantled to build a castle. Still, the games continued until 393 A.D., when Theodosius I banned them by decree. In 426 A.D., Theodosius II ordered the total destruction of the Sanctuary's temples. In the sixth century, earthquakes completed the destruction, but the river Alfios saved the site to some extent—its floods preserved the entire area under sand until 1875, when archaeologists rediscovered Olympia.

The Olympic Games were revived in 1896 by Baron de Coubertin. Except for the two World War periods, the Games have been held consistently every four years in a world capitals, with athletes from almost every nation participating.

Greek Holidays

New Year's Day, Epiphany (Jan. 6), Feast of the Annunciation and Independence Day (March 25), Good Friday, Easter Sunday, Easter Monday, Labor Day (May 1), Assumption (Aug. 15), National Holiday (Oct. 28), Christmas Day, Boxing Day (Dec. 26).

Note: Greece follows the Orthodox religious calendar.

For literature and further information, contact the **Greek National Tourist Organization**. In the U.S., addresses are 645 Fifth Ave., New York, NY 10022 (212-421-5777); 168 North Michigan Ave., Chicago, IL 60601 (312-782-1084); and 611 West 6th St., Los Angeles, CA 90017 (213-626-6696).

About the Author

Margaret M. Johnson, a Massachusetts native of Irish ancestry, currently lives on Long Island (New York), where she teaches high school English. Summer vacations give her time to travel in Europe, and *Festival Europe!* is her effort to lure travelers to enjoy the music, sports, religious, folk, and historic traditions that make Europe one of the world's most exciting and diverse destinations.

More Great Travel Books from Mustang Publishing

Let's Blow thru Europe by Neenan & Hancock. The essential guide for the "15-cities-in-14-days" traveler, this is the funniest, most irreverent, and most honest travel guide ever written. With this book, you can blow off the boring museums and minor cathedrals and instead find the great bars, restaurants, and fun stuff in all the major cities of Europe. *"Absolutely hilarious!"* —*Booklist.* **$10.95**

Europe on 10 Salads a Day by Mary Jane & Greg Edwards. A must for the health-conscious traveler! From gourmet Indian cuisine in Spain to terrific take-out pizza in Italy, this book describes over 200 health food/vegetarian restaurants throughout Europe. *"Don't go to Europe without it"* —*Vegetarian Times.* **$9.95**

Europe for Free by Brian Butler. If you're on a tight budget—or if you just love a bargain—this is the book for you! With descriptions of thousands of things to do and see for free all over Europe, you'll save lots of lira, francs, and pfennigs. *"Well-organized and packed with ideas"* —*Modern Maturity.* **$8.95**

Also in this series:
London for Free by Brian Butler. **$7.95**
DC for Free by Brian Butler. **$6.95**
Hawaii for Free by Frances Carter. **$6.95**

The Nepal Trekker's Handbook by Amy R. Kaplan. This book guides trekkers through every aspect of planning and enjoying a trek through Nepal—one of the world's most magnificent adventures. From medical advice to cultural *faux-pas,* it's an essential guide. *"A must"* —*Midwest Book Review.* **$9.95**

Australia: Where the Fun Is by Goodyear & Skinner. From the best pubs in Sydney to the cheapest motels in Darwin to the greatest hikes in Tasmania, this guide by two recent Yale grads details all the fun stuff Down Under—on and off the beaten path. *"Indispensable"* —*Library Journal.* **$12.95**

Northern Italy: A Taste of Trattoria by Christina Baglivi. For the most delicious, most authentic, and least expensive meals in Italy, skip the *ristoranti* and head straight for *trattorie*, the small, unassuming cafes known only to locals. This guide, describing over 80 *trattorie* from Rome to Milan, is a must for the hungry traveler. ''A tasty tidbit of a tour guide'' —*Quick Trips Travel Letter.* **$9.95**

Bet On It! The Ultimate Guide to Nevada by Mary Jane & Greg Edwards. What does it mean when there's a cup over the handle of a slot machine? When should you buy ''insurance'' in blackjack? Which hotels have the best deals in Las Vegas? Is there good fishing near Reno? **Bet On It!** answers all the questions and more. It's a complete handbook on all the casino games, plus an up-to-date guide to Nevada's best—and best-avoided—hotels, attractions, and tourist activities. A sure bet for anyone going to Nevada! **$10.95**

Mustang books should be available at your local bookstore. If not, send a check or money order for the price of the book, plus $1.50 postage per book, to Mustang Publishing, P.O. Box 3004, Memphis, TN 38173 U.S.A.

Allow three weeks for delivery. For rush, one-week delivery, add $3.00 to the total. *International orders*: Please pay in U.S. funds, and add $5.00 to the total for Air Mail.

For a catalog of Mustang books, send $1.00 and a stamped, self-addressed, business size envelope to Catalog Request, Mustang Publishing, P.O. Box 3004, Memphis, TN 38173.